INSTITUTIONS IN
AUSTRALIAN SOCIETY

Edited by John Henningham

Melbourne

OXFORD UNIVERSITY PRESS

Oxford   Auckland   New York

OXFORD UNIVERSITY PRESS AUSTRALIA

Oxford   New York
Athens   Auckland   Bangkok   Bombay
Calcutta   Cape Town   Dar es Salaam   Delhi
Florence   Hong Kong   Istanbul   Karachi
Kuala Lumpur   Madras   Madrid   Melbourne
Mexico City   Nairobi   Paris   Singapore
Taipei   Tokyo   Toronto

and associated companies in
Berlin   Ibadan

OXFORD is a trade mark of Oxford University Press

National Library of Australia
Cataloguing-in-publication data:

Institutions in Australian society.

  New ed.
  Includes index.
  ISBN 0 19 553663 0.

  1. Social institutions — Australia. 2. Australia —
  Social conditions. 3. Australia — Politics and
  government. I. Henningham, J. P.

  306.0994

Typeset by Syarikat Seng Teik Sdn Bhd
Printed in Malaysia by SRM Production Services
Published by Oxford University Press
253 Normanby Road, South Melbourne, Australia

Contents

ACKNOWLEDGMENTS

The authors and publisher are grateful to the following copyright holders for granting permission to reproduce material in this book:

Active magazine, Women in Sport Unit, Australian Sports Commission for Kathy Watt quotation in *Active*, Spring 1992; table from Active, 1993 (Table 12.1)

ACTU for passage from Bill Kelty, *Together for Tomorrow*, Melbourne, 1991

Allen & Unwin for passage from M. A. Jones, *The Australian Welfare State: Origins, Control and Choices*, Sydney, 1990

Angus and Robertson for two tables from B. Stoddart, *Saturday Afternoon Fever: Sport in Australian Culture*, Sydney, 1986 (Tables 12.2 and 12.3)

©*The Australian* for passage from editorial, 4 August 1991

Australian Government Publishing Service for passages from *Rondel v. Worsley* [1967] 1 QB 443; Peter Cook, 'Address at launch of Industrial Relations at Work, Workplace Australia conference'; *Reserve Bank Act 1959*; *Financial Corporations Act 1974*; Australian Sports Commission and the Office of the Status of Women, *Women, Sport and the Media*, Canberra, 1988; A. Daly, 'Structure' in *Australian Sport: A Profile*, Canberra, 1985; House of Representatives Standing Committee on Finance and Public Administration, *Going for Gold: The first report on an inquiry into sports funding and administration*, Canberra, 1989; for tables from Commonwealth Schools Commission, *Participation and Equity in Australian Schools*, Canberra, 1984 (Table 8.1); Commonwealth Schools Commission, *In the National Interest*, Canberra, 1987 (Table 8.2); figure from Committee on Employment Opportunities, *Restoring Employment: A Discussion Paper*, Canberra, 1993 (Figure 10.1)

Australian Labor Party for passage from ALP policy speech delivered by E. G. Whitlam, Blacktown Civic Centre, 1972

Board of Secondary School Studies (Queensland) for passage from *Aims and Objectives of Secondary Education*, Brisbane, March 1974

R. Broome for passage from 'Professional Aboriginal boxers in eastern Australia, 1930–1979', *Aboriginal History*, 1980

The Courier-Mail (Brisbane) for passage from L. Kavanagh, 'Here beginneth a lesson for the church', 23 July 1988

Curriculum Development Centre for figure from *Core Curriculum for Australian Schools*, Canberra, 1980

John Fahey for passage from the *Australian Olympian*, Spring 1993

Greenwood Press for passage from L. Snyder, *The Meaning of Nationalism*, Westport, 1968

Holmes & Meier for passage from J. Richie, *Australia As Once We Were*, Melbourne, 1975

Donald Horne for passage from 'Cup Fever' in the *National Times*, 30 September 1983

The Law Book Company for figure from G. J. Bamber and R. D. Landsbury (eds), *International and Comparative Industrial Relations, Politics and Law*, Sydney, 1993

©OECD, 1993, *Public Management: OECD Country Profiles*, reproduced by permission of the OECD (Figure 10.2); ©OECD, 1993, *Revenue Statistics of OECD Member Countries*, reproduced by permission of the OECD (Figure 10.3)

Penguin Books Australia for passage from Donald Horne, *The Lucky Country*, Melbourne, 1964

Price Waterhouse for passage from *Price Waterhouse and Co. Centenary, 1874–1974*, Melbourne, 1974

Pan Macmillan for passage from I. Turner, *The Australian Dream*, Sun Books, Melbourne, 1960.

Every effort has been made to trace the original source of all material contained in this book. Where the attempt has been unsuccessful, the authors and publisher would be pleased to hear from the copyright holder concerned to rectify any omission.

INTRODUCTION

John Henningham

Change has become the one constant in all aspects of Australian society. As the twenty-first century approaches, old certainties have disappeared, together with traditions, values, behaviours and ways of looking
at the world that had for generations seemed immutable. In this respect,
Australia simply reflects processes occurring throughout the world,
both in western industrialised societies and in the former communist
countries: challenges to the state and the extent of state regulation, a
rethinking of the welfare state, and economic reorganisation. But other
aspects of Australia's changes derive from the nation's own growing
pains and the uncertainties rooted in its European colonial history and
its Asian-Pacific geography.

To take the latter point first: Australia is derived from a cluster of
British colonies established from the late eighteenth to the early nineteenth centuries. It represents the apogee of the great age of European
discovery and colonisation, differing only from African, Asian and
American equivalents in its paucity of exploitable resources (pre-
mining) or of inhabitants to be exploited as slave labour on a large
scale. Its establishment at the death knell of slavery as an English economic policy spared it that cruelty, although its early decades of convict
labour served an equivalent function, as did the later policy of inden-
tured labour from the Pacific.

Colonists were almost exclusively from the British isles, generating over time an unusual melting pot of English and Celtic races 15 000 kilometres from the homeland where they had warred for centuries. Formal institutions in the new colonial society derived from London-appointed governorships and appointments. Methods of organising the legal system, embryonic government, religion and the economy were all squarely English, forming a mindset in which, even until the mid-twentieth century, England was often referred to as 'home' by Anglo-centric Australians.

Australia's geography — further from its colonists' 'home' than almost any place on earth, and separated by only a narrow sea passage from the 'teeming millions' of Asia — resulted in the development of a xeno-phobic, isolationist world view, in which psychological barriers were erected against near neighbours, and intervention in foreign affairs was only at the behest of Mother England. As immigrants, Continental Europeans were as unwelcome as were Asians and other non-Anglo-Saxons, so that by the time the colonies were federated in 1901, citizens of British Isles origin accounted for 87 per cent of the population. The Aboriginal population, which had roamed the continent for at least 40 000 years, was not considered worthy of inclusion in census counts (nor was it to be until as recently as 1967).

It was only after World War II that the Australian government encouraged large-scale immigration from the European Continent (itself partly a policy to stave off potential emigration from Asia), and the best-known fact about Australia among its northern neighbours was the insulting policy of 'white Australia'. That policy was finally abandoned in the late 1960s and 1970s, resulting in the development of a 'multicultural' immigration policy and the development of ethnic diversity. The 1991 census showed that one in four of Australia's population were born overseas, and of these, 23 per cent were from Continental Europe and 19 per cent from Asia, four times the figure of twenty years previously.

The changing nature of the Australian population is one strand in the current debate about the Constitution, and in particular the system of government that derives the notion of constitutional monarchy from Great Britain. Although in all practical senses independently self-governing, Australia retains the constitutional fiction of being ruled by the prevailing monarch of the United Kingdom, who exercises his or her powers through a local governor-general. The post-colonial oddity of this situation was only partially addressed in the 1970s when the British monarch was also designated Queen of Australia.

Yet the political system that has developed within the framework of constitutional monarchy has proved remarkably stable and for the most part democratic, thus strengthening the case of supporters of the status quo and giving republicans the unenviable task of convincing the majority of the population in the majority of states that an uncertain constitutional future is better than a certain present and past. The key problematic issue is the nature of the relationship between the head of state in a republican system and the government and parliament.

The theme of change recurs throughout the chapters of this book, as authors summarise and analyse the key features of the range of institutions that underpin modern Australia. Institutions reflect a society but also function to mould it: there is a circular process. Just as it is said that we get the politicians we deserve, all our institutions derive ultimately from popular consent. Yet at the same time, they involve rules and understandings that help determine individuals' behaviours, and thus cannot be changed or reformed at will. Processes of evolutionary change occur as society strives through formal and informal, conscious and unconscious processes to remould its institutions.

Before looking at examples of these processes, it is fitting to examine the notion of an institution. Of the dozen distinct meanings of the term identified by the *Shorter Oxford English Dictionary*, one definition comprehensively suits our purpose: 'An established law, custom, usage, practice, organisation, or other element in the political or social life of a people'. The Oxford dates this usage to 1551.

Common to all institutions is their social origin: they derive, in one way or other, from people; they are functions of human organisation, the end products of varying methods of controlling and structuring human interactions. Some, such as systems of government and law, are formal, rule-based structures, deriving their legitimacy either directly or indirectly from popular consent. Others, such as the economy, have regulatory parameters set by government or law, but otherwise function in response to the interplay of market forces. Yet others, as diverse as religion and sport, are primarily cultural, expressing a community's priorities and values in areas of individual and communal self-expression.

The evolving nature of institutions is an inevitable consequence of their existence. Such institutions as the Roman Empire can change no more, but all living institutions must grow and change in some way. For example, Australia's contemporary political system at the end of the twentieth century is markedly different from that of the beginning of the century, despite being subject to the same written Constitution:

power is centralised to a degree that the Founding Fathers, anxious to maintain most functions of government under the control of the several states, could not have imagined; moreover, government is involved in areas of human endeavour, such as welfare, education, health and even sport, where a role for governments was previously either minimal or non-existent.

The evolution of institutions is in some cases gradual and incremental: the increasing power obtained by the Commonwealth government at the expense of the states has been the result of almost a century's development (although national emergencies such as war speeded up the process).

In other cases, change comes about in sudden leaps, at the behest of small groups of 'opinion leaders' or even of charismatic individuals, and the processes are controversial and divisive. Thus, Paul Keating made his mark when achieving the prime ministership in 1991 by promoting the option of a republic (as well as the changing of the national flag), raising the ire of many and the approval of others.

Similarly, industrial relations reform in the early 1990s has been a painful process for many, as the complex statutory structures that have developed throughout the century have begun to give way to systems of enterprise bargaining. Industrial and rural institutions throughout the world have been forced to adapt to international changes in trade policy and protection, expressed in implementation of the Uruguay Round of the General Agreement on Tariffs and Trade (GATT) agreement of 1994, which marks a significant leap towards liberalised trade.

Religion has not been untouched by traumatic change: the Anglican Church's decision in 1992 to ordain women was the result of two decades' intense debate, and its ramifications continue to be discussed, particularly after the English mother church took the same step. Religion is an institution of diminishing influence, yet still of great importance in Australian life. Conflicts between Anglican archbishop Hollingworth and former prime minister Hawke over government economic policy, as well as churches' criticisms of the Opposition's previous consumption tax policy, were major public issues in the early 1990s, indicating that the churches' views still count and that they are recognised as representing a considerable constituency.

Sudden, controversial change has also come to sport as an institution, as commercial considerations have come to the fore. Kerry Packer succeeded in the late 1970s in introducing a whole new form of cricket, again to the accompaniment of much heartache, although his challenge to the cricketing establishment has resulted in a boost for the traditional game. In 1994 Murdoch issued a similar challenge to rugby league, with his proposed 'super league', aimed at boosting pay TV subscriptions. Meanwhile, sponsorship has changed the face of all codes of football played in Australia, even including the once fiercely amateur code of rugby union. The role of governments in funding sport has also changed, especially in Olympic events. Sydney's successful bid for the 2000 Olympics gave Australians an insight into the processes and motives involved in hosting international sport's greatest prize: promotion of trade and tourism, commercial sponsorship and political advantage are major factors that diminish the original, athlete-centred concept of the Games.

This book sets out to give a lucid, introductory account of contemporary institutions that impact on citizens' lives. It is a paradox that the complexity of today's society is matched only by the lack of detailed understanding most people have of that society. As education has become more and more specialised, the need has arisen for more accessible information about how society works.

All of us wishing to be well-informed citizens require some knowledge of the structures and institutions that have developed at national and regional levels. While the mass media give daily accounts of major events initiated by or affecting these institutions, many people find the barrage of information puzzling and difficult to assimilate: they suffer from 'information overload'.

Most problematic is the lack of context that bedevils so much daily journalism: if readers have missed out on the first part of a continuing story, how do they ever manage to catch up? This gap in people's understanding extends to the very foundation of the institutions that affect us. What sense can people make of public events if they have not been schooled in the foundational knowledge required? All of us tend to lack knowledge of institutions outside our immediate spheres of work or interest, but research into knowledge gaps has found alarmingly high levels of popular ignorance about fundamentals in our political, legal and economic systems.

Studies of school leavers matriculating to university have found, for example, considerable haziness about the difference between the House of Representatives and the Senate, or between federal and state government functions, uncertainty about the structure of courts, and next to no understanding of fundamental economics.

Institutions in Australian Society sets out to fill such gaps by providing a comprehensive overview of major institutions in contemporary Australia. It is unapologetic in starting from the basics, on the simple premise that failure to grasp the foundations of any discipline inevitably results in a flawed understanding of the field of study at a more advanced level. But the authors go beyond the basics to discuss current issues and problem areas, giving readers an insight into the challenges posed by a study of each institution.

As politics and the processes of government set the framework for so much institutional activity, we begin with the consideration of the different levels of government in Australia.

In writing about federal government, Ian Ward depicts the workings of the Westminster system in Australia, and in particular the nature of 'responsible government'. Ward demonstrates the theory versus the practice of the 'chain of accountability' in the political system, pointing out that the Westminster theory of responsible government is an 'ideal type' rather than a model of how government really works in Australia. Part of the reason for differences between theory and reality is to be found in the federal system, which results in constitutional limitations to the power of the national parliament. Moreover, the institution of the High Court means that the Australian national parliament lacks the sovereignty enjoyed by its British and New Zealand counterparts.

A century after it was hammered together (at the great constitutional conventions of the 1890s), Australia's Constitution has re-emerged as a controversial issue. Calls for constitutional reform have led to a resurgence of interest in the Founding Fathers' document. In the past unread and perhaps even unheard of by most Australians, the Constitution has during the 1990s even been reproduced in newspapers and magazines. But the road to a republic has already been shown to be a rocky one: unless bipartisan consensus is achieved (which seems unlikely during Keating's premiership), popular consent through referendum to amending the Constitution in order to establish a republic is unachievable.

State government remains a profoundly important sector, despite the increasingly glamorous profile of federal government. Authors of Australia's federation conceived the states as the real power in Australian politics, with the federal government charged only with those responsibilities where it was manifestly more efficient for an 'umbrella' government to have powers. The century since then has seen the drift of powers from the states to Canberra, most notably when the Commonwealth Government gained income-taxing powers from the states during World War II.

But the states remain powerful entities, which, as Brian Costar shows, are likely to long outlive the occasional calls to do away with them:

'they remain deeply embedded both within the federal Constitution and Australia's political culture'. Differences between the states demonstrate the extent to which they reflect regional differences — geographic, historic and cultural. Additionally, Australia's political parties are state-centred organisations: having evolved different procedures and electoral structures, they share a resentment of federal intervention while competing to maximise representation in federal power structures at party and parliamentary levels. Often forgotten in the move towards changing the federal Constitution is the fact that the states each have their constitutions as well, which will require amendment if Australia is to become a republic (unless the somewhat Gilbertian scenario can be sustained of a republican central government in conjunction with monarchical states).

Local government is the Cinderella of the governmental sector, with a general image of rather humdrum albeit essential activities (sewerage, roads) together with authoritarian power ('you can't beat City Hall'), enlivened only by stories of petty corruption and personality-based politics. Yet with its grassroots base, local government can be seen as the most fundamental form of democratic organisation — and indeed, in most countries, undertakes the functions that in Australia are given to the states.

For the student of local government in Australia, life is not made easy by the fact that each state has organised local government differently. Moreover, local government has no constitutional recognition, and is a creature of the states — with the result that state governments can dismiss councils and restructure the local system at will. There is currently enormous change occurring nation-wide, with local government authorities being amalgamated and restructured to improve their efficiency.

As Doug Tucker argues in his chapter, the current shift towards economic rationalism in local government (involving modern managerialist approaches as well as a desire for streamlining and for uniformity) may be at the expense of local government's traditional strength of diversity as well as responsiveness to community concerns.

The legal system is one of those institutions that until recently seemed less changeable than most. Australia accepted and perpetuated the totality of English common law, while precedents from Britain set the parameters for Australian judgments. The adversarial system, which prevails in courts of the UK (unlike the quite different European system), is the basis of the Australian court system. The continuity in legal structures is symbolised by the regalia and ceremonies that mark courtroom practice.

Yet a judiciary that has for centuries been collectively beyond criticism has suddenly attracted comment and scrutiny. Individual judgments have led to a focusing of attention on the social and cultural backgrounds of judges, with suggestions that they are out of touch with contemporary Australian values. This has resulted in calls for judges to be 're-educated' and for the methods of choosing judges to be re-evaluated. These views were endorsed by a Senate report in 1994, 'Gender bias and the judiciary', which also recommended that the Australian Law Reform Commission review laws to eliminate gender bias.

Meanwhile, the High Court appears to be undergoing a transformation from its traditional 'referee' role (although it was never simply that) to a more overt 'law-making' role, involving it in political controversy. This was seen in particular in its Mabo judgment, which necessitated federal legislation to enact the principles of native title established by the Court. At the same time, lawyers' monopolies over legal processes have been challenged by the Trade Practices Commission, and a general shake-up of the state-fractured system of law has been set in train by the federal government.

To understand these changes it is first necessary to understand the principles of the legal system as it is practised in Australia. Donald Gifford's chapter is concerned with explaining and demystifying the processes of law and their impact on those caught up in legal procedures.

The economy is inevitably an area of controversy because of the range of opinions, wants and ideologies that underly people's judgments about appropriate policy and directions for the nation. A vast number of economic institutions, governmental and private, set the parameters for the working of the economy, while debate is continuous about the role and effectiveness of those institutions as well as about the functions they perform. In his overview of the economy, Tony Makin indicates the importance of four major goals of economic policy: full employment, low inflation, external balance of payments and economic growth. To achieve these goals (which can be mutually inconsistent), the chief instruments available to governments are fiscal policy, monetary policy and wages policy. Of these, only fiscal policy is entirely under the command of the federal government, although its policy-making must appease many constituencies and interest groups.

Monetary policy is carried out by the Reserve Bank, notionally independent but subject to considerable influence and direction from the Treasury. As Makin shows, in addition to implementing monetary policy in order to achieve the government's overall policy objectives, the Reserve Bank exercises oversight over the financial system as a whole, including banks as well as other financial institutions (such as insurance companies, credit unions and building societies). Its role has changed considerably as part of the shift towards deregulation of the financial system. Australia's role in the international economy has also changed markedly, with a floating rather than regulated currency, and a future increasingly linked with Asia.

Closely linked with economic reforms have been changes to the labour market and in relations between employers, employees and governments. The 90-year-old, uniquely Australian system of legally sanctioned processes of industrial relations through conciliation and arbitration is giving way to enterprise bargaining. This move, originally promoted by employers, has won the support of the federal government and, most importantly, the Australian Council of Trade Unions — with only the traditional umpire, the Industrial Relations Commission, expressing reservations.

As Greg Bamber and Edward Davis show, the series of Accords struck by federal Labor governments since 1983 have resulted in comparative industrial relations harmony but also, it has been argued, a drop in real wages. Further, unemployment has re-emerged as a major problem, leading Labor to break with tradition in 1994 by endorsing below-award wages for the long-term unemployed.

Agricultural institutions have had to adapt more than most to the changing role of agriculture in Australian society. As in many countries, agriculture is more than an economic activity. The role of farmers and of producers of wool and beef has become an important aspect of Australian culture, as part of the general lore of the bush, yielding such terms and concepts as squatters, selectors, jackeroos and swagmen. Perhaps for this reason, there is much sentiment attached to rural activities, and in particular to the preservation of the family farm. Against this, farming families and those in allied industries often perceive a lack of sympathy from the urbanised majority, especially when rural industries have suffered the consequences of international protectionism of rural products combined with local protectionism of secondary industry.

As Colin Brown and John Longworth point out in their chapter, Australian agriculture is competitive and efficient by world standards, as a result of which the rural sector and the nation should benefit from the historic Uruguay round of GATT trade talks, which lifted many barriers to Australian exports. However, adjustments, many of them painful, will still be necessary within Australia's rural sector, which is character-ised by great heterogeneity of production systems of varying efficiency and viability.

Education is an institution of unequalled importance, as attested by the bumper sticker 'If you can read this, thank a teacher!'. Yet, as Rus-sell Cowie shows in his survey, education has for most of our past been a means of social control. Even the first moves towards increasing edu-cational opportunity were in the context of training people about accept-ing their station in life, or else to safeguard the state from an unlettered electorate. Cowie illustrates how the relative recency of universal edu-cation, particularly at the secondary level, is akin to a miracle: the progress towards giving all people the opportunity to complete their education is now being extended to the concept of high school reten-tion rates approaching double the level of the early 1970s. At the same time, governments that a little over a century ago shunned all respons-ibility for education are now inclined to impose a regulatory frame-work that has undermined educators' autonomy. The amalgamations of tertiary institutions imposed by the federal government and com-plex mechanisms of accountability and review are examples of the new order, while commercial imperatives including privatisation have become features of education.

The obvious importance in maintaining and improving the popu-lation's standard of health render medicine a major institution. Its importance is reflected in political divisions about fair and equitable policies for the funding of health care, as well as such changing factors as increased life expectancy with its consequent ageing population, environmental influences on health, shortages of doctors in non-metropolitan areas, and the impact of new diseases (especially AIDS). As Adrian Bower and John Biggs show, increasing importance is attached to health education, including the role of campaigns to increase people's awareness of risk factors. The new century will also witness the first graduations of doctors trained under the new post-graduate model of medical education.

Social welfare as an institution in the sense of an area of govern-ment policy is very much a twentieth-century invention, and most of the developments in this area in Australia have occurred in the past fifty years. About 28 per cent of the federal budget is committed to welfare (and under a broader definition of services meeting people's health, welfare and educational needs, the total is 60 per cent). Yet the role of governments (at local and state as well as federal level) often detract appropriate recognition of the large volunteer role in welfare work — estimated at approaching two million people. Meanwhile, federal government policy in Australia has moved towards making citizens more responsible for their own welfare — through, for example, compulsory superannuation. John May criticises the direction of contemporary policy, showing the dangers of subverting needy people's needs to economic policy.

The oldest continuing institution in the world is the Roman Catholic Church, and churches, protestant and catholic, took root in Australia with the first colonists. As Ian Gillman demonstrates, however, the manifestly religious basis of the earliest North American colonies was not to be found in Australia's white settlement, whose secular beginnings initiated a tradition of scepticism and materialism that has become part of Australian culture.

But change is evident. Although given new momentum by the women's ordination decision (except in its evangelical and anglo-catholic wings), Anglicanism has lost forever its once dominant role in Australian society, overtaken in numbers by Catholics in the mid-1980s, and with declining church attendance. Fastest growing religions have been pentecostal groups (again, a world trend), while new immigration patterns have meant a rise in non-Christian faiths especially Islam and Buddhism. There is also more understanding of Aboriginal spiritual beliefs.

With Australia's climate and a leisure-oriented culture, sport has become a major preoccupation for many Australians, who in particular cherish the winning of international sporting contests. National pride was near-tangible when Australia won the America's Cup in 1983 (held exclusively by the United States for a century), as it was in 1993 with the awarding of the 2000 Olympics to Sydney. In recent years Australia has achieved world supremacy in cricket, hockey, rugby union, rugby league, golf and netball, as well as posting Olympic achievements in swimming and equestrian events. But as Ian Jobling shows, sport has become far more than a recreational activity: commercial sponsorship and the role of the media have changed sport into a money-making enterprise, which has had an important impact on all aspects of sport including the rules of the game.

Australia's mass media are rarely far from controversy. As the most important means by which people develop their personal images of all the other institutions in society, the media are often judged defective in their representations of what is worth knowing. Often, they are the victims of the 'shoot the messenger' syndrome, but there is also justice in critics' perceptions that the significant often takes second place to the superficial. Contemporary trends and issues include concentration of ownership of the press, foreign ownership, and the challenges posed by the introduction of pay television and other emerging technologies. Daily newspaper circulation is in serious decline, offset to some extent by increased weekend and magazine reading, but the future of the newspaper is linked to the 'paperless' means of delivering print media that is expected to be commercially viable early in the new century. Meanwhile, the foreshadowed availability of hundreds of information channels through a combination of satellites, optical fibre, microwave and digital compression, spell the end of the 70-year-old concept of broadcasting in favour of 'narrowcasting'.

Changes occurring in the structure of media highlight the importance of technical developments in changes to institutions at large. The capacity for people to access vast quantities of information instantly as a basis for their commercial decisions is continuing to transform the functioning of various economic and legal institutions as well as the public sector. But it can be argued that the most important changes in Australian society at the turn of the century flow from a developing consciousness of the opportunities and challenges posed by a combination of natural endowments, the inheriting of a stable (if overprotective) political and economic system, a distancing from colonial ties, a more ethnically diverse population, an egalitarian disposition, and a belated awareness of the Asian-Pacific region.

Some of these challenges are touched on in the chapters that follow, as authors sketch the characteristics and the contemporary responses to change of significant institutions.

There are other institutions we could consider. And there are other ways of looking at institutions. This book shows one approach, based upon individual overviews of key institutions in Australian political, economic and cultural life. Designed to help Australians and those with an interest in Australia to grasp important fundamentals about how the country functions at the institutional level, we hope also to have provided an understanding of the kinds of issues and dilemmas that occupy contemporary Australians.

1

FEDERAL
GOVERNMENT

....

Ian Ward

Since 1988 the nation's capital has had a celebrated new tourist attraction. It is, of course, the hugely expensive new Parliament House, which is bunkered within and atop Canberra's Capital Hill. Visitors to this billion-dollar-plus home to the House of Representatives and Senate may well imagine that parliament is a powerful institution that lies at the very heart of Australian government. But this is not so, as those few tourists who venture into the visitors' galleries of either house may begin to suspect. The national (or Commonwealth) parliament is not the seat of real political power. Yet Australia does have a parliamentary system of government, and parliament itself has a major symbolic importance as indeed the magnificence of its Canberra accommodation suggests.

One aspect of its symbolic significance lies in the definition of parliament found in the Constitution: section 1 stipulates that the federal parliament shall consist of 'the Queen, a Senate, and a House of Representatives'. This formal-legal description of parliament underlines the fact that Australia is a monarchy. Although the republican cause is again gathering strength, Australian laws are enacted and administered with the authority of the Crown and not, as in the United States of America, which is a republic, in the name of the people. Despite this constitutional formality, Australia is commonly seen as a democracy. In practice, most political scientists sensibly treat the parliament as comprising just the House of Representatives and the Senate. Each of these Houses is popularly elected — thus parliament symbolises Australia's democratic system of government. But the full symbolic significance of parliament derives from the theory of responsible government.

A CHAIN OF ACCOUNTABILITY?

The particular form of parliamentary democracy (imperfectly) practised in Australia is known as 'responsible government' (Summers, 1990, p. 12). It is sometimes also described as 'cabinet government' since its distinguishing feature is that the group (or cabinet) of ministers charged with the responsibility of overseeing the various departments of the public service is drawn from within parliament. These ministers, headed by the prime minister, are often referred to as 'the Government' because (unlike parliament itself) they clearly do wield considerable legislative and executive power. Although voters do not directly elect cabinet, parliament is elected and is thus the vital link in a supposed 'chain of accountability' (Figure 1.1), which links electors, parliament, cabinet and the public service. The public service is accountable to a cabinet of ministers. Ministers including the prime minister are, in turn, selected from within, and thus answerable to parliament. Parliament is of course accountable to the voters who periodically elect it, and who may thus change its membership or indeed replace the government altogether.

It needs be emphasised that responsible parliamentary government is *not* a model of how government in Australia actually works. It is a *theory* or a *set of guiding principles* taken from the British (Westminster) parliament that suggest how Australia's government ought to be conducted. Note, however, that the Constitution, which formally sets out the rules governing Australia's national government, makes no direct mention of Westminster theory. Indeed, the important institution of cabinet is not mentioned, let alone its powers defined. Nor does the Constitution define the role of the prime minister. In short, the Constitution presumes rather than prescribes responsible government. (Its nineteenth-century authors were more intent upon writing the rules for federation.)

Westminster theory requires that collective and ministerial responsibility bind members of cabinet; that heads of state act only upon the advice of ministers; and that the public service should be politically neutral and able to serve any government. But it is parliament that lies

Figure 1.1   The Westminster 'chain of accountability'

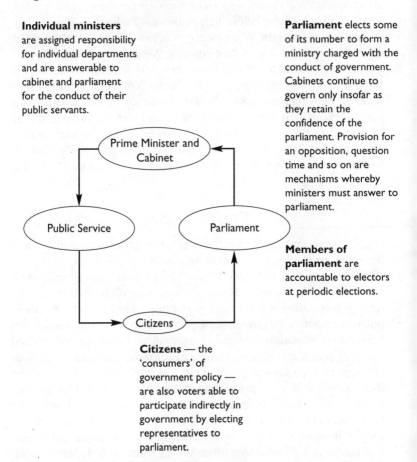

Individual ministers are assigned responsibility for individual departments and are answerable to cabinet and parliament for the conduct of their public servants.

Parliament elects some of its number to form a ministry charged with the conduct of government. Cabinets continue to govern only insofar as they retain the confidence of the parliament. Provision for an opposition, question time and so on are mechanisms whereby ministers must answer to parliament.

Prime Minister and Cabinet

Public Service

Parliament

Members of parliament are accountable to electors at periodic elections.

Citizens

Citizens — the 'consumers' of government policy — are also voters able to participate indirectly in government by electing representatives to parliament.

at the heart of responsible government. It is seen as a popularly elected and representative legislature with the dual role of creating and checking cabinet. Cabinets are entitled to govern only insofar as they retain the support of a majority within the lower house. Parliament's role, and in particular that of the opposition as the alternative government-in-waiting, is to scrutinise the executive actions and legislative initiatives of governments. While its prescriptions are often a poor guide to actual political practice, the theory of responsible government permeates and supplies an organising rationale for much of the business of government in Australia. In particular it explains why parliament as an institution is accorded a special symbolic importance, and is celebrated in the expensive edifice that is the new Parliament House.

For our purposes the Westminster theory of responsible government offers an 'ideal type'. That is, by comparing Westminster theory with Australian practice, and by asking where there are weak or missing links in the chain of accountability, it is possible to develop a picture of how Australia's key national political institutions actually function. One of the major reasons why the national parliament is far less important than Westminster theory suggests is that Australia has a federal system. Counting the Australian Capital Territory and Northern Territory as well as the six original states, there are nine parliaments and not one.

FEDERALISM

Legislative powers are divided between the national parliament and the states (according to a formula originally set out in the 1901 Constitution, but adjusted since by the High Court exercising its own powers of judicial review). Hence the authority of the national parliament is constitutionally limited. For example, hospitals, schools, roads, public transport, local government, print but not electronic media, and universities fall within the legislative province of state parliaments and not the Commonwealth. It is true that since the inception of the federal system the national government has (with the assistance of the High Court, which ruled in its favour in the 1942 and 1957 Uniform Taxation Cases) usurped revenue raising powers that the authors of the Constitution had intended to be exercised by the states. This has enabled the Commonwealth to intervene in areas such as education, transport and health policy by making funds (in the form of 'tied grants') available to the states conditional upon the adoption of measures it wishes implemented. While this gives the national government *de facto* powers in policy areas that formally lie within the constitutional bailiwick of the states, it is still restricted in the areas that it may legislate.

Unlike its British and New Zealand equivalents, the Australian parliament is not sovereign, for the High Court may disallow legislation judged incompatible with that parliament's constitutional powers. This judicial review function makes the High Court a key political institution, although the Court itself would resist this description. Certainly much of its work is non-political. It is the final court of appeal for Australia's judicial system and constitutional cases make up less than 10 per cent of its business. Nowadays it is rare for appointees to the Court to have political backgrounds. Moreover, the Court has nurtured a strong tradition of legalism by paying attention to the letter-of-the-law rather than to the social or political consequences of its decisions. The High Court, like its US counterpart, does not offer advisory opinions, instead confining its role to adjudicating disputes in cases brought before it. Nonetheless, judicial review inevitably has political consequences. And in interpreting the Constitution, the High Court, in effect, defines the powers of the national and state parliaments (along with those of other political actors including the Court itself).

From time to time the rulings of the High Court have had a dramatic political impact (as happened with its decision in the 1992 Mabo case, which fundamentally changed the land rights debate in Australia). However, the High Court's most pronounced political impact has been upon Australia's federalism. That this should have been the case is not surprising for the Constitution of which the Court is custodian is primarily a set of rules for a federal system of government. (For instance, it has no equivalent to the US Bill of Rights.) Its authors were mostly colonial politicians intent upon establishing a federation in which colonies would survive (as states) free from central control by the Commonwealth. They intended a system of coordinate federalism in which the states and the Commonwealth would co-exist as separate and equal jurisdictions.

This legalistic federalist model was flawed from the beginning. The states and the Commonwealth soon found it necessary to establish a series of extra-constitutional bodies to liaise, bargain and negotiate with each other, and to undertake those joint activities needed to make federalism work. These included annual Premiers' Conferences (commenced in 1901 and formalised in 1919); the Australian Loan Council established in 1927–28 to centralise and coordinate government borrowing; and the Commonwealth Grants Commission founded in 1933 to advise on federal government financial grants to states. Aided by a series of High Court rulings, especially in the 1942 Uniform Tax Cases where the Court validated Commonwealth legislation that imposed uniform taxation and deprived states of the power to raise their own income taxes, the Commonwealth greatly extended its revenue-raising powers and thus its dominance of the federal system.

The particular form of federalism that has evolved since 1901 is sometimes dubbed cooperative federalism. This is not because relations between the Commonwealth and state governments are harmonious — frequently they are not. However, much public policy requires co-operation between both tiers of government — especially where the Commonwealth provides finance but states possess the relevant constitutional powers. This may entail joint legislation or coordination and consultation at ministerial and public service levels. The evolution of cooperative federalism has seen a meshing and overlapping of government at the national and state levels. Typically there are, for example, both state and Commonwealth education, transport, welfare, and economic ministers and departments, and this has blurred responsibility in key policy areas. It permits buck-passing between governments and prevents parliaments at either level from holding their ministers accountable. It is arguable that, from the beginning, the mix of federalism and responsible government devised by the nineteenth-century authors of the Constitution contained a tension, since the one divided legislative powers and narrowed those of the national legislature while the other envisaged a sovereign parliament. Certainly the evolution of cooperative federalism with its duplications and blurred lines of responsibility has weakened the chain of accountability.

CABINET

If federalism is a major feature of the Australian political landscape, so too is the dominance of executive government. The Constitution formally vests executive power in the Queen, with the governor-general as her representative. It establishes an executive council, members of which are chosen by and hold office at the pleasure of the governor-general whom they advise. And it provides that the governor-general may appoint persons as executive councillors to administer public service departments who shall be, or become within three months, members of parliament.

Australia's system of cabinet government rests upon a series of unwritten constitutional conventions, the chief one being that the governor-general exercises his or her executive powers only upon the advice of the prime minister (insofar as the prime minister enjoys the support of a majority in the House of Representatives). Thus cabinet comprises selected members of parliament whom the governor-general appoints as executive councillors and ministers of state at the direction of the prime minister. (Ministers are drawn from both houses although most — usually about two thirds — come from the House of Representatives, which is the house in which, by convention, the prime minister sits.) Whereas the executive council is the formal body that gives effect to cabinet decisions — for example, issuing regulations or making appointments — cabinet itself meets separately with the prime minister in the chair. Cabinet is the very engine room of national government, initiating the government's legislative program, coordinating its administrative and policy decisions, and reconciling the conflicting demands that ministers and their departments may make.

The convention that constrains the governor-general to act as the prime minister advises derives from the theory of responsible government. So too do a number of other conventions that apply to cabinet. Chief among these are collective and individual ministerial responsibility. Collective ministerial responsibility obliges all ministers to publicly support cabinet decisions regardless of their own personal predilections, and whether or not they argued a contrary case within cabinet. (A closely related convention requires that cabinet meetings be confidential.) Ministers who cannot agree with cabinet policy should resign. Thus cabinet stands (or falls) together, which is necessary if it is to be answerable to parliament.

Individual ministerial responsibility asks that ministers accept responsibility for their own policies and actions as minister, as well as for those of the public servants whom they oversee. This convention is another link in the chain of accountability. Australian politicians — especially when in opposition — do voice support for the conventions of ministerial responsibility. But in practice neither convention is rigorously practised. Nowadays it is rare for a minister to offer to resign where public servants for whom he or she is responsible err, and unremarkable for ministers to openly signal their disagreements with government policy.

The relaxation of ministerial responsibility is not so much a question of declining standards in public life, but of the changing nature of cabinet and the ministry itself. In 1904 there were just seven Commonwealth public service departments, four of which had fewer than 50 employees. A fifth had only 124 staff and only the Post Master General's Department, with 10 323, approached the size of many modern public service departments. In such a context individual ministers might reasonably have been expected to answer to parliament and to cabinet for the actions of their public servants. Equally a consensus might have been expected among the members of such a small cabinet. Nowadays no minister can have a direct knowledge of much of her or his department's operations. The scale, diversity and technical complexity of modern government has grown enormously since the early 1900s — cabinet has similarly grown in size and complexity. By 1974 there were 37 portfolios making for a large and unwieldly cabinet.

Cabinet has no constitutionally fixed size. Nor is there a limit on the number of ministers who can be appointed. The party in office is free to arrange the size and portfolio responsibilities of its cabinet and ministry in keeping with its own policy priorities and political circumstances. To make cabinet manageable, governments have pursued two distinct strategies. One is to make use of cabinet sub-committees. Different governments have pursued their own particular arrangement of committees with the common aim of coping with the complexity and volume of decisions that need to be made. Potentially this concentrates power within the hands of a relatively small number of ministers who make up the key sub-committees of cabinet, and whose decisions are often routinely endorsed by the whole cabinet. The second strategy involves forming cabinet from an inner group of senior ministers holding key portfolios, and leaving an outer ministry comprising junior ministers who take part in cabinet meetings only when matters pertaining to their portfolio responsibilities are discussed. All governments except the 1972–75 Whitlam government have followed the precedent set by Menzies in 1956 and divided the ministry in this way. Until 1987 the numbers of public service departments meant that this was likely as not to be an arbitrary division that left some important portfolio areas unrepresented in cabinet.

Administrative arrangements introduced by the Hawke Government in 1987 aimed to improve the stability and operation of the cabinet system. It reduced the number of public service departments from 28 to 18 and arranged these into 16 cabinet portfolios each held by a minister sitting in cabinet. Thirteen additional junior ministers were originally also appointed to share the burdens of overseeing the newly-merged 'mega' departments and each was given responsibility for a particular departmental program or section. Although broadly in keeping with Westminster practice, this new arrangement, in which ministers jointly administered departments, muddied the question of ministerial responsibility. But importantly it reduced the flow of material going to cabinet, and enabled it to take a whole-of-government policy perspective to reach decisions informed by a full range of viewpoints (Keating, 1993, p.9).

Keating, Hawke's successor as prime minister, initially continued with the arrangement of the public service into 'mega' departments and with a similar cabinet structure. Following his 1993 election win, he partially reorganised ministerial portfolios and handed responsibility for ten of the 18 departments over to teams of two or more ministers. He also increased the number of quasi-ministerial appointments of parliamentary secretaries from four to ten to reward those supporters he was unable to accommodate in the ministry proper. Faced with a series of ministerial resignations in 1993 and 1994, he made further minor adjustments to his cabinet (including dividing the 'mega' Transport and Communications department into two separate portfolio areas) before finally launching a substantial reshuffling of cabinet in April 1994. In this rearrangement of public service departments and portfolio responsibilities Keating yet again altered the cabinet formula struck by his predecessor in 1987 to accommodate a fresh set of political demands and to impart his own policy stamp and priorities. In the final analysis, the arrangement of cabinet is driven as much, if not more so, by politics than by administrative efficiency.

The Constitution does not fix the structure or operation of cabinet. Cabinet organisation and practice can — and does — vary according to the predilections of the prime minister and party in power. While cabinet is a formal institution of government, it is also a party committee and the chief custodian of the ruling party's electoral fortunes. If the theory of responsible government holds that cabinet is formed within and answerable to parliament, the reality is that it is constituted by the political party (or coalition of parties) with majority support in the House of Representatives. The Liberal Party forms its cabinet and ministry quite differently than does the Australian Labor Party (ALP). The ALP caucus, comprising all Labor members from both houses, elects the full ministry and allows the prime minister only to allocate portfolios. Since the mid–1980s the leaders of organised factions within caucus have negotiated the composition of Labor's front bench. By contrast, the Liberal party room, free of disciplined factions, elects a prime minister and permits that leader to choose the people who will be ministers. As well, Liberal cabinets have always included National Party ministers in accordance with the parties' coalition agreement. Not surprisingly, the internal dynamics of cabinets can widely vary.

There are two basic reasons why real political power is concentrated in cabinet and the ministry (rather than in parliament as the Westminster theory of responsible parliamentary government prescribes). One is that ministers have access to the considerable resources and expertise of the public service, which backbench and opposition members do not. In an era when issues facing governments are often very complex and in which the public service has grown enormously, this is of immense advantage to the prime minister and cabinet in developing policy and legislative programs. Of course the Constitution requires that legislation be passed by both houses of parliament. But ministers introducing legislation can be confident that disciplined voting by all the members of the House of Representatives belonging to their party will ensure its smooth passage through the lower house if not the Senate. For party discipline is the second prop upon which cabinet power rests. Cabinet and the ministry typically comprise the most influential and powerful members of the ruling party (or party coalition) and are able to use this power to control parliamentary proceedings and the legislative process.

PARTIES AND PARLIAMENT

Political parties are groups organised to win the electoral support necessary to capture government and to implement policies that will advantage their supporters. Although there are a great many Australian political parties, only four have any real prospect of regularly gaining parliamentary places. Of these, the Australian Democrats and National Party each command a relatively small following, although the latter (formed in 1920 as the Country Party) has been relatively successful in participating in government through coalition with the Liberals. Thus far the Democrats, founded in 1977, have only been successful in winning seats in the Senate. The dominance of the Australian Labor Party (founded by trade unionists during the 1890s) and Liberals (established in 1944 to give a voice to middle-class Australia) is rooted in an entrenched pattern of party identification, which, although showing recent signs of waning, still means that nine in every ten voters regard themselves as either coalition or Labor supporters. Indeed, three-quarters of Australian voters have always voted for the same party (McAllister and Bean, 1990, pp.164–5). This underlying electoral stability is the basis of party discipline and the power that the leaders of the major parties wield over their parliamentary backbenchers.

Endorsement by a major party is clearly a key to a parliamentary salary and career. The Labor and Liberal parties have different rules and procedures governing preselection. Notably the ALP requires that its candidates pledge to support party policy and caucus decisions, whereas the Liberals do not. Liberal senators and MHRs are ostensibly free to vote as they choose, although in practice they too are subject to forms of party discipline. Both parties will reward loyal party service and penalise those who fail to support agreed party policy in parliament. This means that, with very few exceptions, matters are decided in parliament along party lines. Indeed, party Whips in both houses ensure that their members attend and vote as required. As a consequence legislation introduced by ministers in the lower house is invariably carried. However, in the Senate the governing party (or coalition) is now unlikely to command a majority.

Originally the Senate was intended to be a states' house and a bulwark to federalism. Whereas the majority of the 147 members of the House of Representatives come from the three populous eastern seaboard states, there are 12 Senators from each state (plus two each from the ACT and the NT). Except in the unusual circumstances where both houses of parliament are simultaneously dissolved, half of the Senate is elected every three years, usually in conjunction with lower house elections. Since 1949 the electoral method used for the Senate has been proportional representation, with each state serving as a multi-member electorate. With this method, candidates obtaining a quota of votes cast (a quota is calculated by dividing the number of formal votes by the number of Senators to be elected plus one) are elected. At half-Senate elections minor parties such as the Democrats (and even independent and fringe party candidates) may accumulate the necessary 14.3 per cent of votes cast to gain Senate representation. Under the single member preferential method used to elect the lower house, successful candidates must win an absolute majority. This makes the task of minor parties far harder (except for the National Party, whose electoral supporters are concentrated in rural areas).

The use of separate methods to elect the two houses of parliament results in a different party mix in each. The Senate is no less a party-dominated house than is the House of Representatives. But it is now rare, although not impossible, for the governing party (or parties) to hold a majority in the Senate, and this normally frees it from immediate government control. During the 1980s the Democrats were in a position to frustrate the Fraser and then the Hawke governments by voting with the Opposition. Their electoral fortunes have since slumped. The 1993 election deprived the Democrats of their ability to decide contests between the government and Opposition in the Senate. But it did leave the Keating government without a Senate majority and needing to secure the support of the seven Democrat and two of the remaining three independent and Green Senators in order to enact its legislative program. Loss of the balance of power has checked the influence of the Democrats. Even so, there are still some advantages in this situation for the Democrats and parliament alike. The Senate still provides the Democrats with an important forum and base from which to attempt to halt their slipping electoral fortunes. And it means that the upper house of parliament is not wholly reduced to 'rubber stamping' legislation introduced by the government.

Clearly, as their critics claim, parties have aided the domination of parliament by executive government, and seemingly sheered a major link in the chain of accountability prescribed by Westminster theory. Yet arguably, the discipline that parties bring to parliament is necessary. Without parties it is difficult to imagine how 147 MHRs seeking to advance the particular interests of their own electorates might resolve the complicated and varied issues of public policy that parliament is called upon to address. Equally it is difficult to see how the government of the day might negotiate its legislation through the Senate in the absence of disciplined parties. Of course there can be no doubt that in propagandising, organising, fundraising, recruiting and electioneering in pursuit of the goal of winning elections and thus government, political parties act in their own self-interest. Yet these activities give parties an important role in formulating policies and forging public support for them. Hence it is quite possible to paint political parties, not as undermining responsible government, but as breathing life into parliamentary government and the electoral process. This alternative view has been described as 'responsible party government' (Lucy, 1993).

The question of whether parties facilitate the functioning of the parliamentary system points to a further lesson about political institutions: they should not be viewed in isolation from one another. Consider the extra-parliamentary structure of the major parties as a case in point. The Liberal and Labor parties each consist of a coalition of separate state branches. Members — including affiliate unions in the case of the ALP — join individual state branches and not a national party. State branches (called divisions in the Liberal Party) typically have different rules and organisations as well as different political histories and records of electoral success. Often they focus upon state-level rather than national politics and are dominated by people with parochial rather than national interests. Whereas the national ALP is empowered to intervene in the running of state Labor branches and its biennial National Conference decides party policy, the federal Liberal party organisation exercises (since 1994) limited authority over the various state divisions, which are all formally autonomous. Of course, neither party is divided simply along state–federal lines. Each contains those factional and ideological divisions to be expected in mass parties that assemble diverse interests under the one organisational umbrella. But the parties' state-based organisational structures testify to the shaping influence of Australia's federal system upon them.

PRESSURE GROUPS

The federal system is similarly reflected in the organisation of a great many pressure groups. Pressure groups, or organisations that seek to influence policy decisions without attempting to capture government as parties do, are a ubiquitous feature of Australian politics. There are literally thousands, ranging from large, established national lobbies — for example, the National Farmers' Federation (NFF), the Australian Council of Social Service and the Australian Council of Trade Unions (ACTU) — to relatively small, loosely organised and often transient neighbourhood action groups. The imprint of federalism is most evident upon larger, established pressure groups. For example, most individual trade unions are federations of state-based organisations. Collectively unions form trades and labour councils at state level, and come together at the national level to form the ACTU peak association. Farmers' groups are similarly divided, forming separate state-based organisations, which are united at the national level by the NFF. This federal organisational arrangement, which is typical of many pressure groups, is to be expected of associations that may have to defend their interests by dealing with state governments in some instances, and the Commonwealth in others.

There are many different kinds of pressure groups. Sectional groups such as the Australian Medical Association mostly defend the narrow interests of their members, while promotional groups such as Greenpeace or the Women's Electoral Lobby have broader objectives. Some are wholly political organisations, whereas others (for example the Royal Automobile Club of Queensland and its sister state automobile associations) are not. Some, but not others, are insider groups welcomed by and having regular contact with policy makers. Some (usually promotional) groups will be transient and disappear when their cause is won or lost, while other (usually sectional) groups are permanent organisations. And of course pressure groups vary widely in the financial, membership, media interest and other resources that they can muster. Some wield considerable power. This is especially true of producer groups comprising professional associations and established business, union and primary industry groups whose strategic economic importance has enabled them to forge close links with government.

The influence that pressure groups — especially producer groups such as the Business Council of Australia, Australian Medical Association, Australian Mining Council or ACTU — can have over governments and particular areas of policy-making arguably weakens the chain of accountability. Mostly pressure groups pursue minority, sectional interests. Few are publicly accountable, and their influence over areas of public policy may not always be visible. Thus they can be viewed as exerting undesirable pressure and distorting the processes of representative government. However, pressure groups can also be seen to assist good government. Some may voice alternatives and scrutinise a government's actions, or educate and mobilise popular opinion and involvement in policy-making. Competition between groups to influence public policy can also encourage the representation and reconciliation of diverse interests. Further, pressure groups can be a source of valuable specialist knowledge about the policy areas and questions with which they are concerned, and this explains why groups will cluster around and, in some instances, forge ongoing links with particular public service departments.

THE PUBLIC SERVICE

Westminster theory paints the public service as politically neutral, and able to advise and serve any government regardless of its political complexion. In fact the 18 departments (in which most of Australia's 170 000 federal public servants work) often have policy 'lines' or preferences, which they promote whenever the opportunity presents. The close consultative relations that business, professional and primary industry producer groups have established with individual departments is one reason for this. Departments may voice the interests of sectional groups with whom they consult and work closely. Equally, departmental lines can also reflect the professional judgments that their own officers make. Proposals to change a policy usually spring from public servants' knowledge of its shortcomings while administering it. Against the theory of responsible government, there is no neat division between the making of policy and its implementation, and senior public servants are routinely involved in deciding as well as administering policy. It should not be surprising that firmly held departmental policy preferences will be vigorously defended in the policy-making process against other departments and even against responsible ministers. Although journalists in the press gallery who report federal politics give it too little attention, bureau-cratic politics, in which departments lobby and themselves behave as quasi-pressure groups, often has an important bearing upon the poli-cies that governments adopt.

The sheer complexity of many policy areas and the inevitable reliance of 'amateur' ministers upon the advice of expert public servants suggests a further weak link in the chain of accountability. But again, the picture is more complex. The public service is certainly not monolithic. For example, Treasury, the Department of Finance and the Department of the Prime Minister and Cabinet each have key coordinating roles (see Aitkin, Jinks and Warhurst, 1989, pp.225–8), which often places them in conflict with other departments wishing to press policy changes. Fur-thermore, many policy proposals have implications for a number of departments with cognate administrative areas and are formulated in detail by interdepartmental committees, and hence the influence of individual departments is checked by the involvement of others in the policy-making process itself. Given Australia's federal structure and public service duplication at the state level, policy initiatives may some-times even have to be worked out in conjunction with state public service departments. During the mid-1980s the Labor Government introduced a series of major managerial reforms to the public service. These included the introduction of fixed terms for department secretaries (formerly 'permanent heads') to ensure the rotation of public servant chiefs from department to department, as well as provision for the involvement of ministers (via cabinet) in the appointment of secre-taries with whom they must closely work. A related reform established the Senior Executive Service as a pool of senior officials who, instead of serving out their careers within individual departments, might be switched between departments to encourage service-wide rather than departmental loyalties. The full effect of these reforms remains to be seen, but it is clear that they were aimed at least in part at breaking old public service fiefdoms and restoring the political authority of min-isters vis-à-vis public servants. In 1987 the Government exercised its pre-rogative to arrange the public service into departments suited to its particular policy priorities. Many of the 'mega' departments created were placed under the joint control of senior and junior ministers in a further experiment to bolster ministerial authority. These changes to the public service and its relations with the government underline a further important lesson: political institutions are not immutable and do evolve and change over time.

CHANGE AND REFORM

The tour guides who usher visitors around the new Parliament House are wont to emphasise that it is the people's building — that it houses the people's parliament. However the building has a further, and quite different symbolic significance, which the guides do not remark upon. For example, it has a masculine feel and symbolises the gender imbalance that is a fact of Australian political life. Suits and ties are the common form of dress. The portraits that adorn the building are mostly of men. (There has only been one female Speaker and never a woman prime minister). The doors are heavy. It contains a gym for the use of members but not a childcare facility. The debates, which visitors may see from the galleries — especially in the House of Representatives, and at Question Time — are combative. In fact most of the parliamentarians occupying Parliament House are men. Only 13 of the 147 MHRs elected in 1993 were women. In this sense the House of Representatives is quite unrepresentative of the wider population. So too is the upper house, in which four in every five Senators are male, and inevitably, so is the ministry whose members are drawn from parliament.

Despite the celebrated presence of politicians such as Bronwyn Bishop and Carmen Lawrence, the Liberals and the ALP have in the past been reluctant to endorse female candidates. Both parties now profess to have remedied this and to have in place schemes that should see them stand more women candidates in safe seats. Nonetheless, it is likely to be some time before the gender imbalance in parliament is corrected. The fact that parliament does not mirror the diversity of Australia's multicultural society can also be traced to the failure of the major parties to embrace many of the ethnic communities now found in Australian cities. Of course the major parties are able to act as gatekeepers and to effectively control who sits in parliament only insofar as most Australians continue not to vote for independent and minor party candidates. However, in the 1993 election voters in Wills and North Sydney did return independent candidates to the House of Representatives. But it is unlikely that this rare event marks a new trend, which, were it to continue, would undo the system of responsible party government.

Far more so than in the old building, the layout of the new Parliament House (in which ministers are housed in a separate wing) clearly separates the executive arm of government from the legislative. In a sense this separation symbolises the removal of parliament's influence in the process of government. As we have seen, because of the party discipline that binds most members of the House of Representatives, parliament is largely reduced to rubber stamping cabinet decisions. The development of disciplined mass political parties has expanded the power exercised by cabinet and by the prime minister. Similarly, the great expansion of the public service and its involvement in ever more complex policy-making has also marginalised parliament and consolidated the power of the executive. So too has the proliferation of professional lobbyists and pressure groups seeking to influence policy-makers beyond parliament, and indeed the development of news and current affairs media which have largely usurped parliament's place as the chief forum for public debate of policy issues. The exception remains the Senate in circumstances where the ruling party does not have an upper house majority and cannot control the outcome of its deliberations.

The power wielded by the prime minister and cabinet means in practice that the government, rather than parliament, is the key to political reform. In the House of Representatives the government is able to press through amendments to the Standing Orders as it did in 1994 when it decided to restrict the interrogation of ministers during Question Time to those rostered to attend. Of course some political reforms require legislative change and must be negotiated through the Senate — as were the Hawke government's 1983 amendments to the Electoral Act, which introduced public election funding and created the independent Australian Electoral Commission to administer the electoral system. Very occasionally a government lacking a Senate majority in its own right may be forced to pursue reforms that it might not otherwise have — as happened in 1994 when the Democrats forced the Keating government to introduce new rules for ministerial accountability as a price for their not supporting an Opposition-sponsored Senate inquiry into the 'sports rorts' affair. Nor do governments have complete control over political reforms that require the formal amendment of the Constitution. For these must be put to a referendum and, to be passed, must secure both an overall majority vote and be endorsed by voters in a majority of states. It should also be noted that a government's reform agenda is less likely to be driven by altruism than a search for political advantage. Witness Prime Minister Keating's active encouragement of the republican debate.

A REPUBLICAN AUSTRALIA?

Keating's suggestion that Australia should mark the new century by becoming a republic has transformed the giant Australian flag that flies above the new Parliament House into a symbol of reform — and of resistance. Of course, in the flag's corner is a Union Jack. This is a reminder of historic ties with Britain, which resulted in Australia being formally constituted as a monarchy. Thus the Australian head of state is a governor-general who represents the Queen, the Queen is formally part of parliament, and the constitutional basis of the authority that prime minister and cabinet wield via the executive council is that of the Crown. This is an arrangement in which some Australians find solace — and others a spur to press for changes that would see Australia reborn as a republic.

Transforming Australia into a republic will be no easy task. To make even the minimal republican gesture of replacing the governor-general with a head of state who directly represents Australians will require that extensive changes be made to the Constitution. This will provide ample scope for those who wish to preserve the status quo to find sticking points. And history's lesson is that referenda proposals that do not have bipartisan support (or that stir powerful state premiers to action) are doomed to fail. It is ironic that any attempt to transform Australia into a republic will probably ultimately fail the test of section 128 of the Constitution. For, despite the intensity of debate between monarchists and republicans, Australia is already a de facto republic — in part because of section 128. This constitutionally entrenches the core republican principle of the primacy of popular sovereignty. (It stipulates that arrangement of government set down in the Constitution can only be altered with the express approval of the people voting in a referendum.) And of course, for all its limitations, Australia's present parliamentary system also provides for popular sovereignty in that it allows voters to periodically decide who should govern them.

CONCLUSION

Perhaps the lesson here is that we need to look beyond the formal arrangement of government and behind Westminster theory. Clearly Australia's political institutions have demonstrated both a resilience and a capacity to accommodate change. Parliament is an obvious case in point. In its new abode on Capital Hill it continues traditions and practices with which the politicians who assembled in Melbourne in 1901 to sit as Australia's first federal parliament would have been quite familiar. Yet, despite this continuity with the past, parliament is a much

Figure 1.2 Breakdown in the 'chain of accountability'

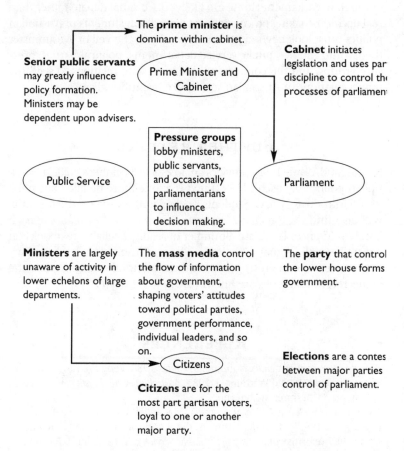

changed institution. It now dances to the tune called by prime ministers and cabinet — not vice versa. It is now dominated by disciplined political parties which ensure that governments are no longer made and unmade with the ease of former colonial parliaments and federal parliament during its first decade.

Theoretically, parliament is a principal link in the chain of accountability that connects the various key political institutions at the heart of Australia's national government. In practice, parliament has a lesser and largely symbolic importance. In short it is a vehicle through which the exercise of political power is legitimised, rather than a locus of power itself (see Figure 1.2). Just as the visitors to the public galleries of the new Parliament House are likely to see ritual debate rather than real decision-making processes being played out, students of Australian politics must look beyond parliament and past the veil of Westminster theory into cabinet, public service departments, political parties, pressure groups, and the complexity of federal–state relations to see how power relations in Australian society are institutionalised.

FURTHER READING

Stewart and Ward (1992) provides an accessible 'beginner's guide' to Australian politics. Jaensch's (1992) text is a little more detailed but still a useful introductory text. Students reading in this area for the first time will also find the *Penguin Macquarie Dictionary of Australian Politics* a handy reference. There are a number of readily available textbooks on Australian politics that examine parliament, cabinet, federalism, parties, pressure (or interest) groups and the electoral system. Two of the better recent textbooks are Smith (1992) and Lucy (1993).

REFERENCES

Penguin Macquarie Dictionary of Australian Politics 1988, Penguin, Ringwood, Vic.
Aitkin, D., Jinks, B. and Warhurst, J. 1989, *Australian Political Institutions*, 4th edn, Longman Cheshire, Melbourne.
Jaensch, D. 1992, *The Politics of Australia*, Macmillan Education, Melbourne.
Keating, M. 1993, 'Mega-departments: the theory, objectives and outcomes of the 1987 reforms', in *Reforming the Public Service*, eds, P. Weller, J. Forster and G. Davis, Macmillan, Melbourne.
Lucy, R. 1993, *The Australian Form of Government*, 2nd edn, Macmillan, Melbourne.
McAllister, I. and Bean, C. 1990, 'Explaining Labor's victory', in *The Greening of Australian Politics*, eds, C. Bean, I. McAllister and J. Warhurst, Longman Cheshire, Melbourne.
Smith, R. (ed.) 1992, *Politics in Australia*, 2nd edn, Allen and Unwin, Sydney.
Stewart, R. and Ward, I. 1992, *Politics One*, Macmillan, Melbourne.
Summers, J. 1990, 'Parliament and responsible government in Australia', in *Government, Politics and Power in Australia*, 4th edn, eds, J. Summers, D. Woodward and A. Parkin, Longman Cheshire, Melbourne.

2

STATE GOVERNMENT

....

Brian Costar

With the collapse of the Soviet Union and the tragic breakdown of the former Yugoslavia, Australia belongs to that shrinking band of nations whose political system is based on the federal principle — the others include the United States, Canada, Germany, Malaysia, India, Switzerland and Mexico.

Federalism involves a division of powers between a central government and regional governments where each tier of government retains certain functions on which it makes 'final decisions' (Riker, 1975, p. 101). The mere occurrence of two levels of administration does not alone create federalism: the United Kingdom has a central government and local government authorities but is a unitary state (the opposite of federalism) because the parliament at Westminster can exercise ultimate power over local government. Similarly, despite the fact that they too operate two tiers of government, the Australian states are not mini-federations because their local authorities are ultimately subservient to their state cabinets and parliaments. A minimum requirement for federalism is that both tiers of government must retain a degree of autonomous decision-making. Debates as to the appropriate boundaries of the relative autonomies have been central to the history of Australian federalism.

When Australia's tortuous journey to national unity ended with federation in 1901, the then six self-governing 'colonies' of New South

Wales, Victoria, Queensland, South Australia, Western Australia and Tasmania attained the status of 'states'. The option to dissolve the colonies as political units and to remodel the structure of regional government was never seriously contemplated. Rather, the constitutional apparatus of the colonies was transferred to the states to operate contiguously with the new central parliament and government. What did change was the allocation of certain specific powers to the new Commonwealth parliament by way of section 51 of the Constitution. While the scope of those, originally very limited, powers was to expand dramatically throughout the century, the physical contours of the Australian Federation have, by contrast, altered little since 1901.

The Commonwealth relieved South Australia of the burden of administering what is now the Northern Territory in 1911 and the Australian Capital Territory was excised from New South Wales to provide both the national capital and the permanent home of the federal parliament — which moved there from Melbourne in 1927. Despite the preamble to the Constitution speaking of 'one indissoluble Federal Commonwealth', the electors of Western Australia voted in 1933 in favour of that state seceding from the union, only to be thwarted by legal and constitutional technicalities. Section 121 of the Constitution provides for the creation of new states but none has yet emerged. Northern Queensland has long sustained a new state movement and in 1965 a concerted effort to establish a new state in the New England area of New South Wales controversially failed to win support at a plebiscite. The only foreseeable change to the geography of Australian federalism is the possibility that the Northern Territory might be granted statehood. If it were, it would not be an 'original' state in the terms of the Constitution and thus would not be entitled to a minimum of five members in the House of Representatives or to an equality of Senate representation with the other states.

STATE POLITICAL HISTORY

It is axiomatic that the contemporary politics of the states are much influenced by their economies, demographies and political histories. Space does not permit detailed accounts of the histories of the six states, but a comparison of Victoria and Queensland reveals just how much diversity is possible within a basically similar constitutional context.

Tables 2.1 and 2.2 provide data on the formation and defeat of governments in Victoria and Queensland for the period stretching from the First World War to the present. Some startling contrasts are evident. Before the 1950s, Victorian politics was chronically unstable with no government possessing an absolute majority on the floor of the Legislative Assembly between 1923 and 1952; whereas, in Queensland, every government has achieved such a majority — remembering that between 1957 and 1983 it required a coalition between two parties to

Table 2.1 Victorian Governments 1914–94

Years	Majority government	Minority governments	Coalition governments
1914–15	Peacock(LP)		
1915–17		Peacock(Lib)ALP	
1917–18	Bowser(Nat)		
1918–23	Lawson(Nat)		
1923–24			Lawson/Allan(Nat/CP)
1924		Lawson(Nat) + CP	
1924		Peacock(Nat) + CP	
1924		Prendergast(ALP) + CP	
1924–27			Allan/Peacock(CP/Nat)
1927–28		Hogan(ALP) + CPP	
1928–29		McPherson(NAT + CP)	
1929–32		Hogan(ALP) + CP	
1932–35			Argyle/Allan(UAP/CP)
1935–43		Dunstan(CP) + ALP	
1943 (4 days)		Cain(ALP)	
1943–45			Dunstan/Holloway (CP/UAP)
1945		MacFarlan(LP) + CP	
1945–47		Cain(ALP) + CP	
1947–48			Hollway/McDonald (LP/CP)
1948–50		Hollway(LP) + CP	
1950–52		McDonald(CP) + ALP	
1952 (3 days)		Hollway(ERL)	
1952 (2 months)		McDonald(CP)	
from 1914–52 (38 Years)	*6 years*	*22 years*	*10 years*
1952–55	Cain(ALP)		
1955–72	Bolte(LCP/LP)		
1972–81	Hamer(LP)		
1981–82	Thompson(LP)		
1982–90	Cain(ALP)		
1990–92	Kirner(ALP)		
1992			Kennett/McNamara (LP/Nat)
from 1952–92 (40 years)	*39 years*	*0 years*	*2 years*

Notes: ALP — Australian Labor Party
CP — Country Party
CPP — Country Progressive Party
ERL — Electoral Reform Liberals
LP — Liberal Party
LCP — Liberal and Country Party (the Victorian Liberal Party's name 1949–65)

Nat — Nationalist Party
UAP — United Australia Party
+ ALP(etc) — refers to the party giving regular support to the government. Governments of very brief duration often lacked such support.

Table 2.2 Queensland Government 1914–94

Year	Majority governments	Minority governments	Coalition
1911–15	Denham(LP)		
1915–19	Ryan(ALP)		
1919–25	Theodore(ALP)		
1925	Gillies(ALP)		
1925–29	McCormack(ALP)		
1929–32	Moore(CPNP)		
1932–42	Forgan Smith(ALP)		
1942–46	Cooper(ALP)		
1946–52	Hanlon(ALP)		
1952–57	Gair(ALP)		
1957–68			Nicklin(CP/LP)
1968			Pizzey(CP/LP)
1968			Chalk(LP/CP)
1968–83			Bjelke-Petersen(NP/LP)
1983–88	Bjelke-Petersen(NP)		
1988–89	Ahern(NP)		
1989	Cooper(NP)		
1989–	Goss(ALP)		
81 years	*55 years*	*0 years*	*26 years*

Notes: CPNP — Country Progressive National Party
NP — National Party
The Liberal Party had so many leaders in 1957–83 space does not permit their listing, but Gordon Chalk (1965–76) was the longest serving.

do so. Before 1952 Victorian party politics was both complex and unstable. All three major parties, the Labor Party, the Liberal Party (and its predecessors) and the Country Party were schismatic and were often involved in ideologically bizarre alliances within parliament. The Country Party was a major beneficiary of the inability of any one party to dominate the political scene and was often supported in government by the Labor Party.

In Victoria before the 1950s, while all parties shared in government at one time or another, the Labor Party fared badly: it was in office for relatively short periods, dependent on the support of the Country Party and not able to form a government in its own right until 1952. Queensland politics during the same period was dominated by the ALP, which governed continuously from 1915 to 1957, save for a brief non-Labor interlude from 1929 to 1932. Despite these stark differences, the 1950s were to be a watershed in both Victorian and Queensland politics. Serious splits occurred within the Victorian ALP in 1954–55 and in the Queensland ALP in 1957, which terminated the governments of John Cain Snr and Vince Gair and ushered in long periods of conservative party dominance in both states.

But again differences were obvious: the Victorian Liberal Party ruled alone as a majority government from 1955 to 1982, whereas Queensland was governed by a Country/Liberal Party coalition from 1957 until 1983 when the Country Party (renamed the National Party from 1974) formed a majority government in its own right. The Bjelke-Petersen, Ahern and Cooper governments (1983–89) are the only examples of Country/National Party majority governments in the history of the Australian states.

STATE CONSTITUTIONS

On the eve of Federation (1901) the states had the status of self-governing colonies within the British Empire. They possessed written constitutions derived from that granted by Britain to the colony of New South Wales in 1855. The act of federation wrought no major changes to the states' constitutions and they continued to evolve structurally if not functionally independent of the Australian federal Constitution.

Generally, the states' constitutions are less well-known and attract much less media attention than does the federal Constitution. This is not only because the federal parliament and government are now appreciably more powerful than the states, but also because the state constitutions are, unlike the Commonwealth's, relatively easy to amend. When colonial politicians debated and drafted the federal Constitution in the 1890s, the majority were determined to render it difficult to amend so as to protect 'state rights' against central encroachment. What emerged was section 128, which requires that for the text of the Constitution to be amended a plebiscite (referendum) must be approved by a majority of electors in a majority of states.

The state constitutions, by comparison, are much more flexible documents, amendable in the most part by legislative action alone. To alter the wording of a state Constitution, a suitably drafted Bill must pass both houses of parliament by absolute majorities. There are some exceptions to this flexibility: in New South Wales the Legislative Council may not be abolished unless approved by a popular referendum, whereas in Queensland the upper house cannot be restored save by a similar process.

Also, when the Queensland government wished to extend the duration of parliament from three to four years in 1990 it was required to put a referendum to the electors who rejected it. By contrast, parliamentary terms were extended in Victoria and New South Wales during the 1980s without the need to directly consult the people. The requirement to amend some sections of some state constitutions by referendum is referred to as an 'entrenchment' provision. Once adopted, such an entrenchment cannot itself be amended by legislation alone. It must be put to referendum.

One similarity between the state and federal constitutions is that, unlike their United States equivalent, they enshrine relatively few positive rights or liberties. Queensland, however, has recently been the most active state in the area of constitutional review. The Electoral and Administrative Review Commission (EARC) in 1993 issued a Report on Consolidation and Review of the Queensland Constitution which advocated the establishment of a Constitutional Convention to draft a new constitution and, in the same year, completed an extensive inquiry recommending the adoption of a wide-ranging Queensland Bill of Rights.

In the future the state constitutions will certainly require alteration in the event that Australia adopts a republican form of government. Federal republicanism might not, however, automatically devolve to the states. Elizabeth II, as well as being Queen of Australia, is also Queen of New South Wales, Tasmania and so on. It may be technically possible then for one or more states to utilise their constitutional autonomy to continue as micro-monarchies within a republican federal structure. Politically this seems unlikely. First, if a republican referendum were to succeed in all states it would be difficult for the government of any of them to retain monarchism. Second, the republican referendum could contain a clause that compelled the states to abandon the practice whereby the Queen appoints governors. Finally, in the event that the Commonwealth and a majority of states opted for republicanism, neither the British monarch nor the British government would relish being embroiled in domestic Australian politics by being seen to support one or two 'rebel' monarchical states.

Political impediments aside, state transition to republicanism could be achieved relatively easily: even the current entrenchment of the office of governor in Queensland and Tasmania is not an insurmountable problem. While of doubtless symbolic significance, the adoption of 'minimalist' republicanism would not significantly alter the essentials of the machinery of state government (Republic Advisory Committee, 1993, ch. 8).

POLITICAL PARTIES

Not only do the states possess their own competitive party systems, but also the federal party system itself remains in many respects state-based. If Hague and Harrap (1987, p.146) are correct in their contention that whoever controls candidate selection in competitive parties controls the party as a whole, then the power brokers of the Australian parties are to be found in the state organisations. This is particularly true of the Liberal and National Parties whose federal instrumentalities struggle to exert more than moral pressure on the state organisations' prerogatives in selecting both federal and state parliamentary candidates. Only in the Labor Party, which was for long the most 'federalist' of the parties, has its federal executive effectively intervened in state branches to influence candidate selection.

Perhaps because Australian federalism is structurally and not culturally based, persistent, distinctly regional parties are not features of our political system. The federal contest between the Labor Party and a coalition of the Liberal and National Parties (or the Liberal Party acting alone) is replicated in the states, though with some discernible regional variations. New South Wales most closely resembles the federal pattern with government alternating between Labor and the Coalition. A similar pattern is evident in Victoria, although the Coalition agreement dates only from 1990, before which the Liberal and National Parties were keen competitors. Western Australia also has a long history of competition between Labor and the Coalition.

The remaining three states, however, exhibit significant deviations from the norm. Tasmania has not possessed a viable Country/National Party at state level since the 1920s and in South Australia the non-Labor parties blended into the Liberal Country League in 1932. While the Country Party re-emerged in that state in the early 1960s, it did not prove electorally successful with the current party contest in South Australia being between Liberal and Labor. Queensland, of course, is the most interesting exception to the national pattern, since from 1957 to 1983 the senior Coalition partner was the National (Country) Party and when the Coalition broke up in acrimony in 1983 it was the

National Party that emerged as the government — albeit assisted by the defection of two Liberal politicians. Despite being the major non-Labor party federally and in all other states, the Liberal Party in Queensland with only nine members in a parliament of 89 remains very much a minority party.

The current uniformity of party competition in the states as shown in Table 2.3 was not always so and earlier party systems were much more complex. This complexity was often the product of party schisms and gave rise to distinctly state-entitled parties. For example, during the mid-1940s and early 1950s the 'Liberal Party' was sometimes named the Queensland People's Party in Queensland, the Democratic Party in New South Wales, the Liberal and Country Party in Victoria, the Liberal Country League in South Australia, and the Liberal Party in Western Australia and Tasmania. The Country Party also operated under different names in different states and even as late as 1974 was known as the National Country Party in the federal parliament, the National Party in Queensland, Victoria and Tasmania, the National Alliance in Western Australia and the Country Party in New South Wales.

Labor, while more uniform in title, has also contributed in the past to the diversity of state party systems. A split over economic policy in 1931 produced the Lang Labor Party, which was influential in New South Wales politics for more than a decade. The more serious schism of the mid-1950s produced the Democratic Labor Party, which remained

Table 2.3 Status of parties in Australia's lower houses as at latest general election

	Election	ALP seats	LP seats	NP seats	Other seats
Commonwealth	1993	80	49	16	2
New South Wales	1991	46	30	19	4
Victoria	1992	27	52	9	0
Queensland	1992	54	9	26	0
South Australia	1993	10	37	0	0
Western Australia	1993	24	26	6	1
Tasmania	1992	11	19	0	5
Northern Territory	1994	7	17*	0	1
Australian Capital Territory	1992	8	6	0	3

*These seats are held by the Country Liberal Party

robust in Victoria and Queensland until the 1970s and contributed significantly to Labor remaining out of government in those states and on two occasions (1961 and 1969) its second preferences denied Labor federal office.

Organisationally the major parties operate broadly similar structures in each state, tempered by relatively minor local variations. Typically, the ALP possesses a state conference comprised of 60 per cent of delegates from affiliated trade unions and 40 per cent from party branches. An administrative committee or state executive meeting monthly attends to the functioning of the party between conferences. A full-time secretary, supported by assistants and organisers, operates the day-to-day affairs of the party. Factionalism is endemic in the state branches of the ALP and, while in all states it is based on a left versus right ideological contest, the factions are not uniform across all states. Victoria, long regarded as possessing the most highly organised factional system, has four factions — Labor Unity, Socialist Left, Pledge and Independents. Factional titles and structures reflect both the efforts of the ALP's federal executive to restructure branches and local political conditions. For example, in Queensland the Australian Workers Union is sufficiently powerful to be a dominant factional player in its own right. Even the development of 'national factions' within the federal ALP caucus has not prevented the state branches from maintaining their own distinctive factional arrangements.

The Liberal Party's extra-parliamentary organisation has proved unable to exercise consistent control over its parliamentarians, though its state branches have enjoyed more success than has its federal executive. Typically, a state division of the Liberal Party possesses a conference or state council meeting at least once a year and a state executive assembling on a more regular basis. The usual office bearers — president etc — are supplemented by a paid state director who fulfils the functions of party secretary. One issue that has divided state divisions of the Liberal Party over the past decade is the preferred method of candidate selection. Traditionally the Liberal Party has devolved the power to select parliamentary candidates to local branches. Provoked by poor electoral performances federally and in a number of states, some Liberal divisions sought to extend the influence of the state executive over candidate selection. The issue proved divisive as local branches used their status at state conference/council to thwart the would-be reformers. After a prolonged battle and much compromise, the Victorian division adopted procedures that gave the statewide organisation greater influence in candidate selection. But not all other divisions have followed suit, and the issue remains particularly contentious in New South Wales.

The National Party has historically sought to tread a middle path between Labor and Liberal on the issue of organisational control of politicians. Annual National Party state conferences are large gatherings with executive functions being discharged by central/state councils. Candidate selection remains very much in the hands of locals and the National Party generally lacks the ideological diversity evident in the other major parties, though the Queensland branch in the 1980s stands out as an exception to this generalisation with 'Country Party' traditionalists doing battle with neo-conservative, moral-majoritarians.

ELECTORAL PROCEDURES

Elections and electoral systems are central to a representative democracy and the Australian states have, at various times, employed a wide variety of electoral systems for their parliaments. Australia's federal electoral system involves 147 single-member constituencies for the House of Representatives and a multi-member, proportional representation system for the Senate. Voting is compulsory for Australian citizens 18 years and older and a preferential method is employed for both chambers.

The essentials of the federal systems are present in many of the states, but variations are also observable. All states require compulsory voting (at 18 years) for both their upper and lower houses. The Liberal government in South Australia (elected in 1993) has introduced a Bill for voluntary voting; however, it is unlikely to pass the Legislative Council, which is controlled by the ALP and the Australian Democrats. Also New South Wales Liberal premier, John Fahey, indicated in 1994 a desire to revert to voluntary voting in an attempt to reduce the number of independents in the New South Wales parliament. His motives were perceived as rather too partisan and no legislation has been introduced. Soon after his election in late 1992, Liberal premier Kennett of Victoria was also eager to abolish compulsory voting, but retreated in the face of strong opposition from Coalition backbenchers uneasy about the electoral effects of the proposed change.

Preferential voting is employed by the six states, but New South Wales and Queensland require voters to number only as many squares on the ballot paper as there are places to be filled (optional preferential voting) whereas the other states require the rank ordering of all candidates. New South Wales, Western Australia and South Australia elect their Legislative Councils by proportional representation methods broadly similar to the Senate's. Despite five separate attempts by Labor governments in the 1980s, Victoria retains a compulsory preferential method for its upper house, electing two members each from 22 electoral provinces for staggered, eight-year terms.

Tasmania has long been the deviant state in regard to electoral procedures. Since 1907 it has employed a quota preferential, proportional system to choose its lower house. Moreover, it employs the five federal electoral divisions as state boundaries (as did Victoria from 1953 to 1965) with seven members chosen from each. Ironically, Tasmania operates a non-proportional, preferential system for its upper house. Liberal premier, Ray Groom, provoked controversy in late 1993 when he proposed legislation to reduce the size of the House of Assembly from 35 to 30. Groom's objective, like Fahey's, seems to have been to enhance the likelihood that the parliament would always be under the control of one of the major parties. The strength of Green and Independent support in Tasmania sustained a public campaign against the proposed reduction and it has been shelved.

Perhaps the most prolonged controversy involving state electoral systems has been the practice of all of them (except Tasmania) to submit to the temptation to over-represent rural areas in their parliaments. Known as malapportionment, this practice involves allocating smaller numbers of voters to electorates in rural areas than in urban areas. Its clear and often partisan objective is to create more rural electorates than would occur under a system in which every electorate contained an equal (or near-equal) number of voters. One popular method of ensuring rural vote weightage has been to divide a state into different electoral zones and then to allocate those zones different quotas of voters to be included in each seat. Historically, South Australia and Victoria were the worst offenders in regard to malapportionment, but by the 1980s most attention was centred on Queensland.

Since 1949 Queensland has operated a complex and controversial system of electoral zones, which first were said to benefit the ALP and later the National Party. The so-called Queensland 'gerrymander' was identified with the controversial premiership of Joh Bjelke-Petersen and was trenchantly criticised by Commissioner Tony Fitzgerald in his 1989 report dealing with police and political corruption in Queensland. One problem for those keen to criticise the Queensland zonal system was that, on the first occasion since 1956 that the ALP won an absolute

majority of votes (1989), it won a landslide victory — a victory replicated in 1992 under completely revised electoral procedures. This evidence suggests that the partisan impact of the Queensland zonal system
was not as great as some imagined and that preferential voting was
more important to successive National Party victories.

Before the 1989 state election all three political parties pledged to legislate the outcome of an EARC review of Queensland's electoral procedures. Predictably EARC recommended the abolition of the electoral
zones and their replacement by a single, statewide quota of electors for
each seat. Less predictably (and controversially), EARC permitted a small
level of vote weightage for remote electorates that exceeded 100 000
square kilometres in area. Queensland's electoral boundaries were then
substantially redrawn, but this neither advantaged nor disadvantaged
the Labor Party, which repeated its 1989 result at the 1992 election.

Currently only Western Australia (despite reforms in the 1980s) now
malapportions its lower house to any significant degree, but recent election results do not support the charge that any major party is system-
atically disadvantaged; though Labor's 1993 defeat was less severe than
it might have been because of the party's retention of mining and pastoral seats that are the beneficiaries of rural weightage. One may contrast the 1993 Western Australian result with the 1993 South Australian
election where, in the absence of serious vote weightage, the Labor
government was defeated in a landslide.

PARLIAMENT

The legislatures of the states (colonies), simply because they long pre-
dated federation, provided the model for the new central legislature
created in 1901. The colonial parliaments, in turn, had been created
as antipodean versions of Westminster, although they soon adopted
some procedures different from those of the British parliament. By
1901 all the state legislatures were bicameral — that is, they consisted
of an upper and a lower house — and were elected by limited popular suffrage (though many of the upper houses were decidedly less
democratic than the lower houses, with the New South Wales Legislative Council not adopting direct elections until as recently as 1978).
They also manifested the Westminster tradition of 'responsible government', whereby the political executive consisted of that group of
ministers which could assemble majority support on the floor of the
lower house.

Modern state parliaments are beset by many of the problems that are encountered in the federal arena. Executive dominance of the lower chamber (generally called Legislative Assemblies in the states) is a perennial complaint. By definition, state governments must be capable of 'controlling' their lower houses. This means that they are able to utilise their majority status to constrain parliamentary — in practice Opposition — scrutiny of executive action. The traditional methods by which the legislature may hold the executive accountable such as question time, grievance debates, censure and no confidence motions are provided for in the standing orders of most state parliaments, but their effectiveness is often limited, provided the government's parliamentary majority is secure.

While it is true that state premiers of all political persuasion will readily sacrifice parliamentary conventions in favour of political expediency, the very real problem of executive dominance needs to be kept in perspective. Excessively strong legislatures can be as problematic as domineering executives. To hark back to Table 2.3, the period from 1945 to 1952 was a highly unstable one in Victorian politics since no group could permanently secure a parliamentary majority and governments were regularly defeated on the floor of either the Legislative Assembly or Council. Contemporaries complained that this excessive alternation of government impeded sustained, consistent policy development and administration, and transferred too much power to the bureaucracy.

Also it cannot always be assumed that the government of the day always enjoys a lower house majority in its own right. Until recently, majoritarian electoral systems and robust party discipline seemed to have rendered minority governments a thing of the distant past in Australian politics. Yet in 1992 the New South Wales, Western Australian, South Australian and ACT governments all depended on independent members' votes to maintain them in office, thereby making them more than usually sensitive to parliamentary scrutiny. If the picture is widened to encompass political alignments in the upper houses, only the Queensland and Northern Territory governments 'controlled' their parliaments in 1992.

While conceding that this is not usual for Australian parliamentary politics, it does serve as a reminder that governments often dominate the Assemblies but face hostile majorities in the Councils. Legislative Councils were adopted by all colonies in the nineteenth century to represent property interests and to curb 'radical democratic' legislation passed by the Assembly. Modern upper houses have altered their rationale to being 'houses of review', yet they remain powerful players in state politics in two major respects. First, the Legislative Councils of Victoria, Western Australia, South Australia and Tasmania have the power to impede supply (money) bills in ways that may force a dissolution of the lower house. The last time a Legislative Council did so was in 1952 (in Victoria), but the threat has been issued to effect on a number of occasions since.

Legislative Councils have displayed much less reticence in exercising their powers to amend or reject general government legislation of which they disapprove. In such contests between state governments and upper houses, it is usually the latter that holds the whip hand, largely because no state Constitution contains an exact equivalent of the federal double dissolution provision by which a premier might threaten a truculent upper house with an early election. (The South Australian Constitution contains a 'double dissolution' provision, but the Assembly and Council may only be simultaneously dissolved following a separate Assembly election.) In this respect, at least, the Legislative Councils are more powerful than the federal Senate.

The premier of Queensland is alone in not having to cope with a Legislative Council because the Labor government of Ted Theodore abolished the upper chamber in 1922. No other state has followed suit, but a Labor administration in New South Wales sponsored a referendum to abolish the Council in 1961 which failed to pass. It is interesting to note that when the federal parliament established the legislatures of both the Northern Territory (1978) and the Australian Capital Territory (1988), a unicameral structure was chosen in preference to a bicameral one.

The most significant recent change in the balance of power between the upper and lower houses of the state parliaments has occurred in Victoria. Before 1937, Victoria had no constitutional provisions for resolving deadlocks between the two houses: in that year it adopted a set of procedures that was so complex and so favoured the Council that it was never utilised. In 1984 the Cain Labor government, with the support of the Liberal and National Parties, reformed the deadlock provisions by extending the maximum term of the Legislative Assembly to four years, the first three of which were fixed in such a manner that Council rejection of 'supply' would not produce an early election. Given the history of bicameral relations in Victoria this was a major reform, though it retained the power of the Council to reject or amend other Bills and leaves uncertain the powers of the Council to force an Assembly election during the fourth year of its term.

EXECUTIVE GOVERNMENT

Powers of governors

The structures of the executive arms of government in the states are, in most major respects, identical to those operating at the federal level. A non-elected governor discharges official functions on the advice of ministers possessing the confidence of the lower house. The premier is the chief minister and is, in effect, the head of government. Ministers convene regularly in cabinet meetings to consider draft legislation and to coordinate the overall political strategy of the government.

Governors, while legally central to both the executive and legislative operations of the states, have become largely ceremonial in function. However, as the dismissal of Prime Minister Whitlam by Governor-General Kerr in 1975 revealed, governors-general, and by extension governors, retain significant uncodified reserve powers. These powers relate to the appointment and dismissal of ministers and the granting, or not granting, of dissolutions of the lower houses. Controversy arises as to whether and when it is constitutionally proper for a governor to decline the advice of his/her premier and to act independently. Governor Game dismissed New South Wales premier Jack Lang in 1932 and in the late 1940s and early 1950s Victorian governors were regularly required to exercise independent discretion in deciding whether to grant dissolutions and whom to appoint as premier. Yet, as party systems in the states stabilised, governors were only rarely called upon to exercise more than their ceremonial functions. However, two recent case studies from Queensland and Tasmania highlight the potentially complex relationship among governors, premiers and parliament, and illustrate that governors remain more than mere figureheads.

Adverse publicity from the Fitzgerald Inquiry into police corruption combined with a bungled attempt to enter federal parliament in 1987 severely undermined the leadership of long-term Queensland premier, Sir Joh Bjelke-Petersen. In order to stave off a leadership challenge, Sir Joh sought to placate his National Party critics by reluctantly agreeing in October 1987 to resign on 8 August 1988 — the twentieth anniversary of his accession to the premiership. This action appeared to diffuse the situation, but in late November 1987 Sir Joh visited the governor, Sir Walter Campbell, seeking to have five of his senior ministers dismissed from their portfolios. Sir Walter requested that the premier provide him with more information and, utilising extended powers granted to him in 1986 by Bjelke-Petersen, consulted other senior ministers. Eventually, only three ministers were replaced.

Sir Joh's provocative actions precipitated a leadership challenge: he was defeated in the party room as leader of the National Party by Michael Ahern on 26 November 1987. Sir Joh, however, declined to follow convention and resign as premier. Rather, he declared his intention to call parliament in an attempt to secure a majority vote of support. Ahern was adamant that Sir Joh should resign the premiership in his favour and forwarded to the governor a document signed by all National Party members of parliament (except Sir Joh) supporting his leadership. Official letters later made public (*Age*, 17 December, 1988) revealed that Governor Campbell at one stage of the crisis warned Sir Joh that he might not recommission him as premier if he proceeded with a strategy to resign and to reconstruct his ministry by excluding his opponents. The firmness of the governor apparently played a major part in Sir Joh's eventual resignation on 30 November 1988 and the ex-premier bitterly denounced him in his memoirs. The Queen, however, commended Sir Walter for his dextrous handling of the crisis in which he resisted calls to dismiss Sir Joh but, at the same time, facilitated the change in leadership desired by the majority party in parliament (*Australian*, 18 April, 1990).

Tensions between Tasmanian Liberal premier, Robin Gray, and governor Sir Phillip Bennett arose in the wake of the 1989 state election. The incumbent Liberal government lost its majority on the floor of the House of Assembly in an election made notable by the election of five independent Green members who declared publicly their intention to support a minority Labor administration.

Premier Gray refused to resign his commission and convinced the governor to allow him to meet the parliament in a month's time. Speculation ensued that the premier was considering advising the governor to call another election in an attempt to regain his majority. This did not occur: parliament assembled on 28 June, 1989, and debated a no-confidence motion in the government. Robin Gray continued to imply that, despite the likely outcome of the confidence vote, he was still considering advising an early election. The no-confidence motion was carried in the early hours of 29 June; the governor was not required to exercise his prerogative powers to dismiss ministers because Gray tendered his resignation and advised Sir Phillip to commission the Labor leader as premier. Had Gray not resigned at the last minute, the governor would have been within his constitutional rights to dismiss him and commission Michael Field as premier.

Women in executive roles

In recently appointing or electing women to senior positions, the state executives have proved much more progressive than their federal counterpart. Carmen Lawrence became Australia's first female premier in 1990 and was followed a short time later by Joan Kirner in Victoria. While both their Labor governments were severely defeated (Western Australia 1993, Victoria 1992) opinion polls consistently showed them to be much more popular than the parties they led. Earlier, Rosemary Follett had become the ACT's inaugural chief minister in 1989. In March 1994 Carmen Lawrence won the federal seat of Fremantle and was immediately elected to the ministry. The South Australian government in 1991 appointed Dame Roma Mitchell as Australia's first female vice-regal office holder, and Queensland appointed Leneen Forde as its second in 1992. We await the appointment of the first female governor-general and the election of the first female prime minister.

Statutory corporations

A final, important element of the executive and administrative machinery of state politics involves statutory corporations. A statutory corporation is established by parliament to discharge a specified administrative function such as the production and distribution of water, gas or electricity, to name just a few. Traditionally these bodies, while under the ultimate direction of a minister, have enjoyed a greater degree of independence from ministerial control than a normal government department. The rationale behind this arrangement was to lessen the likelihood of inappropriate political interference in the operations of the corporations, particularly those now known as Government Business Enterprises (GBEs), which engage in commercial operations.

One consequence of this arrangement was that some corporations in a number of states grew into large and powerful bodies capable of autonomous political activity — not always to the benefit of the government of the day. Tasmania's Hydro-Electric Commission (HEC) became so dominant in that state's economic and industrial policy-making process that it was often described as the 'real' government of Tasmania. The determination of the HEC in the early 1980s to proceed with the building of a dam on the Franklin River produced a political crisis, which led to the electoral defeat of the Labor government of Doug Lowe. Similarly, the high level of autonomy traditionally accorded the State Banks of South Australia and Victoria allowed them to pursue unsound lending policies, which, in turn, produced financial crises in the early 1990s and contributed significantly to the defeat of the local, Labor state governments. Many state governments are now keen to 'privatise' their GBEs by selling them to private investors.

CONCLUSION: THE FUTURE OF THE STATES

All genuine federal systems involve tension between the central and regional spheres of government. In Australia's case this has occasionally led to calls to abolish the states. Traditionally those most hostile to the states have been on the left of the political spectrum and have expressed frustration at the constraints federalism imposes on national policy-making. More recently, the critics have included so-called 'economic rationalists', impatient at the alleged over-government of Australia and the additional expense caused by the existence of two tiers of admin-istration. While it is undeniable that the states have surrendered to the Commonwealth a great deal of their original economic independence, and with it a significant amount of political power, they remain deeply embedded both within the federal Constitution and Australia's politi-cal culture.

It is difficult to imagine a future federal government risking the polit-ical backlash that would be provoked by a serious campaign to abolish the states. Similarly, it is unlikely that the states will be able to reverse the trend of the past fifty years and recover their former financial inde-pendence. In this regard, at least, the foreseeable future is likely to be rather similar to the present and recent past.

FURTHER READING

Bennett (1992) provides an up-to-date, general account of politics in the states and territories. Galligan's (1986; 1988) more detailed texts deal-ing with both politics and policies are less contemporary than Bennett. Lumb (1991) is a formal, legal analysis of the state constitutions and is best read after Bennett or Galligan. Considine and Costar (1992), Parkin and Patience (1992) and Stevens and Wanna (1993) provide detailed analyses of three recent state governments and contain general mater-ial concerning the processes of state politics.

REFERENCES

Bennett, S. 1992, *Affairs of State: Politics in the Australian States and Territories*, Allen & Unwin, Sydney.

Considine, M. and Costar, B. (eds) 1992, *Trials in Power: Cain, Kirner and Victoria*, Melbourne University Press, Melbourne.

Galligan, B. (ed.) 1986, *Australian State Politics*, Longman Cheshire, Melbourne.

—— (ed) 1988, *Comparative State Politics*, Longman Cheshire, Melbourne.

Hague, R. and Harrap, M. 1987, *Comparative Politics and Government: An Introduction*, Macmillan, London.

Lumb, D. 1991, *The Constitutions of the Australian States*, 5th edn, University of Queensland Press, St Lucia.

Parkin, A. and Patience, A. (eds) 1992, *The Bannon Decade: The Politics of Restraint in South Australia*, Allen & Unwin, Sydney.

Republic Advisory Committee 1993, *An Australian Republic: The Options* (vol. 1: 'The Report'), AGPS, Canberra.

Riker, W. 1975, 'Federalism', in F. I. Greenstein and N. W. Polsby (eds), *A Handbook of Political Science*, Addison-Wesley, Reading.

Stevens, B. and Wanna, J. (eds) 1993, *The Goss Government: Promise and Performance of Labor in Queensland*, Macmillan, Melbourne.

3

LOCAL GOVERNMENT

....

Doug Tucker

Concentration of power and officialdom in our national and state capital cities is one of the distinguishing features of Australia's federal system of government. Many other countries allocate operational responsibility for important functions such as education and policing to local governments. In Australia, state governments retain direct, day-to-day control of these activities.

Hence it is not surprising that one of Australia's most distinguished political scientists asserted decades ago that the characteristic talent of Australians is for bureaucracy, which operates on a 'massive scale' (Davies, 1958, p.1). Another has warned that 'the most clamant need for Australian democracy is to develop a determination to break away from the stranglehold of centralisation' (F. A. Bland, quoted in Kandel, 1961, p.57). In similar vein, Reid asserts that the only means of checking the power of the Australian bureaucracy is 'somehow to decentralise political power' (1975, pp.111–12). He adds that local government is 'the jewel in the governmental crown in Australia . . . simply in virtue that we still have a system where representatives can be policy makers' (Reid, 1976, pp.12–13).

Local governments, like universities, are important diversifying institutions in society: they express and accommodate the varying needs, values and aspirations of local communities. This is an important role in Australian society where the state, with its centralised, bureaucratic apparatus, the mass media, the major professions, and other homogenising and increasingly powerful pressure groups, including chambers of commerce and the unions, emphasise uniformity and 'minimum standards' — for example, of services, of construction, of treatment, of working conditions, and of educational curricula.

Diversity is increasingly devalued as something that gets in the way of efficient operations. British political scientist Bernard Crick (1964, p.68) notes that 'in almost nothing is totalitarian doctrine more remarkable than in its hatred of diversifying groups and institutions', adding that 'the theory of democratic centralism robbed men more and more of any intimacy with institutions small enough to be known, worked and loved'. The eminent philosopher of science, the late Professor Sir Karl Popper (1960, p.159) has also warned that 'if the growth of reason is to continue, and human rationality survive, then the diversity of individuals and their opinions, aims, and purposes must never be interfered with . . . The mainspring of evolution and progress is the variety of the material which may become subject to selection'. The United States, with its population of 250 million, boasts more than 83 000 local governments to govern its many diverse communities (Dye, 1991, p.258). Australia, with a population of 17 million, has only about 770 local governments, and efforts are currently afoot to reduce this number.

Local government in the 1990s is in the midst of unprecedented change around Australia (Pensabene & Beirouti, 1993; Tucker, Morton & Edwards, 1993). This extraordinary phenomenon, in the level of government that has historically been largely overlooked or ignored, is the outcome of a number of mutually reinforcing influences.

First, from the late 1980s through to the early 1990s, the election to government of state parliamentary oppositions previously consigned to the political wilderness for lengthy periods created the conditions for 'reform' in various directions. (This was particularly true in an era in which previous state governments were widely perceived as having been corrupt, or grossly incompetent, or both.)

Second, the importation from overseas, especially the United Kingdom, of the ideology of managerialism in the public sector in the early 1980s was still filtering down from the Commonwealth level through the states and, currently, to local government.

Third, many of the ideas and theories collectively referred to as 'economic rationalism', almost all of which are compatible with the ideology of managerialism, were still enjoying a large measure of bipartisan support.

Fourth, the economic recession of the early 1990s, exacerbated as it was by other circumstances such as decline in export earnings, drought, and mismanagement of state finances, compelled incoming governments to seek to economise in public spending.

Fifth, the increasing efforts by Aborigines and Torres Strait Islanders to enhance their role in Australian society during this period impacted both on mainstream local government and on local government in Aboriginal and Islander communities.

Mention must be made, finally, of the Australian Capital Territory, which is a hybrid type of state (or territory) and local government. In other words, Canberra is the one major urban centre that, unlike national capitals in many other countries, lacks specifically municipal government: there are mayors of Washington, London, Paris, Moscow and Beijing, but there is no mayor of Canberra. Located in the Australian Capital Territory, Canberra enjoys territory government with municipal functions tacked on: it thus boasts a chief minister, who leads the ACT government, the members of which are drawn from a 17-member Legislative Assembly. Despite Canberra's modest population size (about 310 000), the ACT government's total outlay of approximately $1.2 billion for the 1991–92 financial year far exceeded the corresponding amount for the Greater Brisbane City government, although Brisbane City has a population of 777 280. This is due to the ACT government's state-type responsibilities (such as education and police), as well as significant trading enterprises such as electricity supply, added to which are ordinary local government functions.

THE LEGISLATIVE FRAMEWORK

Like other public authorities, local governments are the creations not (as is often claimed) of state governments, but of state parliaments. Senior state politicians and bureaucrats sometimes adopt a condescending attitude to local governments on this account — until they are reminded that state governments are also the creations of state parliaments. Local government, however, has long felt itself at a disadvantage in that while it has recognition and some degree of protection in state constitutions, its right to exist is not acknowledged in the Commonwealth Constitution, where it is not even mentioned. The Australian people rejected a proposal to include recognition of local government in the Constitution in a referendum (along with three other unrelated proposals) as recently as 1988.

Nevertheless, local government's push for greater recognition, and its criticism of the state Local Government Acts under which it had to operate, prompted most state governments around Australia to replace these very old and much amended statutes. In a foreword to a discussion paper on the issue published by the New South Wales government, the minister remarked that 'Local Government reform in New South Wales is long overdue. There has been no comprehensive review of the legislation since 1919. The current Act inhibits effective government at the local level by being unduly prescriptive. This restricts freedom for councils to react to, or reflect, community needs' (Peacocke, 1991). In the event, the New South Wales Act was not especially generous in granting power and autonomy to local government in that state, whereas recent Queensland and Tasmanian legislation is quite liberal.

From 1993 on, a spate of new local government legislation has been enacted in the four eastern states of Australia, with more to come in Western Australia in 1995. The new acts are much more 'user friendly' than those they supersede. The provisions of these statutes are mostly couched in clear, simple prose. The New South Wales Act, in particular, is outstanding for its clarity and approachability — a valuable attribute in a statute often consulted by elected local government members. The Act is divided first into chapters with headings like: 'What are the purposes of this Act?'; 'What is a council's charter?'; 'How can the community influence what a council does?'. Section 6 of the Act states: 'Introductions to chapters, notes, charts and diagrams are explanatory notes and do not form part of this Act. They are provided to assist understanding'. A diagram depicting the local government system in Chapter 2 of the Act is reproduced below in Figure 3.1.

Queensland's local government legislation is unusual in two respects. First, the *City of Brisbane Act 1924* constituted Australia's only 'greater' capital city scheme. Inspired in part by the consolidated metropolitan government schemes adopted nearly three decades earlier in New York and London, this legislation became feasible after the abolition of Queensland's upper house of parliament, the Legislative Council (Tucker, 1988). Second, amendments to the *Community Services (Aborigines) Act 1984* and the *Community Services (Torres Strait) Act 1984* enacted in 1990 transformed the 31 Aboriginal and Torres Strait Islander ('ATSI') councils into genuine local governments (Tucker et al., 1981, p.6). These ATSI councils therefore constitute a separate, parallel stream of local government in Queensland. However, the legislation was not, at the time of writing, being administered by the minister responsible for mainstream local government in Queensland.

Figure 3.1   The system of local government in New South Wales

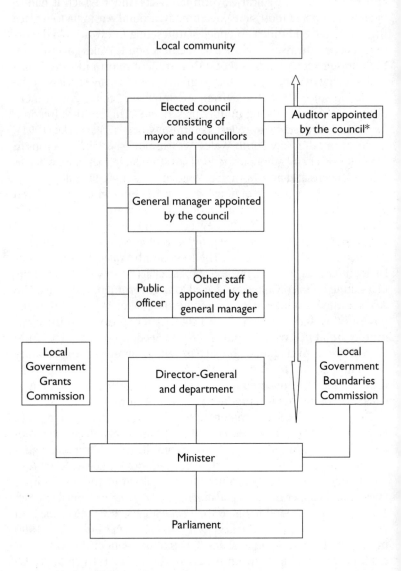

* The auditor's report is made public and a copy goes to the Minister.
Source: New South Wales *Local Government Act 1993*

TERRITORIAL STRUCTURE

Traditionally, local government areas (LGAs) have been categorised as urban (variously called cities, towns or boroughs) or rural (called shires or districts). Soon after World War II, however, rapid urbanisation in a number of LGAs began to create 'urban overspill' — the spread of residential areas across town and city boundaries into neighbouring shires. Because many shire councils resisted the inclusion of the new urban pockets in expanded urban LGAs (such a change would have deprived the shires of rate revenues from the new residential estates), many shires adjacent to expanding cities have become hybrid, or mixed, urban-rural areas. Victoria's *Local Government Act 1989* identifies the existence of what are now three types of LGA rather than two. Section 4 of that Act recognises cities, rural cities and shires, and stipulates that cities be 'predominantly urban in character', that rural cities be 'partly urban and partly rural in character', and that shires be 'predominantly rural in character'. Regrettably, however, the 'rural city' class was scarcely used to the end of 1994. Current indications are that few, if any, local governments in Victoria will be classified as rural cities in future.

In addition to the long-established classes of LGA, new classes of LGA have been created to recognise the emergent self-governing Aboriginal and Torres Strait Islander communities. The Northern Territory Local Government Act recognises such LGAs in the form of Aboriginal communities controlled by community governments (Wolfe, 1989). However, separate legislation recognises Aboriginal Associations in the Northern Territory and Aboriginal and Islander communities in Queensland. Table 3.1 shows these details.

The 1990s are an era in which significant structural changes are taking place, ostensibly to prepare Australian local government for the challenges of the twenty-first century. New South Wales led the way in mergers when the Wran Labor government legislated to reduce the number of LGAs by twenty-one by means of amalgamations in 1980 (see Table 3.2). The Tasmanian government implemented state-wide mergers in 1993 as part of that state's local government modernisation program. In 1993 and 1994 Queensland's Local Government Commissioner (1994, p.13 ff.) proposed, and the state government approved, seven separate mergers, reducing total LGAs in Queensland by nine. The Western Australian government decided without warning in October 1993 to divide Perth City into a smaller city and three new towns. An advisory committee will report to the government in November 1995

Table 3.1 Types of local government area by state/territory, November 1994

Type of LGA	NSW	Vic	Qld	SA	WA	Tas	NT
Cities	40	35	18	27	19	6	1
Towns	–	–	3	–	13	–	5
Rural Cities	–	2	–	–	–	–	–
Municipalities	27	–	–	9	–	23	–
Shires	110	68	107	–	110	–	1
Districts	–	–	–	82	–	–	–
Aboriginal communities[1]	–	–	14	5	–	–	25
Aboriginal 'associations'[1]	–	–	–	–	–	–	31
Torres Strait Islander communities[1]	–	–	17	–	–	–	–
Total	177	105[2]	159[3]	123	142	29	63

Sources: Australian Bureau of Statistics, State Grants Commission annual reports, State Departments/Offices of Local Government, and State Local Government Associations.

Notes: [1] Indigenous communities are included only if eligible for grants from the Local Government Grants Commission in their state or territory.
[2] Mergers were expected to reduce this total to about 78 by 31 January 1995.
[3] Mergers were expected to reduce this total to 156 by 31 December 1994.

on possible structural change in local government, but not on council amalgamations (*West Australian*, 28 October, 1994). In South Australia, significant reductions in numbers of LGAs are likely, but the process will be controlled by local government and facilitated by state government (Brown, 1994).

Victoria, however, is the state where a sweeping program of amalgamations has been put in place. It began when the government led by premier Jeff Kennett brought down special legislation in mid–1993 to create a new Greater Geelong City from six LGAs and the urbanised parts of two others. The city councils of Ballarat and Bendigo then called for similar action in their districts: these were confirmed by a newly created Local Government Board. Meanwhile, the government had also secured the enactment, in October 1993, of the City of Melbourne Act, alteration of the city's boundaries by the Act, dismissal of the Melbourne City

Table 3.2 Number of local government areas in Australia 1910–94

Year	NSW	Vic	Qld	SA	WA	Tas	NT	Total
1910	324	206	164	175	147	51	–	1067
1923	320	192	170	187	142	49	–	1060
1931	319	196	146[1]	196	147	49	–	1053
1946	289	197	144	143	148	49	–	970
1956	236	205	134	143	147	49	–	914
1967	224	210	131	142	144	49	1	901
1977	209	211	131	130	138	49	2	870
1980	199	211	134	129	138	49	4	842
1982	175	211	134	127	139	49	4	840
1986	175	211	134	124	140	49	6	872
1990	176	210	165[1]	121	139	46	60[2]	918
1994	177	78[3]	156	123	142	29	63	768

Sources: Australian Bureau of Statistics, Advisory Council for Intergovernment Relations, State Grants Commission annual reports, State Departments/Offices of Local Government, and Local Government Associations.

Notes: [1] Aboriginal and Islander councils became fully recognised local governments in 1990 following legislation authorising them to approve their own budgets.

[2] NT community government councils and 'association' councils recognised for purposes of distribution of federal assistance grants.

[3] Approximate total only, pending completion of restructuring in 1995.

Council without consultation, and the appointment of commissioners to govern the rearranged CBD area. In mid-December, the government directed the Local Government Board to inquire into the areas and boundaries of 21 LGAs in the inner Melbourne area. The Board's interim report in April 1994 recommended that nineteen of these LGAs be merged into nine cities (Local Government Board 1994a, pp.273–4). However, this was varied slightly in the Board's final report in June. The Board estimated that the mergers would produce administrative savings of at least $65 million and perhaps as much as $94 million (Local Government Board, 1994b, p.4).

The Kennett government subsequently directed the Board, in a series of references, to review the structure of local government elsewhere in Victoria in order to enhance its efficiency and effectiveness. By mid-November 1994, it was clear that the final number of LGAs in Victoria on completion of the reviews would be about 78.

POWERS AND FUNCTIONS OF LOCAL GOVERNMENT

Local governments, unlike appointive statutory authorities such as the Australia Postal Commission, university senates, and harbour (or port) authorities, are democratically elected assemblies with powers of taxing property owners in their LGA. Because of the public representative character of local councils, British and Australian courts have been inclined since the late nineteenth century to interpret local government statutory powers generously. Beginning in 1924 with the newly created Greater Brisbane scheme, the Queensland Parliament departed from the tradition of enumerating the council's powers in detail, and opted instead for a general power to govern, or 'general competence power' (Tucker, 1988). This meant that the council could do whatever it wished, so long as its proposed actions were not inconsistent with Commonwealth and state law. In 1936, the Queensland Parliament conferred this power on all other councils in Queensland. Both the Tasmanian and Queensland Local Government Acts of 1993 contain this power and there are hopes that the Western Australian statute expected in 1995 will do so too.

The 1993 New South Wales statute failed to grant a general competence power to local government, which keeps local government in that state more dependent on the state government than is the case elsewhere. Unlike local governments in other states, those in New South Wales have no power to make by-laws (or 'local laws'), but may make 'local policies', which achieve a similar result, though formally they are less powerful than local laws.

The activities or 'functions' of local governments are so many and varied that it is helpful to group them in two ways for purposes of explanation. The first is by process — whether the function takes the form of services, regulation, planning, or administration. Services include such functions as garbage collection, sewerage, drainage, road maintenance, and provision of parks. Regulatory functions include various types of health inspection (including restaurants, boarding houses and places of public entertainment), building inspections (to ensure compliance with building standards) and traffic control (through provision of traffic lights, roundabouts and traffic signs). Planning (discussed more fully below) involves thinking ahead for the community to ensure that decisions made today by public and private bodies do not destroy or threaten the sort of community that residents want it to be in five, ten or twenty years' time. Administration involves the mobilisation and deployment of resources (revenue, human resources, buildings and equipment) needed to carry out other functions.

The second way of grouping functions is by content, which cuts across the process method. The content of functions may be treated in different ways, but some convenient headings are health, recreation, mobility and social welfare. Health, for example, may encompass services such as immunisation, fluoridation of water, drainage and pest destruction. It would also encompass regulatory activities such as noise abatement measures, planning activities such as projected expansion of sewerage and projected upgrading of sewage treatment facilities, and administrative activities such as raising loans for new drainage works. Recreation covers the provision of a multitude of community facilities (for instance, art galleries, museums, libraries, swimming pools, and parks) for both passive and active recreation. Mobility involves services such as road maintenance and municipal transport, regulatory activities such as traffic control and monitoring of on-street parking, planning of future capital works such as road and bridge construction, and administrative activities such as the recruitment of qualified civil and traffic engineers.

The best method of distinguishing the more important functions from the less important is to ascertain how much the local community, through the local government of the area, is prepared to spend on each of them. Traditionally, capital-intensive functions such as road construction, drainage, water supply, sewerage and other engineering-based functions have gobbled up the lion's share of available resources, although local government's responsibilities in these areas vary markedly from state to state (see Table 3.3). However, a shift towards the softer, human services has been noticeable in recent decades: Victorian local government has long been the most active in this direction and Queensland (preoccupied with distance between its settlements, and directly responsible for town water supply) has been least concerned with human services. The increased emphasis on human services during the decade to 1992 is indicated by the following comparison: against an overall increase of around 13 per cent in total outlays, local government spending on human services (health, social welfare and public order) increased by about 40 per cent.

Local governments in Australia are now involved in an extensive range of human services, although there is great interstate and intrastate variability in their provision. They include: the Commonwealth-funded Home and Community Care Program (HACC) for frail aged and those with disabilities; a wide range of services for children and youth;

Table 3.3 State and local government gross fixed capital expenditures on water supply and sanitation and protection of the environment, 1991–92

State	Level of government	Water supply ($ million)	Sanitation and protection of the environment ($ million)
NSW	state	311	328
	local	83	83
Vic	state	143	233
	local	–	16
Qld	state	14	1
	local	120	146
SA	state	44	42
	local	–	24
WA	state	85	93
	local	–	15
Tas	state	4	–
	local	9	15
NT	territory	10	11
	local	–	–

Source: Australian Bureau of Statistics, Catalogue no. 5512.0

provision of neighbourhood centres; provision and management of public housing; participation in labour market programs; initiation of community relations programs that target disadvantaged groups such as Aboriginal and Islander groups; community development programs, especially in locations where communities have been rapidly formed (for example, new mining towns); and social planning activities.

Town (or land use) planning

A well-arranged town or city may be likened to a well-designed house. Compatible activities take place in adjacent areas; incompatible activities are separated. Movement between areas is easy and swiftly achieved. The general design harmonises with both the topography and climate of the area. In short, the layout works well and is pleasing.

Unlike most homes, a city develops as a result of the inspiration and activities of many different people. If there is no overall plan to which its development must generally conform, serious problems may emerge. The purpose of a town plan, then, is to guide people wishing to build new homes or facilities so that the city as a whole develops in accordance with some unifying vision of what the city should be like in the future.

Town planning is centrally concerned with the allocation of land to one use among the many that might be feasible. Hence, some people prefer the term 'land use planning' to 'town (and country) planning'. The town planner's task, however, is often difficult because of severe competition among different uses for particular parcels of land. In such cases, the final decision involves many considerations, some technical and straightforward (for example, the land may be subject to periodic flooding); and some evaluative (that is, value judgments in which conflicting ideals are traded off against one another in the search for an acceptable compromise). In representative democracies such value judgments, or political choices, should be made by elected representatives of the community after hearing the views and recommendations of the council's specialist town planners.

Town planning is probably local government's most prominent responsibility, not least because it is often highly controversial. For instance, modern societies generate a great deal of waste, which ideally should be disposed of safely, economically, and without inconveniencing anyone. But the disposal of waste — particularly toxic waste — is almost certain to cause problems for some citizens, who may then form resident action groups to oppose the plans and the councillors who favour them. (This is often dubbed the NIMBY ('not in my back yard') syndrome.) However, councillors know that they cannot please everyone: hostile criticism is sometimes unavoidable no matter how conscientiously they make their decisions.

While planning and environment legislation in most states recognises the democratic right of local communities to develop their own town plans through the local government of their area, that recognition is qualified by other considerations. For example, metropolitan areas around the country (other than Brisbane) are governed by a multiplicity of councils with differing views and priorities, which forces state governments to find some means of developing a coherent plan for the entire metropolis. Again, the objectives of individual councils, responding to the wishes of local citizens, may conflict with those of the state government, which mostly takes a state-wide view of emerging issues. Such conflict might centre on a quiet seaside resort whose residents oppose development, while the state government — anxious to boost the overall economy of the state — favours proposals to build five-star hotels and other facilities attractive to tourists. State governments therefore insist on retaining overall, or strategic, control of the land use planning process.

Although such control is unexceptionable, the means chosen for that purpose may create controversy. If, for example, a council refuses a developer permission to do something that is contrary to the government-approved town plan, the government can expect vigorous criticism if it intervenes and reverses the council's decision. Such intervention makes a mockery of the town plan and, of course, awakens suspicions of government corruption. This situation arose on a number of occasions in Queensland during the Bjelke-Petersen premiership.

Another legitimate complaint against state government arises if the government does not bind its own agencies to government-approved town plans, which are binding on everyone else. An approved town plan may set aside a parcel of land on the outskirts of an urban centre for public open space. A government agency — say the Education Department — may then decide to acquire that parcel for a school, irrespective of the fact that costly local government services to the land such as sealed roads, drainage, water mains and sewerage mains do not exist. While such arbitrary departmental action occurs less often now, it plays havoc with council plans and resources if it does occur. The best solution is for state governments to bind their own agencies, along with everyone else, to conform with approved town plans.

ELECTED COUNCIL MEMBERS

Local governments, like other organisations, depend for their success largely on the efforts of people. Citizens elect councillors to articulate community desires and aspirations. Councillors often come from different backgrounds and ideally will reflect the varying shades of opinion that exist among their constituents. Even in quite homogeneous communities, differences in age, gender, education, occupation and income give rise to different views; and the extent to which these differences are represented among elected councillors depends on the local government electoral system, the number of council members, and perhaps the LGA's demographic characteristics. In this latter regard, the presence of ethnic minority groups in an LGA may make an otherwise fair electoral system unfair in terms of adequate representation on the council.

As to the electoral system, the New South Wales Local Government Act has much in its favour. First, it makes voting compulsory for residents but optional for non-resident ratepayers, occupiers and ratepaying lessees. Elections are held at four-yearly intervals under a preferential system (whenever one or two positions must be filled) or a proportional system (whenever three or more positions must be filled). This voting system gives maximum weight to citizen preferences, unlike the first-past-the-post system adopted in most Queensland LGAs, where successful candidates may obtain a plurality of votes (more than their opponents) but not an overall majority. The second and lower-order preferences of citizens voting for unsuccessful candidates are simply ignored in first-past-the-post voting, while the New South Wales arrangement takes them into account — arguably, a fairer procedure.

A further point in favour of the New South Wales system is that it enhances the opportunity of minority groups and women to be represented on councils. This is especially true in LGAs where all councillors are elected 'at large' and the method of proportional representation (PR) is the voting system used. In Commonwealth and state parliamentary (lower house) elections where one member is returned per electorate, the arrangement favours the major parties and male candidates (Rule, 1987). Local government's use of proportional representation in undivided New South Wales LGAs illustrates how local government can fulfil its role as a diversifying institution: it enables minority interests otherwise shut out of the governmental arena to win seats and legitimacy at the local government level.

The New South Wales electoral system is flexible in various ways — for example, in the election of mayors. Mayors are to be popularly elected, that is, by all voters in each LGA, as in Queensland. However, the citizens of any LGA can, by constitutional referendum, change the system to enable the councillors to choose the mayor annually from among their number, as in Victoria. Popularly elected mayors tend to be high-profile, strong-willed leaders who may serve in that capacity for a number of consecutive terms. Owing their position directly to the citizens, they may clash with their fellow council members on various issues. By contrast, mayors elected by councillors from among their number usually have lower profiles, and they tend to emphasise harmony and teamwork. In Victoria, attachment to the traditional English practice of electing mayors for one year only has led in many LGAs to the emergence of a 'roster' arrangement, whereby mayoral candidates 'queue up' (usually in seniority order) for their one-year stint. Such an arrangement transforms the mayor into a purely ceremonial figure, while senior officials manage council operations.

Remuneration of council members is quite strictly controlled in all states except Queensland. In New South Wales for example, a

Remuneration Tribunal must determine no later than 1 May each year the maximum and minimum fees to be paid during the following year to mayors, councillors and a number of county councillors, having regard to criteria set down in the Act. In Queensland, by contrast, after parliament removed the remuneration 'cap' of $4 000 in 1978, members of some larger urbanised councils (other than the (Greater) Brisbane City Council, whose members have drawn salaries since 1925), began to pay themselves large allowances.

This is undesirable for three reasons. First, as these councillors gradually become full-timers, civic-minded citizens wishing to serve on a part-time basis are squeezed out as they cannot compete with full-timers for voter support. Second, full-time councillors try to involve themselves in the detail of day-to-day administrative and technical matters for which they lack qualifications and expertise. The cost in time of senior salaried officials who have to 'defend their turf' or simply explain technical points to under-employed councillors can be very high indeed. Third, some Queensland councils have successfully sought reduced numbers of councillors in the process of moving from part-time to full-time councillors: this, however, decreases the likelihood that most shades of community opinion will be represented in council.

Formal council meetings usually take place every fortnight, but large councils may meet each week and small councils may meet less often. Larger councils form standing committees to meet between council meetings and bring recommendations to the next council meeting. Standing committees specialise in matters such as health, recreation, works, finance and so on. Councils may also form ad hoc committees to deal with some specific issue outside the ambit of the standing committees.

MANAGERIALISM, THE CORPORATE APPROACH, AND PRIVATISATION

Since the 1960s in Great Britain and the 1970s in Australia, much debate has focussed on the issue of managing local government activities. This raises further questions about the appropriate division of responsibilities between the mayor and chairpersons of standing committees of council; between the mayor and the traditional town or shire clerk; between the council committee chairperson and the departmental head concerned; between elected council members and salaried staff and other employees; and between the clerk and the heads of the various council departments. Every local government has at some time experienced bitter controversy over one or more of these questions, especially as state legislation has mostly been silent on them (although local laws may clarify some of them).

During the 1970s and 1980s, individual councils began to absorb and apply 'managerialist' arrangements that were widely adopted in Great Britain. Some important tenets in British local government's managerialist ideology were, first, that each department's tendency to operate in isolation from other council departments had to be overcome by a corporate (or whole-of-council) approach to community services. Second, a corporate approach could best be achieved if salaried departmental heads were formed into a corporate team under the dynamic leadership of a general manager or chief executive officer (CEO) who, unlike the traditional town or shire clerk, would be the undisputed head of the council's salaried organisation. Such an approach, borrowing heavily from private-sector models of company management, could arguably secure the coordination of departmental activities so often missing in traditional arrangements.

The new local government legislation in Australia embraces these managerialist ideals, making it obligatory for councils to appoint a chief executive. Section 335 of the New South Wales statute makes the general manager 'responsible for the efficient and effective operating of the council's organisation and for ensuring the implementation, without undue delay, of decisions of the council'. The same section specifically vests responsibility for appointing, controlling and dismissing staff in the general manager, except that he or she must consult with the council before appointing or dismissing senior staff (section 337).

By contrast, the mayor's role, ceremonial activities aside, is to preside at council meetings, to exercise policy-making functions in cases of necessity between council meetings, and to exercise such other council functions as the council determines (section 226). Very similar provisions are contained in sections 60 to 64 of Tasmania's *Local Government Act 1993* and in sections 705 to 707 in Queensland's *Local Government Act 1993*, except that Queensland uses the title 'chief executive officer' instead of 'general manager'.

Each statute obliges councils to develop three-year or five-year corporate (or 'strategic') plans, which must be updated each year after appropriate opportunities have been provided for public input. The Tasmanian and Queensland statutes also require the preparation of yearly operational plans consistent with the current corporate or strategic plan.

Each Act requires the chief executive to report to the council at quarterly or four-monthly intervals on the extent to which performance targets specified in the relevant plans have been achieved.

The other British legacy dating from the privatising Thatcher years is the imposition on local government of compulsory competitive tendering (CCT). In this form of privatisation, local governments provide services by contracting with private (or, sometimes, in-house) suppliers to produce the services required. The Victorian Local Government Board recommended that the government bring down amending legislation to require councils to put activities to the value of 20, 30 and 50 per cent of their budget out to tender in each of the first three years respectively. Tender guidelines should ensure consistent and fair rules for the preparation and consideration of in-house bids (Local Government Board 1993, p.i). The board, the government and a number of councils considered that this measure would force local government to become more efficient.

FINANCING LOCAL GOVERNMENT

The traditional source of local government revenue in Australia and many other countries is what Americans call the 'property tax' and what British and Australian people call the 'rate'. The rate is a tax or compulsory levy applied to the value of real (or immovable) property. Thus if a council decides to raise revenue by taxing real property in its LGA at the rate of one cent in the dollar, the owner of a property valued at $25 000 will be legally liable to pay the council $250 per annum.

Councils obtain funds for their activities from rates, user charges, loans, grants from Commonwealth and state governments, and some miscellaneous sources such as interest earned from investment, and surpluses from trading and entrepreneurial activities. Revenues from rates and charges have increased steadily as other sources of funds — especially government grants — have declined from the late 1980s on. A Commonwealth government-funded report recommending that financial rewards and penalties designed to encourage councils to be more efficient (Australian Urban and Regional Development Review, 1994, p.xiff.) seemed unlikely to be implemented at the time of writing.

Local government legislation empowers local governments to raise revenue by rating properties in various ways. Councils may levy general, or ordinary, rates to finance general local government activities for which specific charges would not be feasible, or appropriate. The costs of street-lighting, maintaining parks and roads, and similar services that benefit the entire community are usually financed from general rate revenues. In addition, services provided to specific properties may be financed by special rates such as water rates (where water supply is a local government responsibility).

In recent decades, councils have turned increasingly to user charges as a means of financing particular activities. Not only are they seen to be fairer than requiring ratepayers to meet the costs through rates, regardless of whether and to what extent they use the services, but user charges are also seen to promote environmental values and economic efficiency, as paying users are mostly deterred from using the services in question unless they really need to. In future, for instance, as garbage disposal in heavily populated cities becomes increasingly expensive, residents may be charged according to the weight of garbage collected. This would prompt them to avoid producing excessive waste, by purchasing unpackaged or lightly-packaged goods. Again, electronic sensing devices on busy roads may automatically charge motorists for using roads (as already happens in Hong Kong), thus discouraging unnecessary trips on very busy roads and reducing traffic congestion and pollution.

Local government is sometimes assailed by critics for its indebtedness. In fact, gross debt as a percentage of gross annual outlays declined between 1982/83 and 1991/92. Local government's emphasis on debt reduction strategies during that period largely accounts for this. In general, local governments' gross debt situation is more favourable than that of state governments. Figure 3.2 shows the relative debt position for both state and local government on a state-by-state basis. It will be noted that because Queensland local government is responsible for the capital-intensive functions of water supply and sewerage, the state government looks even better than its counterparts elsewhere and local government looks worse. However, when net indebtedness is considered, the Queensland government is unique among state governments in being debt-free.

CONCLUSION

Critics of local government generally fall into one of two groups. There are those who would bypass it completely and create non-elected statutory authorities, or 'quangos', to provide important community

Figure 3.2 State and local government debt 1992

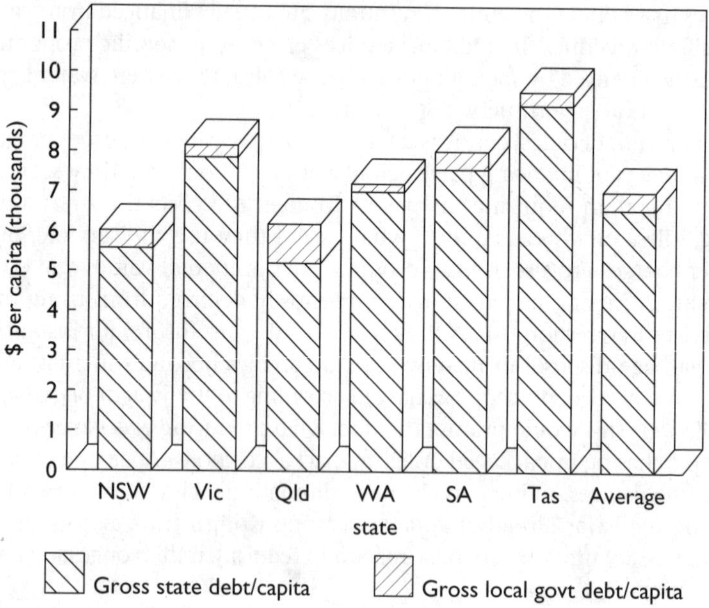

Source: Australian Bureau of Statistics, Catalogoue no. 5513.0

services such as fire fighting, community hospitals, ambulances, electricity supply and so on. These critics have been influential in the past, and local government has little to do with such services in Australia. The second group are those who concede that general-purpose elective councils should control community services, but argue that LGAs should expand to permit better area-wide planning; to harvest economies of scale; and to enable twentieth and twenty-first century approaches to management to replace nineteenth century approaches.

These critics have exerted a dramatic influence during the 1990s by promoting amalgamations and managerialist practices throughout local government. That influence will undoubtedly continue into the twenty-first century with further amalgamations, the introduction and spread of compulsory competitive tendering, and the adoption of other measures of contracting out and privatisation currently being promoted by the Victorian state government.

These changes put at risk the view so eloquently articulated by de Tocqueville (1945 [1835]: I, p.61) that the smallest units of government are the most fundamental units in a free democratic society. With the advocates of rationalisation and uniformity winning out against the champions of diversity, the latter may eventually have to turn to voluntary associations to develop civic virtues in young citizens, and to protect and defend the diverse needs, local aspirations, cultural traditions, and values so important to a lively, informed and active society.

FURTHER READING

Jones (1993) provides an informative introduction to the changing local government scene in Australia during the 1990s. For a detailed, state-by-state analysis of Australian local government, which is now a little dated but is otherwise very useful, see Power, Wettenhall and Halligan (1981). The most informative and detailed history of local government generally is Larcombe's three-volume history of New South Wales local government. The most comprehensive history of Australia's largest local government is Greenwood and Laverty's (1959) centennial history of local government in Brisbane.

REFERENCES

Australian Urban and Regional Development Review 1994, 'Financing local government: a review of the Local Government (Financial Assistance) Act 1986', *Discussion Paper 1*, Australian Urban and Regional Development Review, Melbourne.

Brown, D. 1994, 'Local government reform', Ministerial Statement to South Australian House of Assembly, 26 October.

Crick, B. 1964, *In Defence of Politics*, revised edn., Penguin, Harmondsworth, Middlesex.

Davies, A. F. 1958, *Australian Democracy*, Longmans, Green and Co, London.

De Tocqueville, A. 1945 (1835), *Democracy in America* (2 vols), ed. P. Bradley. Alfred A. Knopf, New York.

Dye, T. R. 1991, *Politics in States and Communities*, 7th edn, Prentice Hall, Englewood Cliffs.

Greenwood, G. and Laverty, J. R. 1959, *Brisbane 1859–1959: A History of Local Government*, Oswald Ziegler for the Brisbane City Council, Brisbane.

Jones, M. 1993, *Transforming Australian Local Government: Making It Work*, Allen & Unwin, Sydney.

Kandel, I. L. 1961, *Types of Administration*, Australian Council for Educational Research, Melbourne.

Larcombe, F. A. 1978, *A History of Local Government in New South Wales* (3 vols), Sydney University Press in association with Local Government and Shire Associations of NSW, Sydney.

Local Government Board 1993, *Compulsory Competitive Tendering: Final Report*, Local Government Board, Melbourne.

Local Government Board 1994a, *Inner Melbourne Review: Interim Report*, Local Government Board, Melbourne.

Local Government Board 1994b, *Inner Melbourne Review: Final Report*, Local Government Board, Melbourne.

Local Government Commissioner Queensland 1994, *Annual Report 1994*, Local Government Commissioner, Queensland, Brisbane.

Murphy, D. 1994, 'Last days of chez nous', *Bulletin*, 11 January, pp.20–1.

Peacocke, G. B. 1991, *Reform of Local Government in New South Wales: Proposals for Legislation*, Department of Local Government and Co-operatives, Bankstown.

Pensabene, T. and Beirouti, R. 1993, *The Pace of Reform: Victorian Local Government Initiatives*, Municipal Association of Victoria, Melbourne.

Popper, K. R. 1960, *The Poverty of Historicism*, 2nd edn, Routledge & Kegan Paul, London.

Power, J., Wettenhall, R. and Halligan, J. (eds) 1981, *Local Government Systems of Australia*, ACIR Information Paper 7, AGPS, Canberra.

Reid, G. S. 1975, 'Discussion on Mr Uren's paper', *Public Administration*, Sydney, 34 (1): pp.111–12.

Reid, G. S. 1976, 'The physical structure of local government', in *Local Government — The Changing Scene: Proceedings of the Fourth National Seminar*, Institute of Municipal Administration, Canberra, 11, pp.12–13.

Rule, W. 1987, 'Electoral systems, contextual factors and women's opportunity for election to parliament in twenty-three democracies', *Western Political Quarterly*, 40, pp.477–98.

Tucker, D. 1988, 'Charles Edward Chuter: an architect of local government in the twentieth century', *Queensland Geographical Journal*, 4th Series, 3, pp.61–70.

Tucker, D., Morton, A. and Edwards, L. 1993, *Queensland Local Government: Moving Ahead. Interim Report*, Local Government Association of Queensland, Brisbane.

Tucker, J. D. et al. 1981, *Local Government in Queensland*, vol. 1, AIUS Publication no. 94, Australian Institute of Urban Studies, Canberra.

Wolfe, J. 1989, *'That Community Government Mob': Local Government in Small Northern Territory Communities*, ANU North Australia Research Unit, Darwin.

4
LAW

....

Donald Gifford

Law is an officially recognised, enforceable system of rules, governing
the relations of human beings in society. On a desert island there would
be no need for law and the sole inhabitant could behave as he or she
pleased, subject only to the natural consequences of irrational conduct.
Such behaviour would carry a risk of starvation or other disaster, but
would not incur legal penalties. Law, then, relates to social interactions,
but it is not the only body of rules applicable in such circumstances.
For example, the rules laid down within a family to establish which
chores each young child shall undertake, and a 'gentleman's agreement' between an employer and a trade union (not a contract, and
not forming part of any relevant award) are not legally enforceable,
though breach might carry unpleasant consequences.

Similarly, while the rules of law and of morality overlap, they are
not the same thing. Some laws are morally neutral — for example, it
does not matter whether everyone drives on the right hand or on the
left hand side of the road, so long as everyone in the area chooses the
same side. While it is not morally neutral that such a law exists, the
side of the road chosen has no moral significance. Laws can even be
actively immoral, such as the system of enforceable racist restrictions
known as apartheid, or the mediaeval maximum wage laws. These
wage laws were the exact opposite of current practice: it was a crime
to pay workers more than a set wage.

It is true that the legal system as a whole cannot afford to differ too markedly from generally accepted views of morality, because the costs of having a policeman standing behind each citizen 16 hours a day are simply too great to be borne. Any society must rely on the voluntary compliance of the great majority of its citizens with (almost) all its laws (almost) all the time. Should a legal system or any structure of public authority fall into disrepute, then even the most tyrannical regime is in great danger of collapse, as the collapse of communism in Eastern Europe bears witness.

Even in the case of an individual law within a legal system generally regarded as just, persistent breach can undermine that law and may eventually lead to its repeal. An example is the spread of Sunday bread sales in Victoria in the 1960s. The law forbade it, and individual sellers were successfully prosecuted; nonetheless the public flocked to buy and so many shops became willing to sell that the authorities gave up and repealed the relevant regulation. (This was only in relation to bread, however, with the result that similar problems arose years later in regard to other kinds of shops.)

The test for the validity of a law has nothing to do with its wisdom, expediency or morality. Nor does a law disappear when the beliefs underlying it have been discredited — the laws against witchcraft survived in England until World War II, and in the nineteenth century a notorious murderer escaped justice by coming armed to court and demanding trial by battle — a mediaeval survival that parliament had never thought to get rid of. (Parliament did act to prevent a repetition of this absurdity.)

An Act of parliament (or statute) is recognised as valid if it is constitutional, and subordinate legislation if it is made under the authority of the relevant parliament. The courts (in addition to developing the common law on their own account) have the duty of deciding whether particular legislation, or a particular legislative provision, is valid or not, and they have the power and duty to impose penalties on lawbreakers.

HISTORY OF LAW

Various states in the ancient world had codes of law. The Roman empire had a very extensive legal code, in its later days a very harsh one, imposing what was effectively serfdom on the bulk of the population as well as liability to judicial torture. With the fall of the empire in the West, this legal code collapsed as well, and in England was replaced by the customary laws of the Anglo-Saxons. These laws were not initially laid down by the various kings, whose authority at first was rather tenuous. By the time of Alfred the Great it was well-established that the King had the right to issue a code of laws, but not any laws he pleased — the code was supposed to conform to the laws of God, and with generally accepted notions of justice. Some of these laws look strange by modern standards — for instance the payment (in lieu of punishment) of 'weregeld' by the relatives of a murderer to the relatives of the victim, the amount payable varying with the victim's social status. Nonetheless, in the social circumstances of the time, such laws not only were acceptable, but met a vital social need.

Even after the Norman conquest the King's courts had to compete with local jurisdictions such as the court of the lord of the manor, and with the courts of the (Roman) Catholic Church, which at that time dominated intellectual as well as religious life and exercised immense political and social influence throughout Western Europe. The victory of the royal courts was a very gradual process, culminating in the Reformation, which broke the power of the Roman Catholic church in England. (Church courts did survive, subject to the supervision of the common law courts. Indeed, until the nineteenth century the limited equivalents of divorce were available only from the church courts unless, like Henry VIII, you could get a special Act of parliament.)

The royal courts themselves were not monolithic. The judges of the various courts lived on the proceeds of fees paid by litigants, and so had an incentive to provide more effective remedies and to expand their area of operation in competition with each other. Various legal fictions were invented for this purpose. The most important of these jurisdictions arose when the common law courts became overly rigid and technical and the courts of equity developed to mitigate the harshness of the common law rules. For example, at common law a trustee had the legal estate and could keep it for himself regardless of the beneficiary: the latter could appeal to the courts of equity, which could order the trustee to do his duty, on pain of imprisonment for contempt of court if he disobeyed. The courts of equity and of common law were amalgamated in the nineteenth century (in New South Wales, not until the 1970s). However, the Commonwealth government in Australia has introduced a system of federal courts in addition to the pre-existing state courts, so that the problem of overlapping and conflicting jurisdictions has now been revived.

When the first settlers reached Australia from Britain more than 200 years ago, they brought with them a highly developed system of law, the result of centuries of development. However not every aspect of this law could be applied immediately to Australian conditions: for example, the jury system could not be adopted as long as most of the population were convicted criminals and most of the rest were soldiers under stringent military discipline. As the proportion of free settlers increased, so the various Australian colonies (still with no legal connection with each other, save through the British government) increasingly adopted the Westminster system of government. (This system does not involve the separation of powers except [in Australia] for the judiciary. In England the Lord Chancellor exercises judicial, executive and legislative functions, all at the highest level.) Australia improved on the Westminster model — it led the way in the establishment of universal manhood suffrage, elected upper houses, the vote for women, and the secret ballot. The Australian colonies also adopted the traditional judicial system as a protection for the citizens' liberties. The colonies (renamed states in 1901) eventually formed a Federation at the beginning of this century. A unitary state, with only a central government, was never a possibility — as it was, New South Wales joined only on the second ballot and New Zealand refused to join at all. Western Australia voted in favour of secession as late as the 1930s. Although interpretation of the Commonwealth Constitution by the High Court has greatly increased the power of the Commonwealth as against the states, there remain very real limits to the legislative power of any Australian parliament (especially the Commonwealth parliament) and it is essential in the interests of liberty that these limits should be strictly enforced by the courts.

SOURCES OF LAW

The original source of law was custom. Custom has had a deep influence on the development of the law of merchants (sale of goods, etc.) and of the law of meetings, but is now the least important of the four sources of law (although Aboriginal customary law has now been recognised by the High Court). Custom can still be said to exercise a major influence on the law of torts through the test of the 'reasonable man': the test of whether a person should be held liable for negligence is whether or not what was done (or what there was a failure to do) would be regarded by the ordinary reasonable person as negligent in the circumstances.

The best-known source of law is statute law — that is, the Acts of parliament (state, territory or Commonwealth). The power of each parliament to pass laws is limited. For example, the parliament of Queensland has no power to pass a valid law governing the behaviour of Tasmanians in Western Australia, if there is no connection between that conduct and the good rule and government of Queensland. Also, no parliament can pass valid laws infringing freedom of religion or freedom of interstate trade, contrary to the Commonwealth Constitution (as interpreted by the High Court). The Commonwealth parliament cannot pass laws outside the heads of power set out in the Commonwealth Constitution, and the state parliaments cannot pass laws contrary to valid Commonwealth legislation.

Despite the prominence in the public mind of statute law, and the large number of statutes passed in recent years, Acts of parliament take third place after the common law and delegated legislation as a source of legal rules.

Delegated legislation (also known as subordinate legislation) consists of laws passed not by parliament but under the authority conferred by some statute. The delegated legislation must remain within the authority conferred by that statute on pain of being struck down as invalid by the courts. Local councils, for example, get their authority from parliament and a bylaw (in some states, 'local law') purportedly passed by such a council on a topic not authorised by parliament, or without following the prescribed procedure, is null and void even though it might have popular support.

Other examples of delegated legislation are railway bylaws, regulations made by government departments and town planning schemes. The various Australian governments, together with local government and statutory authorities, have for years been producing a flood of delegated legislation. The flood of delegated legislation provides large corporations with a substantial (though unintended) advantage, because of their ability to readily seek legal advice, but makes it effectively impossible for the small business owner to know whether or not he or she is a criminal, thereby undermining respect for the rule of law itself. Since delegated legislation tends to be amended frequently, it is not enough to consult a lawyer once and then obey the rules as they were at that time — if the rules have subsequently been changed, ignorance of the law is no excuse.

The tragedy is that much of this regulation is unnecessary. Some years ago an attempt was made to introduce a new kind of jam, with a low sugar content. People concerned about their weight would probably have been happy to purchase it, but they were never given the opportunity — regulations in the various states prescribed a minimum amount of sugar that 'jam' was required to contain. No question of protecting the public was involved — the jam's low sugar content was to be its selling point.

Another problem affecting subordinate legislation is that once made it remains in existence (subject to any sunset clause or explicit repeal) even though times and customs have changed. One memorable example is the bylaw made by a Victorian council and still not repealed in the late 1950s: it prohibited bathing unless the bather was completely covered from neck to ankle. In Queensland in the late 1950s a council making a new set of bylaws was retaining one that prohibited swimming in view of any bridge or highway unless all *limbs* were completely covered.

Even today, the greatest source of legal rules is the common law. The common law consists of the legal principles laid down in the decisions of the superior courts (Supreme Court and upwards to the High Court of Australia). More precisely, it consists of the reasons for judgment on which those decisions are based. However, if the outcome of a case is based purely on a factual issue, with no development of the legal principles involved, that case will not contribute to the growth of the common law.

The passing of a new statute can make a wrenching change in the law. The common law usually develops gradually, over a considerable period, by means of a series of legal decisions involving different parties and different judges. New developments can therefore be tested against a variety of actual fact situations before a proposed principle gains general acceptance. The development of the common law is therefore organic, like the growth of a tree, whereas statute law may be compared to the abrupt erection or reconstruction of a building. Whether the building is soundly designed or not may be difficult to demonstrate until it has been occupied and cracks appear in the walls: the common law, while slower to develop, is more likely to endure. Another advantage of the common law is that, as cases are brought before the courts by the decisions of litigants, not the whims of the judges, the growth points of the common law centre around those issues that most concern people at the particular time.

Despite the prominence of statute law and delegated legislation in the public mind, the common law courts continue their labours, and their decisions continue to contribute more to the development of legal rules than any other source of law. Legal textbooks and articles are not in themselves a source of law until the arguments put forward are adopted by some superior court — and even then it is the court's reasons for judgment, not the source of them, that are important.

THE COURT SYSTEM

The courts of an Australian state are arranged in a hierarchy, with the lower courts in the hierarchy bound by the reasons for decision of the higher courts (that is, those courts to which there is a right of appeal from the lower court). A simplified version of the hierarchy is set out in Figure 4.1.

There are various other courts and quasi-judicial bodies, which fit into the hierarchy at different levels (the name and level depend on the state legislation) — for example, the town planning appeal and the liquor licensing bodies. There is also the hierarchy of federal courts and tribunals such as the Federal Court itself and the Family Court. Even courts fulfilling the same functions and with similar names can be found at different levels in the hierarchy in different states: the Land and Environment Court of New South Wales is a court of superior court status,

Figure 4.1   The Australian Courts Hierarchy

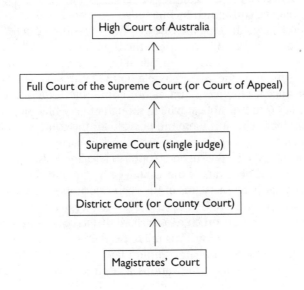

but the South Australian Environment, Resources and Development Court and the Queensland Planning and Environment Court are of District Court status, while the Victorian Administrative Appeals Tribunal Planning Division is only a tribunal.

The various levels of tribunals and courts are differently constituted, and handle different kinds of problems. The lower levels of the hierarchy, such as magistrates' courts, handle problems in which issues of fact are usually more to the forefront in the litigation than are issues of law. The criminal cases they have to decide usually relate to the less serious crimes. Also, the amounts of money at stake are usually less than in litigation before the higher levels of the hierarchy. What is needed is a practical commonsense approach — provided that parliament only entrusts cases of such a nature to this level of the hierarchy. Unfortunately, parliament does not always observe the distinction.

In the superior courts (of state Supreme Court status and higher) the judges tend to deal with either important matters of law, the more serious criminal cases, or larger sums of money. Also, they hear appeals (in many cases restricted by parliament to questions of law) from the lower levels in the hierarchy.

Tribunals and courts of less than superior court status may develop bodies of principle governing specialised fields, but these rules are not treated as part of the common law.

Single judges of the superior courts are not bound by each other's reasons for decision — though they are likely to find them persuasive. (A court may be constituted by one judge — a 'single judge' — or by two or more judges hearing the case jointly.) Any conflict can be sorted out on appeal, in the Full Court or in the High Court of Australia. The various state hierarchies are independent of one another so that a single judge sitting in Queensland, while bound by the decisions of the Court of Appeal of Queensland, is not bound by those of the New South Wales Court of Appeal which, though of very high status, is in a different hierarchy. It is therefore possible for the courts in different states to fall out of step — a tendency checked partly by the careful consideration given by the superior courts to relevant decisions in other states (as well as decisions of the United Kingdom and New Zealand courts) and partly by the status of the High Court of Australia.

The High Court is the highest court in the hierarchy of each state and of the federal court structure as well, so that its reasons for decision bind every court throughout Australia. It is therefore a force for consistency within the Australian common law; but of course it cannot prevent the parliaments of the various states from passing legislation, the provisions of which differ from one state to another. Thus, if a large supermarket chain wishes to hold an Australia-wide promotion in which customers may win prizes, lawyers have to check the legisla- . tion of every state and territory to see whether the particular proposal might not offend against the gambling and lottery laws. Indeed, as the laws currently stand, a Victorian customer reading the conditions has to buy from the company and also complete the form issued by the company in order to enter the draw, while a South Australian can enter the draw without buying anything or completing the form.

In addition to reasons for decision, the judgments of the superior courts may include *obiter dicta* — statements of legal principle not essential to the decision in the particular case. A judge might state, for example, that should the facts of some later case differ in a particular respect, the principle on which his or her present decision was based would not apply. Such *obiter dicta* are persuasive but they are not binding, even on lower courts in the same hierarchy.

In any legal system, consistency is vital. First, a welter of conflicting decisions must necessarily send litigants away dissatisfied; and second, lawyers must be able to give their clients accurate advice. Most of the disputes brought to a solicitor's attention are settled by agreement between the parties rather than litigated to the bitter end; if this were not so, the courts would be overwhelmed. Such settlements depend on objective advice from the lawyers on both sides to their respective clients setting out that client's prospects should litigation ensue.

It is therefore vital that the courts should provide clear and consistent guidance, and this is only possible while the courts rely on the rules of precedent rather than on judicial whim. Also, in many cases a client will approach a lawyer not because a dispute has arisen but because a clear agreement is required, which will forestall the possibility of future disputes between the parties. Again, such consultation is only useful while the courts maintain the principles clearly established in prior decisions: those principles may be modified and developed, but they should not be lightly departed from. The High Court of Australia has developed an increasing tendency to alter the law (note particularly the Mabo case on Aboriginal land rights). This creates uncertainty and can make it difficult for people to arrange their affairs; it also opens the possibility that High Court judges will be chosen on the basis of their political views rather than for their legal expertise.

Courts and quasi-judicial bodies are required to act in accordance with the principles of natural justice. Indeed, these basic principles are being applied ever more widely, so that clubs and administrative bodies may be affected, at least to some degree. Natural justice imposes a requirement of procedural fairness (what Australians would call 'a fair go' for both sides). There are two basic rules. The first is that the decision-maker must not appear to be biased (except in the case of clubs and other bodies deriving their authority from contract, in which case actual bias is necessary for invalidity; also, the decision-maker must not have any pecuniary interest in the outcome. The second is that he or she must hear both sides.

The second rule entails knowledge of any charges made against you, an adequate time in which to prepare your defence and a proper opportunity to put your case in reply. Outside a court situation it generally does not involve the right to an oral hearing (the body concerned may decide on the basis of written argument and evidence), legal representation or cross-examination. Of course, if one party is allowed to cross-examine, the other parties must be allowed the same right. Even in the absence of a right of appeal, if a decision is reached in breach of natural justice, the courts will intervene.

THE LEGAL PROFESSION

Law students, like medical students, require high academic results in order to obtain entry to a law school, but there are no other barriers to entry. Legally trained relatives may help a student by discussing difficult areas of the law, but are in no sense essential to success. Originally all male, the student body is now much more balanced as regards sex.

Words are a lawyer's weapons — mastery of English is essential. When drawing up a contract the difference between precise and sloppy language may be the difference between a satisfied client and a dispute leading to litigation. Hard work is another essential. Integrity is the most important quality of all.

Lawyers are given a monopoly of audience before the superior courts (except for litigants in person) because of the special duties they owe to the law and to the court, duties that override even the duty owed to the client. In an adversary system, the lawyer is expected to do his or her best to win the case, but not to win by any means:

> As an advocate he [the barrister] is a minister of justice equally with the judge. He has a monopoly of audience in the higher courts. No-one save he can address the judge, unless it be a litigant in person. This carries

with it a corresponding responsibility. A barrister cannot pick or choose his clients. He is bound to accept a brief from any man who comes before the courts. No matter how great a rascal the man may be. No matter how given to complaining. No matter how undeserving or how un-popular his cause. The barrister must defend him to the end. Provided only that he is paid a proper fee, or, in the case of a dock brief, a nominal fee. He must accept the brief and do all he honourably can on behalf of his client. I say 'all he *honourably* can', because his duty is not only to his client. He has a duty to the court which is paramount. It is a mistake to suppose that he is the mouthpiece of his client to say what he wants: or his tool to do what he directs. He is none of these things. He owes allegiance to a higher cause. It is the cause of truth and justice. He must not consciously mis-state the facts. He must not knowingly conceal the truth. He must not unjustly make a charge of fraud, that is, without evidence to support it. He must produce all the relevant authorities, even those that are against him. He must see that his client discloses, if ordered, the relevant documents, even those that are fatal to his case. He must disregard the most specific instructions of his client, if they conflict with his duty to the court. (*Rondel* v. *Worsley* [1967] 1 Q.B. 443 at 502 per Lord Denning M.R. (English Court of Appeal); affirmed, [1969] A.C. 191 (House of Lords).)

These ethical duties are strictly enforced, and any lawyer who persistently breaches them can expect before long to be 'struck off' the rolls — that is, to be excluded from the profession. In practice exclusion is for life, as such an individual will not be able to convince the court that he or she is a fit and proper person to be re-admitted to the profession.

Not all law students go into practice: combined degrees are common, such as arts/law, commerce/law, economics/law and even science/law. There are various openings in business and in government service. Practising lawyers are admitted as barristers or as solicitors (in some states it is possible to be both). The most senior barristers are known as Queen's Counsel.

The client comes first to the solicitor, who gives legal advice, draws up contracts and wills, and handles the preliminaries to litigation. The barrister gives advice on matters referred to him or her by a solicitor, and handles litigation. A client cannot come directly to a barrister, who is instead 'briefed' by the solicitor. The solicitor handles clients' trust moneys: the barrister never does. The solicitor is paid directly by the client: the barrister is paid by the solicitor. Solicitors (especially in large city firms) may be expert in particular fields of law — the barrister's expertise is in litigation.

Some barristers specialise in particular branches of law: others, like many solicitors, are generalists. Except in Victoria, a barrister is required to accept a brief sent to him or her by a solicitor for a proper professional fee. It therefore does not follow that the barrister believes his or her client to be in the right or (in a criminal case) not guilty — that is a matter for the court to decide. This ethical rule was adopted so that unpopular people would not be deprived of their rights by being denied legal representation.

THE TRIAL OF A CIVIL CASE

Procedure, especially in relation to the preliminary documents, varies as the inferior courts are less formal, and different names are given to the initiating documents. However, in a superior court the action is commonly initiated by the issue of a writ (or sometimes by a summons, or a notice of motion). A writ is a formal document issued by an officer of the superior court on which the plaintiff (person bringing the action to court) is required to provide a brief statement of the cause of action. The writ is supplemented (then or shortly after) by a statement of claim setting out the facts (but not the evidence) on which the plaintiff relies as well as the remedy sought.

The defendant, on being served with the writ, has a limited time in which to respond by filing an appearance — a formal document stating the defendant's intention to defend the case. If no appearance is filed, the plaintiff may obtain judgment by default. The defendant responds to the statement of claim with a defence — a document which sets out whether the defendant admits or denies each of the allegations in the statement of claim as well as indicating any further relevant facts. Should the defendant assert that he or she should be the one suing the plaintiff rather than the other way about, a counterclaim may be delivered to which the plaintiff in turn will deliver a defence. A party who contests the facts set out in the other party's defence will do so in a document known as 'a reply'. All of these documents together are called 'the pleadings'. Their purpose is to establish which facts are common and which are in dispute between the parties, and thereby to save time at the trial.

Other procedures designed to save time include 'Interrogatories', consisting of a series of questions asked by one party, which the other is required to answer on oath. In a motor accident case, for example, the answers can be used to establish when and precisely where the other party claims the accident occurred and at what speed he or she was driving, etc.

'Discovery' is also used in order to obtain copies of relevant documents (if not privileged) possessed by the other side. Should disputes arise about these or other matters, raising issues that need to be settled before the trial, there can be interlocutory proceedings. Once the case is ready for hearing a 'certificate of readiness' is given so that the case may be set down in the list.

In court each party presents its case in turn. The barrister 'opens' the case by explaining to the court what the case is about and outlining the evidence that the witnesses for his or her party will give. Each witness for that party is then called in turn and gives his or her evidence either on oath or, if there is a religious objection to the taking of an oath, by affirmation. The evidence given to that stage of the trial is known as 'evidence-in-chief'. Each witness on completing his or her evidence in chief may be cross-examined by the barrister for the defendant to test the evidence. After cross-examination the barrister for the party whose witness has been cross-examined then has the right to ask that witness further questions (known as 're-examination'). However, those questions are confined to matters arising out of the cross-examination.

The judge, of course, has the right to ask questions of a witness at any stage of the proceedings. However, usually a judge only asks those questions that he or she feels have not been asked by the barristers and that would assist in determining the case. It is an established principle that the judge must not ask so many questions as to disrupt the presentation of the case by the parties.

The system of evidence-in-chief, cross-examination and re-examination of course relates to evidence given orally. Evidence may also be given in writing. Known as documentary evidence, this may be given in addition to or in substitution for oral evidence. Some cases are tried solely on documentary evidence. For example, a case in which the court only has to interpret a contract may not involve any oral evidence: the contract can be placed before the court by agreement, or it can be annexed to an affidavit. There is an increasing tendency to require the evidence of expert witnesses to be given in typed form, exchanged between the parties, and filed with the court in advance of the hearing; the written evidence can then be supplemented by oral evidence. Both types of evidence are then subject to cross-examination.

In a case heard by both judge and jury, the judge decides issues of law and the jury issues of fact. In the absence of a jury, the judge decides issues of both law and fact.

The trial of a criminal case differs from the trial of a civil action. The most important difference relates to the standard of proof: the plaintiff in a civil case must prove his or her case on the balance of probabilities; the prosecution in a criminal trial must provide proof beyond reasonable doubt. For the trial of a criminal case, and further details about civil actions, see Gifford and Gifford (1983).

Problems in the judicial system

Someone wishing to consult a doctor or dentist may well experience delays if previous patients require longer than their allotted time. But delays before the courts are much worse, partly because the courts are not subject to the sort of competition that requires business people and media reporters to make themselves readily available. Not only are there lengthy delays in getting a hearing: once the case is set down for trial the parties, their lawyers and the witnesses cannot rely on the case being heard on a stated day. If a previous case is settled, they could find themselves called early, but if an earlier case drags on, they might be told to come back in another month.

Another problem affecting any judicial system is its cost. Poor people on legal aid, together with rich people, large companies and public authorities can afford to litigate and, if they lose at first instance, to appeal. However, people on average incomes may find themselves financially crippled by the costs of superior court litigation, even if they win. Furthermore, the compensation provided to witnesses and jurors for their time and trouble in being brought (under compulsion) before the court is generally much less than the earnings lost. Procedural reforms to shorten the hearing of cases can help with this problem, but they cannot eliminate it.

The common law is concerned to uphold individual rights. It is irrelevant to the common law whether a person is by descent a Greek or a Turk, a Serb or a Croat, a Jew or a Muslim. The citizen naturalised last week has the same rights and duties as a fourth- or fifth-generation Australian. Prejudice and discrimination are not in themselves penalised at common law (as opposed to sex and race discrimination legislation) so long as there is no violence or incitement to violence. The person who refuses to employ certain suppliers and workers, or to sell to potential customers, on the ground of prejudice merely disadvantages him or herself against more enlightened competitors. (This is one reason why apartheid in South Africa had to be established by legislation: prejudice in itself was not enough.)

Judges do not represent their own sex and racial group — they are there to apply the law. The interests of litigants demand strong and competent judges, not judges of any particular ethnic complexion. In a dispute between a Serb and a Croat, the Serb would object to a judge who was a prominent member of the Croatian community; similarly the Croat would object to a Serbian judge. The rules of natural justice would force such a judge to stand aside once reasonable suspicion of bias was established, even though the judge was in fact impartial. Justice must not only be done; it must be seen to be done.

Judges are expected to give reasons for their decisions, and if those reasons showed that a decision had been reached on the basis of sex or race prejudice rather than on the facts and the evidence before the court, that decision could be set aside on appeal, thereby giving warning to other judges.

THE RULE OF LAW

Throughout most of human history, governments have not been subject to the rule of law. It is no accident that people living under such governments have been exploited and subject to oppression. The only societies in which a decent standard of living for all can be maintained are those in which the rights of the individual are protected by independent and impartial courts, not only against criminals, but especially against governments.

For purposes of protection, governments are given a monopoly on the use of legalised force — but so great a power must be carefully scrutinised, lest the authority given for the protection of our rights should be used instead to limit, and eventually to destroy them. Parliament was in its origins a check upon government, in that it could refuse to grant the King taxes until grievances were remedied and justice was done. However, parliament's very success in establishing that only those who had its confidence could be ministers has led to parliament's decline: now that the ministers are themselves the leading members of the dominant political party it is not very likely that parliament will call them to account. Between elections, there are two checks on the behaviour of those in power: the courts, which see to it that the government's actions remain within the boundaries of the law, and the scrutiny of a free press.

FURTHER READING

A general introduction to the law in Australia is D. J. and K. H. Gifford 1983, *Our Legal System*, 2nd edn, Law Book Company, Sydney, while Geoffrey Walker 1988, *The Rule of Law: Foundation of Constitutional Democracy*, Melbourne University Press, Melbourne, fully explores the theme introduced in the last section of this chapter.

5

THE ECONOMY

Tony Makin

The term 'economics' derives from the Greek word *oikonemia*, meaning the management of a household or a nation. That part of the study of economics that treats the nation as the unit of analysis is macroeconomics. Many daily news items concern macroeconomic issues, such as reports on the latest statistics on inflation, unemployment, national production, interest rates, exchange rates and the balance of payments with the rest of the world. Not only are these facts regularly reported, but equally important are interpretations of how, or even whether, the federal government should respond to them using instruments of macroeconomic policy. Such issues are always central to national political debate.

For instance, we may know that the Australian Bureau of Statistics has measured unemployment at 10 per cent. Economists then ask: What has caused it? And how can the federal government use the levers, or instruments, of macroeconomic policy to reduce it? Similarly, does rising foreign debt mean the nation is losing control over its own affairs and to what extent has previous government policy been to blame? Economic events tend to receive so much attention that it takes a major natural disaster or outbreak of war to dislodge them from the front page of major newspapers. Even so, the very events that can overshadow the economy invariably have secondary economic implications, for instance, in terms of their impact on production and the government's budget.

Economics addresses important issues and to understand the subject in depth, it is necessary to become familiar with economic theory. Economic theory aims to build a framework of analysis to help us understand why different economic phenomena may occur. By and large, this is achieved by making generalisations about which economic variables affect other economic variables. In summary then, economics is about relating facts, which describe the economy's performance, through theory, which posits relationships between economic variables, to policy, which is about using various instruments to affect those variables that most concern us as a nation. This chapter does not attempt to survey economic theory as such, but instead focusses on some basic facts and, more importantly, on the institutions that are central to economic policy-making in Australia.

THE MAIN GOALS OF ECONOMIC POLICY

Economic policy-making is ultimately the responsibility of the federal government, which must constantly be making choices about how to use the policy instruments at its disposal to achieve end goals.

Most economists, policy-makers and voters would agree that the following goals or targets of policy are desirable:

1 Full employment: in practice, over the past decade this has meant trying to achieve an unemployment rate of less than about 7 per cent.
2 Stable prices: more recently, this has meant keeping the inflation rate under 2 per cent.
3 External balance: this refers to policy-makers' preferred state of the external or balance of payments accounts.
4 Economic growth: positive growth in the real output of goods and services (the nation's Gross Domestic Product, or GDP) implies a rising standard of living for the average household.

Why are these goals important? Taking unemployment first, it is obvious that, even though unemployment benefits are available, whenever there are workers who are after a job, but unable to get one, there will be disappointment and hardship. At a broader level, however, high levels of unemployment are a concern because the economy is not producing as much as it could if everyone was working. There is also a potential cost to the social order in terms of the distress, social unrest and crime that high unemployment can generate, particularly among special groups such as teenagers.

Inflation, defined as the increase in the overall level of prices of all goods and services, is unacceptable because it erodes everybody's purchasing power. Whereas the cost of unemployment directly impacts on the unemployed themselves, the effects of inflation are more widespread. In terms of public perceptions, this generally means inflation is considered a greater threat than unemployment. Nonetheless, it is often forgotten that once people become used to inflation, they can insulate themselves against its effects. Hence, when inflation is anticipated, wages, pensions and other contracts such as loans can be adjusted or indexed to inflation to offset the loss of purchasing power. On the other hand, when there is uncertainty about inflation, which always exists to some degree, it becomes difficult for the private sector to plan ahead and this limits the economy's ability to operate at its full employment level.

The nation's balance of payments, or external accounts, can also be a matter of concern to policy-makers to the extent that total payments received from other nations for what we produce fall behind total payments made by Australian firms and households to other nations. The state of the external accounts as well as the level of foreign debt has been a major issue in Australia since the mid-1980s and has generated heated debate among economists. Some argue that the state of the balance of payments accounts is worrisome because it reflects Australia's poor competitiveness or ability to trade successfully in the world. Others argue that the balance of payments accounts and level of foreign debt are indicative of increased liberalisation of international financial flows and the greater willingness on the part of foreigners to help fund development in Australia. Arguments about the economics of this issue are quite complex. Though academic economists tend to think Australia does not have a balance of payments problem, the federal government and the public at large tends to think it does. What the balance of payments actually means is discussed more fully shortly.

Economic growth, the fourth goal of economic policy, is a far less contentious ideal. Economic growth is simply the rise in the economy's capacity to produce goods and services. This is more of a longer term objective, for a consistent pattern of economic growth only becomes evident over extended periods of time — as long as decades. Increasing productivity (the quantity of goods and services produced per worker) is the key to a nation's successful growth performance, and this is largely determined by technological change. Economic growth is generally welcomed because it brings with it higher living standards. For instance, sustained economic growth in Australia has meant that colour television sets and video cassette recorders are affordable and commonplace, whereas an earlier generation had to be content with black and white sets, and the generation before that, just happy with radios. Though the benefits of growth seem obvious, not all agree. For instance, environmentalists highlight that the costs of growth, which include the possible depletion of non-renewable resources, ecological damage and pollution, largely outweigh the benefits and that growth should only proceed at 'sustainable' levels.

Furthermore, there may be other policy goals that have a more social, as opposed to strictly economic, dimension, such as achieving a more equitable income distribution that minimises the size of the disparity between the rich and the poor. Some of the macroeconomic goals discussed above may also be incompatible. For instance, expansionary policies that promote economic activity and hence employment may lead to a sharp rise in total spending on imports, which would worsen the trade balance and hence conflict with the goal of external balance. Similarly, it is widely recognised that a conflict exists between policy attempts to increase employment levels while keeping inflation and the current account deficit low.

Table 5.1   The state of the economy

	1989/90	1990/91	1991/92	1992/93	1993/94
Inflation	8.1%	5.3%	1.9%	1.0%	1.8%
Unemployment	6.2%	8.4%	10.4%	11.0%	10.5%
Current account deficit	$21.6b	$15.6b	$12.1b	$15.4b	$16.4b
GDP growth	3.6%	−0.8%	0.3%	2.8%	3.9%

Sources: Reserve Bank of Australia, *Bulletin*, various.

As Table 5.1 shows, there can be significant year-to-year changes in these macroeconomic variables, as for instance occurred in 1990/91 with the sharp drop in GDP growth, marking the beginning of the recession of the early 1990s.

THE FEDERAL GOVERNMENT AND THE ECONOMY

The federal government implements its economic policies through advice and action from a range of economic institutions in Australia.

In broad terms, the economic instruments/targets schema shown in Figure 5.1 below.

Figure 5.1   Instruments and targets

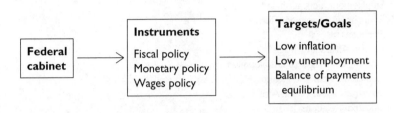

The overall economic policy stance is agreed upon by the federal cabinet, which allows the prime minister, the federal treasurer and a number of special ministerial committees, most notably the expenditure review committee, considerable discretion to implement it. Decisions made by cabinet on the full range of economic policies are often made in response to proposals and professional advice tendered by the key economic departments in the federal public service, all of which are located in Canberra. The most important of these are the Departments of the Treasury; Prime Minister and Cabinet; Finance; Industry, Science and Technology; Employment, Education and Training; and Foreign Affairs and Trade.

The federal treasurer is primarily responsible for manipulating the policy instruments and the Treasury Department is normally the major source of economic advice within the federal bureaucracy, for it explicitly has responsibility for:

- assessing current economic conditions and advising on appropriate fiscal, monetary and wages policies;
- providing advice on the structure and functioning of financial institutions;
- advising on industry structure and development;
- managing government spending and receipts as well as the public debt.

In general, the other federal departments have responsibility for administering a host of policy programs previously initiated by federal governments. Table 5.2 below lists all federal government departments responsible for administering government programs.

Table 5.2 Federal government departments

Administrative Services
Attorney General's
Communications and the Arts
Defence
Employment, Education and Training
Environment, Sport and Territories
Finance
Foreign Affairs and Trade
Housing and Regional Development
Human Services and Health
Immigration and Ethnic Affairs
Industrial Relations
Industry, Science and Technology
Primary Industries and Energy
Prime Minister and Cabinet
Social Security
Tourism
Transport
Treasury
Veterans' Affairs

FISCAL POLICY AND THE PUBLIC SECTOR

Nearly all economic decisions taken by the federal government have implications for the federal budget to the extent that they affect public expenditure or revenue. As with any budget, the federal budget itemises expenditures and receipts over the fiscal year, which runs from 1 July to 30 June. Discretionary changes made by the government to public spending, such as commitments to spend more on hospitals, bridges and dams or spend more on welfare, education and defence, affect the outlays side of the budget. Decisions to change income taxes, company taxes or duties on petrol, beer or cigarettes influence the receipts side.

The main components of federal spending include social security payments, health, defence and payments to state governments. On the receipts side, most revenue comes from individual and company income taxes, with the remainder from excise and sales taxes. The federal budget is in deficit if receipts fall short of outlays, and in surplus if revenue exceeds outlays. Federal budgets must eventually be approved by the federal parliament and often reflect the influence of a range of industry and special interest groups, which lobby elected representatives for particular concessions and programs. Examples of these groups include the Metal Trades Industry Association, the National Farmers Federation, the Australian Mining Industry Council, various social welfare groups and taxpayer associations.

Each year the budget is presented to the parliament with much fanfare by the federal treasurer. Also included in the budget are a set of economic forecasts put together by the federal treasury, which predict the likely outcomes over the coming year for the major economic variables discussed — inflation, unemployment, economic activity and the balance of payments. Financial markets and business at large keenly await this information as it has implications for other important economic variables, particularly interest rates and exchange rates. With the information contained in the budget, the business and household sectors have a better idea of future prospects and hence are better able to plan ahead.

The major items in the federal budget for recent years are shown in Table 5.3.

Federal budgets invariably attract great attention simply because every citizen can be affected, at least potentially, by government initiatives to establish new industry support or welfare programs or by government decisions to abolish existing schemes. Over the past decade, for example, major changes have been announced affecting tertiary students through changes to Austudy, the unemployed through changes in entitlements to unemployment benefits, home owners through changes in assistance for purchasing their first home, senior citizens through changes in benefits for pensioners, farmers, mining companies and manufacturers, through changes in taxation rules for companies, and all wage earners, through changes in tax rates on their income.

The governments in the states, the Northern Territory and the Australian Capital Territory also bring down annual budgets each year, which reflect their spending and revenue raising priorities. By and large, however, these governments depend heavily on the allocation of funds from the Commonwealth and their focus is on more parochial concerns.

Apart from federal and state government departments, the public sector in Australia also includes many public enterprises. Many every day services such as electricity, water, communications, and transport are provided by public trading enterprises such as the various state rail authorities, Australia Post, Qantas, and Telecom. These enterprises are ultimately subject to some form of government control and regulation and are important economic institutions because they provide a substantial proportion of national income each year.

Table 5.3 The federal budget ($m)

	1993/94	1994/95
Outlays		
Defence	9 800	9 637
Education	9 705	10 056
Health	16 303	17 275
Social Security and welfare	41 939	43 449
Housing	1 124	1 196
Culture and recreation	1 124	1 351
Economic services (incl. public utilities, assistance to industry, etc.)	7 692	8 781
General public services	7 779	8 014
Not allocated to function		
• Payments to or for the states, the Northern Territory and local government authorities (not elsewhere classified)	15 479	15 165
• Public debt interest	6 496	8 386
• Other	−2 928	−2 678
Total outlays	114 513	120 633
Receipts		
Taxation revenue		
• Customs duty	3 280	3 290
• Excise duty	11 030	12 270
• Sales tax	10 350	11 150
• Income Tax – Individuals	50 260	54 390
– Companies	12 950	13 860
– Other	4 560	6 520
• Other taxes, fees and fines	1 741	1 845
Total taxation revenue	94 171	103 325
Interest, rent and dividends	6 749	5 581
Total receipts	100 920	108 906
Deficit (−)/Surplus (+)	−13 593	−11 727

Source: Federal Treasury, *Budget Statements 1994–95.*

MONETARY POLICY, THE RESERVE BANK AND FINANCIAL INSTITUTIONS

Monetary policy is under the general direction of the federal treasurer and is implemented by Australia's central bank, the Reserve Bank of Australia (RBA), which is located in Sydney.

From 1945 until 1960, the Commonwealth Bank of Australia actually performed central banking functions for the federal government before the existing RBA (sometimes referred to in financial markets as 'The Bank') was established by the Reserve Bank Act, which became effective in January 1960. Since then, the RBA has operated under a governor with its own board and staff.

The RBA operates with some degree of independence from the federal government, but is required to report regularly to the treasurer on monetary and banking policy. Moreover, since the secretary of the Treasury Department is a member of the RBA Board, along with the governor, deputy governor and other members from industry, unions and academia, there is close liaison with the Department of the Treasury. RBA officers also interact frequently with the Department of the Prime Minister and Cabinet, the Department of Finance and the Australian Bureau of Statistics about current and prospective national and international economic institutions.

Broadly speaking, the RBA formulates and implements monetary and banking policy. The main objectives of monetary policy are outlined in the *Reserve Bank Act 1959*:

> It is the duty of the Board, within the limits of its powers, to ensure that the monetary and banking policy of the Bank is directed to the greatest advantage of the people of Australia and that the powers of the Bank under this Act, the Banking Act 1959 and the regulations under that Act are exercised in such a manner as, in the opinion of the Board, will best contribute to:
> (a) the stability of the currency of Australia;
> (b) the maintenance of full employment in Australia; and
> (c) the economic prosperity and welfare of the people of Australia.

The objectives broadly correspond with the goals of macroeconomic policy as outlined earlier, once it is realised that 'stability of the currency' actually means minimising inflation.

The RBA also performs important functions in accordance with the *Financial Corporations Act 1974*, which states:

The object of this Act is to assist the Australian Government to achieve effective management of the Australian economy by providing a means for:

(a) the examination of the business activities of certain financial and trading corporations; and

(b) the regulation of those activities for the purpose of contributing to economic stability, the maintenance of full employment, the efficient allocation of productive resources, the ensuring of an adequate level of finance for housing and the economic prosperity and welfare of the people of Australia.

Hence not only does the RBA, at the peak of Australia's financial system, implement monetary policy to influence overall economic activity, it has an important role as a prudential overseer of the system as a whole to ensure its efficiency and stability. Figure 5.2 provides a summary picture of the structure of the financial system. The system is essentially a network of financial institutions, which by and large simply act as intermediaries, or go-betweens, for savers and investors in the economy.

Figure 5.2   The Australian financial system

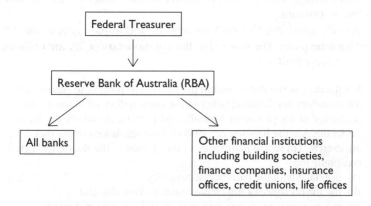

Other functions of the RBA include acting as major banker to the federal government, some public authorities and state governments, acting as banker to the banks themselves and some other financial institutions, and printing the paper notes that circulate as money. It also distributes the coins minted by the Federal Mint in Canberra, which operates under the auspices of the Treasury. At the international level, the RBA retains Australia's official reserves of gold and foreign exchange as well as intervening from time to time in the foreign exchange market to dampen excessive exchange rate volatility.

The framework for the conduct of monetary policy has changed markedly over the past decade as a consequence of the widespread deregulation of Australia's financial system, which has led to rapid structural change within the financial system. In terms of the operation of monetary policy by the central bank, the most significant change has been a shift away from a credit rationing approach, which was implemented via techniques to decrease or increase the amount of funds that the commercial banks could lend, to what is called 'open market operations'. This approach involves the RBA entering the funds market directly to change the supply of funds in circulation.

Both domestic and international financial transactions were tightly controlled in Australia until the early 1980s. For instance, at the domestic level there were quantitative limits on bank lending, deposit and lending rates were controlled and bank reserves were subject to strict regulatory arrangements, whereby trading banks had to lodge a proportion of their deposits with the RBA. A number of restrictions also previously impeded international capital inflows and outflows. For example, whenever the authorities considered capital inflows excessive, embargoes on short-term offshore borrowing were often implemented, and foreign investment in Australia was strictly monitored.

Historically, the process of financial market integration began gathering pace worldwide from the mid-1970s with the relaxation of capital controls in the United States and Canada. By the end of the 1970s, the United Kingdom had abolished all exchange controls and throughout the 1980s Japan gradually relaxed restrictions on foreign outward investment by institutional investors. Liberalisation of Australia's financial markets was virtually complete by the mid-1980s and institutional barriers impeding the movement of financial capital within the entire developed world have now largely disappeared.

Deregulation proceeded apace in Australia essentially because there was widespread acceptance that microeconomic efficiency gains could be realised by removing domestic interest rate distortions and by fostering increased competition between financial intermediaries. Deregulation was also expected to improve the effectiveness of monetary policy as a macroeconomic stabilisation instrument. Accompanying the deregulatory changes were strengthened prudential supervisory arrangements. Capital backing of banks was the basis of prudential regulation and guidelines consistent with international banking practice were issued by the RBA in 1988. These set out the appropriate ratio of capital reserves that banks were obliged to hold against risk weighted assets and were intended to strengthen the capitalisation of banks and hence the security of the financial system.

In an overall sense, the abolition of official restrictions on financial transactions transformed the Australian financial system from being heavily regulated and segmented, into one that was lightly regulated and internationally integrated. Access to international financial capital and services increased greatly, due in particular to the abolition of exchange controls in Australia and the entry of foreign banks. Combined with the removal of capital controls abroad and the development of the Eurodollar market, this boosted resident firms' borrowing opportunities and implied that international money movements increased significantly.

With enhanced international mobility of funds, there is now a closer correspondence between domestic and foreign interest rates. Funds flow virtually instantaneously across country borders to maximise returns, after allowing for expected exchange rate movements. Further, improved international capital mobility makes it easier to finance domestic expenditure, particularly investment, with foreign savings.

The question of how monetary policy should be conducted is one of those perennial issues in economics that generate strong disagreement among economists and policy-makers. The view that governments are responsible for stabilising the economy is founded on the assumption that events like the Great Depression of the 1930s happen frequently and regularly, and that discretionary macroeconomic reactions are generally both effective and timely.

Views about discretionary macroeconomic policy intervention usually depend on whether one judges the interventions, of themselves, to have stabilised or destabilised the cycle of economic activity. Over recent years, the monetary policy implemented by the RBA under the general direction of the federal treasurer has been aimed mainly at containing inflation and managing Australia's cycle of economic activity.

In the macroeconomic interventionist tradition, monetary policy in Australia over past decades has treated various aggregate fluctuations as unique phenomena, and reacted quite differently from one event to another. But the evidence suggests that monetary activism has not always smoothed the peaks and troughs of the business cycle. In fact, a common view of the behaviour of the Australian economy over recent years is that the boom in the late 1980s was mainly due to the easing of monetary policy following the worldwide stock market crash of 1987. The severe recession of the early 1990s was precipitated by a very tight monetary stance, which was essentially driven by official concern about the level of Australia's foreign debt.

More recent discussion about the conduct of monetary policy in Australia has raised the question of central bank independence as a means of avoiding undue political influence over the conduct of monetary policy. Such influence may be exercised by federal governments seeking to improve their chances of re-election. Those countries noted for the stability of their monetary policies, such as New Zealand, Switzerland and Germany, have central banks that are quite independent of direct government control. At the other end of the scale, countries with notoriously unstable monetary policies, such as Brazil, have central banks completely under the control of the government. (See Makin, 1993, for further discussion of whether a more independent RBA is necessary to improve the conduct of monetary policy in Australia.)

WAGES AND INCOMES POLICIES

Wages and incomes policies can take many forms and over the past quarter century, government controls of one sort or another have been imposed on wages or prices in many countries including Canada, the United States, Ireland, Denmark, Sweden, Norway, Italy, the United Kingdom and Australia.

Such measures basically recognise the important role trade unions can play in generating inflation by means of their influence on the level of wages. Put simply, if trade unions raise inflation by pushing up wages, then some agreement or 'accord' needs to be negotiated between unions and the government to alleviate inflationary pressures from this particular source.

Trade unions represent employees seeking higher wages and improved working conditions. Unions achieve their objectives by bargaining with employers at the enterprise or industry level, by presenting argument to legally constituted arbitration tribunals, or by means of strike action.

Australia's union movement had its beginnings in the early 1800s when 'craft guilds' were formed to provide benefits for groups of skilled workers. Initially, efforts to improve working conditions and pay were minimal, but this changed after the gold rushes of the 1850s. In the 1870s and 1880s wages rose as a result of collective bargaining or direct negotiations between unions and employers and the average working week was also reduced to 48 hours over six days.

By 1885 there were more than 100 unions in Australia representing a vast range of unskilled and skilled workers and by the 1890s union power was put to the test. Consequently, the economy witnessed some crippling strikes by shearers, miners and stevedores, which encouraged the formation of the Australian Labor Party and also the establishment of new conciliation and arbitration mechanisms.

In the twentieth century, union membership in Australia has been high and with over half of all employees registered as union members, Australia has one of the most powerful union movements in the world. The Australian Council of Trade Unions (ACTU) was formed in 1927 as the peak body of unions in Australia and is integral to the Australian industrial relations framework. Employers have also grouped into associations to present a common voice on industrial relations and other economic policy matters. The most important of these are the Australian Chamber of Commerce and Industry and the Business Council of Australia.

Various types of wages policy have been implemented by federal governments in Australia since 1980. For instance, the Fraser government initiated a wages pause in late 1982 as a means of reducing inflation, which had risen to around 12 per cent. When the Hawke government came to power in March 1983, a key weapon in its economic policy armoury was the Prices and Incomes Accord, designed to restrain wage rises while allowing the government to implement expansionary fiscal policy aimed at reducing the high level of unemployment (it had jumped to 10 per cent).

The Accord struck between the ACTU and the government depended on common agreement, or consensus, being reached on the nature and extent of the nation's economic problems and the union movement's willingness to curb its wage demands. Hence it was recognised that frequent consultation and liaison was necessary between ACTU officials and the government.

The Accord also recognised the need for monitoring prices in the economy and to this end, the Prices Surveillance Authority (PSA) was established in 1984. The PSA has no powers to set prices, but acts by publicising instances where price rises in particular industries seem excessive.

It is generally accepted that the Accord has succeeded in alleviating wage pressures, but there have been several significant modifications to the original Accord. Following a slump in Australia's export prices in the mid-1980s, the ACTU accepted that wages had to be discounted to assist the nation's competitiveness. Other important modifications to the structure of the original Accord include provisions for extending superannuation entitlements and shifting to more flexible wage fixing criteria, including enterprise bargaining, which are expected to increase workplace efficiency and hence boost economic performance. The Industrial Relations Commission, which conciliates and arbitrates disputes between unions and employers, nonetheless remains central to the wage determination process.

Apart from the evident restraint in wages growth, the Accord has undoubtedly been responsible for reducing the number of working days lost due to industrial disputes. Indeed, under the Accord, industrial relations in Australia have been relatively harmonious by the standards of the 1960s and 1970s.

AUSTRALIA'S BALANCE OF INTERNATIONAL PAYMENTS

Any discussion of the Australian economy must refer to the nature and significance of the balance of payments accounts, which record all economic transactions of Australian residents with the rest of the world. The following section on the meaning and significance of the balance of payments accounts draws on material in Makin (1989).

Individual Australians are linked every day to the rest of the world through the prices and quantities of goods and financial assets they buy and sell, their travel, communication and relations with foreign governments. Whenever funds are exchanged between residents and foreigners, the transactions are recorded in Australia's balance of payments, or external accounts, as well as, but with opposite sign, in the corresponding accounts of the non-resident's country.

The 'balance of payments' as such does not refer to the notion of the balance of payments as understood before the exchange rate, the value of the Australian dollar in terms of other currencies, was allowed to float in the early 1980s. Under the now defunct Bretton Woods system of exchange rate management set up after World War II, balance of payments problems for Australia and other developed countries most often involved unsustainable rundowns in the central bank's holdings of foreign currency assets. Such holdings were necessary to peg the value of the currency in the face of a shortfall between residents' demand for foreign currency arising, for example, as a consequence of the demand for imports, and the supply of foreign currency provided to residents by foreigners, as occurred when exports were sold.

Under that system, which prevailed for around a quarter of a century, when international capital markets were far less sophisticated, balance of payments deficits usually arose for current account reasons. (The current account balance is the trade balance less interest and other income paid to foreigners.) These deficits were the manifestations of rundowns in official foreign exchange reserves required to meet short-falls in foreign exchange. The availability of such reserves represented the ultimate external constraint on an economy's performance.

In contrast, the present floating exchange rate system, which has operated internationally since the early 1970s and for Australia since 1983, almost by definition does not depend on direct intervention by the monetary authorities to maintain any particular exchange rate. Under the purest of floats, the overall balance of payments should in practice be zero with the exchange rate itself bearing all the pressure of external adjustment.

Taken as a whole, Australia's international transactions must always balance. Under a floating exchange rate regime, exchange rates themselves move to eliminate any excess demand or supply of currencies on the foreign exchange market, whereas the central bank manages the exchange rate through intervention under a fixed exchange rate regime. If some force tends to raise or lower the balance in one category of external transactions, a process is automatically set in motion that leads to an offset in other categories.

For example, if there is a surge in foreign demand for Australian financial assets, the additional foreign investment will raise the capital account surplus, which may strengthen the exchange rate and worsen the trade balance. Similarly, a sudden influx of foreign tourists would raise the value of credits recorded in the current account. To the extent that this strengthens the currency and national income, higher merchandise imports would raise current account debits. The current and capital account imbalances of the external accounts are jointly determined at the point where the net demand for foreign funds on one side matches the net supply on the other, with the exchange rate performing the balancing role.

However, what usually attracts most scrutiny is not the international capital or financial flows, but the matching current account deficit. There has been prolonged debate about whether Australia's persistent current account deficits and level of foreign debt are really problematic or not. For conflicting views, see Makin (1988) and Moore (1990).

AUSTRALIA IN THE WORLD ECONOMY

Australia is a relatively open economy in that a sizeable share of its national output is influenced by international economic activity. One measure of openness is the share of exports and imports in GDP: this stands at around 40 per cent. A more comprehensive concept of openness (though difficult to measure accurately) is the share of potentially tradeable goods and services. This measure would include Australian production, which does not actually cross foreign borders, but which is nonetheless subject to international competition (for example, Tasmanian hops sold to make Queensland beer).

Within the tradeable sector of the Australian economy, manufacturing industries account for the bulk of importable products. These are goods whose domestic output falls short of total domestic demand as manifested in net imports, such as the textile, clothing, footwear, pharmaceutical, cosmetic, white goods, electronics and motor vehicle industries. On the other hand, exportable industries — industries whose domestic production exceeds domestic demand and gives rise to net exports — are largely the agricultural and mining industries such as wool, wheat, beef, coal, iron ore, bauxite and gold.

What determines whether industries are by nature exportable or importable is the long-accepted principle of comparative advantage, as reflected in the relative cost structures of different industries. Comparative advantage is one of the most fundamental concepts of international trade theory, yet is often forgotten in public debate on the optimal make-up of Australian industry. A major determinant of relative costs is the concentration of factor endowments. For instance, in relative terms, Australia has an abundance of productive land and natural resources relative to working population. These resources can be extracted, harvested, or, in the case of visiting foreign tourists, simply observed for pleasure.

In contrast, the economies of our trading partners, such as Japan, have an abundance of labour relative to natural exploitable resources. Those countries find it advantageous to employ the relatively abundant factor in adding value to imported primary products through manufacturing activity. So relatively natural resource-intensive economies such as Australia and relatively labour-intensive ones like Japan are complementary to one another.

Traditional trade theory stresses the mutual benefits conferred on nations when they exchange, through international trade commodities that each can produce at least cost. As the famous British economist and philosopher, David Hume, pointed out in the eighteenth century, 'Nature, by giving a diversity of geniuses, climates and soils, to different nations, has secured their mutual intercourse and commerce, as long as they all remain industrious and civilised'. The English economist, David Ricardo, and many modern international trade theorists later transformed this idea into the modern economic theory of comparative advantage. In his famous example, Ricardo argued that England and Portugal could raise their national incomes through the increased trade made possible if England specialised more in cloth production and Portugal specialised more in making wine.

The Australian economy is less industrialised today than it was 20 years ago. Over this period the mining industry, particularly energy-intensive sectors, and services, such as construction, retail trade, transport and public administration, have grown significantly. As in other developed economies, for many decades the production of services has dominated other forms of economic activity. Australia has enjoyed relatively rapid growth over recent decades by broadly adhering to the Humean/Ricardian prescription. Indeed, Australia's real economic growth over the 1980s exceeded that of most other OECD members, including the USA, New Zealand, Canada, Denmark, France, Germany, Ireland, Italy, Netherlands, Spain, Sweden, Switzerland, United Kingdom, Greece and Portugal.

Ever since Federation most of Australia's exports have been basic or semi-processed commodities. Today, more than three-quarters of all merchandise exports fall into just five commodity classifications: cereal grains, metal ores, coal, minerals and meat. In contrast, more than three-quarters of imports are manufactures such as transport, machinery, textiles, chemicals and processed foods. Oil is the most significant commodity import. Australia has sustained its comparative advantage in primary production mainly because productivity has grown impressively in the rural and mining sectors.

An important source of export market shocks to small commodity-exporting nations is the business cycle in the large industrialised economies. If economic activity in these countries falls, the demand for Australia's raw materials also falls, depressing commodity prices relative to the prices of manufactured goods. However, the international transmission of business cycle fluctuations would not be any less disruptive for a small economy like Australia if manufactured goods made up a greater share of its exports. For if aggregate demand in the industrialised world falls, demand for manufactured exports from Australia could also be expected to fall accordingly.

Australia's relative international ranking in the GNP or income-per-head league tables, fell dramatically after World War II from third highest in 1950 to tenth in the early 1990s. In part, this was due to protectionist measures adopted by previous federal governments of all political persuasions, which sought to shut Australia off from the forces of international competition, to Australia's ultimate cost. More recently Australia has become more integrated with the rest of the world as a result of the financial market liberalisation discussed earlier, as well as the growth in international trade in goods and services. It is a simple fact that if smaller economies like Australia tend to be more open to international trade, then national incomes tend to be higher.

The pace of internationalisation of the economy will be further boosted by recent global and regional initiatives aimed at promoting free trade in goods and services, such as the conclusion of the Uruguay round of General Agreement on Tariffs and Trade (GATT) and moves to establish Asian-Pacific Economic Cooperation (APEC).

An important characteristic of the Australian economy in the future will be its strong trading orientation toward the industrialising countries of Asia, now experiencing much higher growth rates than the developed countries of Western Europe, which traditionally have been Australia's major trading partners.

CONCLUSION

This chapter has aimed to provide the reader with a basis for understanding the institutional framework through which macroeconomic policy is devised and delivered in Australia. Macroeconomic issues and the federal government's policy responses to them will always attract widespread attention and generate passionate debate simply because they affect each and every citizen in one way or another. Consequently, it seems everybody has an opinion about what the biggest problems are and what should be done.

Different issues make the economic agenda every day. For example, should manufacturing exports be subsidised? Or, should financial markets be reregulated to reduce foreign debt? Some more fundamental issues always seem to be with us, particularly the threat of inflation and high unemployment levels.

Finally, a good reason for following the big economic issues of the day is that rarely is there full agreement between economists, politicians and commentators on such questions as whether a particular shift in economic policy has been taken at the right time, whether the shift is big enough, or indeed sometimes, whether the right instruments have actually been used to meet the targets in question.

FURTHER READING

Jackson & McConnell (1994) provide an elementary treatment of macroeconomic principles with applications to Australia. Some of the economic policy issues raised in this chapter are covered in more depth in a book of readings on the Australian economy edited by Maxwell & Hopkins (1993). Those especially interested in the financial sector of the Australian economy could also consult Lewis & Wallace (1993), which, among other things, describes the institutional features of Australia's financial markets including its stock markets, bond markets and foreign exchange markets. Short, and usually very readable, articles on macroeconomic policy-making in Australia also regularly appear in the RBA Bulletin, which is published every month.

REFERENCES

Hume, D. 1963, *Essays Moral, Political and Literary*, Oxford University Press, London.

Jackson, J. and McConnell, C. 1994, *Economics*, 4th Australian edn, McGraw Hill, Sydney.

Lewis, M. and Wallace, R. 1993, *The Australian Financial System*, Longman Cheshire, Melbourne.

Makin, A. 1988, 'Targeting Australia's current account: a new mercantilism?', *Economic Analysis and Policy*, 18 (2), pp.199–212.

Makin, A. 1989, 'The external imbalance: burden or blessing?' *Australian Quarterly*, 61 (3), pp.337–43.

Makin, A. 1993, 'Reserve bank independence or a money growth rule?', *Policy*, 9 (4), pp.9–12.

Maxwell, P. and Hopkins, S. 1993, *Macroeconomics: Contemporary Australian Readings*, Harper Educational, Melbourne.

Moore, D. 1990, 'Foreign debt: Is it still a problem?' *Australian Economic Review*, 3rd quarter, pp.17–34.

Reserve Bank of Australia, *Bulletin*, various.

Reserve Bank of Australia 1987, *Reserve Bank of Australia: Functions and Operations*, RBA, Sydney.

Ricardo, D. 1817, *On the Principles of Political Economy and Taxation*, John Murray, London.

Federal Treasury, *Budget Statements* (annual), AGPS, Canberra.

6

INDUSTRIAL RELATIONS

....

Greg Bamber and Edward Davis

Industrial relations are often front page news and prominent in radio and television bulletins. Some of the news and commentary veer towards the sensational, with debate concentrated on perennial issues such as strikes and union power. More recently, attention has been paid to the link between industrial relations and enterprise performance. This chapter examines the Australian industrial relations context, details characteristics of key players and explores industrial relations processes, industrial conflict and pay determination. Included is a discussion of trends and debates about industrial democracy and employee participation, equal opportunities and industrial relations reform.

The Australian states were separate colonies until 1901 when they federated to become an independent country within the British Commonwealth. But these states still wield considerable power over many issues, including industrial relations. Under the Australian Constitution, the federal government appeared to have only limited industrial powers and was able to make laws only on conciliation and arbitration for the prevention and settlement of industrial disputes extending beyond the limits of any one state (section 51, xxxv). Industrial relations reforms implemented in 1994 have challenged this traditional interpretation of the powers of the federal government, which aims to increase its influence in industrial relations, as discussed later.

Having earlier rejected the notion of compulsory arbitration, unions changed their stance after some disastrous defeats during a wave of strikes in the early 1890s. The *Conciliation and Arbitration Act 1904* encouraged employers to recognise unions registered under the Act, and empowered these unions to make claims on behalf of all employees within their coverage. Under the 1904 Act then, unions could ensure that employers were called to court (later a commission) even if they were unwilling to negotiate. Once the court had made an award (a decision on pay or other terms of employment), its provisions were legally enforceable. Although employers were initially hostile to the federal Court of Conciliation and Arbitration established under the Act, they later found that they could use the procedures to their advantage and generally supported them.

There has long been a high degree of state intervention in the Australian labour market, by contrast with Britain, which has often been characterised as having a voluntary approach and relatively little state intervention (see Bamber and Lansbury, 1993, ch. 2). The advent of arbitration was a significant departure from the British traditions that had been important in Australia before the 1890s, when the foundations of Australia's twentieth-century industrial relations system were established.

THE POLITICAL AND ECONOMIC ENVIRONMENT

Australian labourism (Hagan, 1981, p.45) differs from that in Britain and other industrialised market economies. There were at least three special characteristics of Australian labourism. First, the 1904 Act and its provision for compulsory arbitration was a key element of Australia's initial 'social contract' (Frenkel, 1990). A second element was a law restricting immigration, thereby limiting the supply side of the labour market. The 'white Australia' policy aimed to keep out Asians, in particular, who were seen as threatening union strength and union members' living standards. The third element involved creating a regime of tariffs to protect domestic products from the threat of cheap imports. All political parties maintained such characteristics at least until the post-1945 period.

In the context of protectionist policies, most manufacturing has been oriented to domestic markets. High tariff barriers, however, have not prevented the decline of manufacturing employment. Between 1981 and 1991, manufacturing employment declined from 23 per cent to 18 per cent. The proportion of employees in agriculture fell from 7.6 per cent to 5 per cent, but aspects of employment in the service sector increased — for example, the percentage employed in finance rose from 7.6 per cent to 10.3 per cent (ABS, 1993a).

The tariff policy was originally designed to help create employment for an expanding population. It also enabled commissions to determine wages more on social and equity grounds than in accordance with productivity and market forces. Many protected industries, anticipating the chill winds of unrestricted competition, tenaciously lobbied governments to retain high tariff levels. The move of the Whitlam Labor government (1972–75) to reduce tariffs by 25 per cent 'at a single stroke', was strongly criticised by employers and by unions as leading to increased levels of unemployment, especially in industries vulnerable to overseas competition.

Australia is a welfare state, which provides unemployment benefits, for example, to a greater extent than the USA or Japan. Nevertheless, Australia's welfare arrangements are less developed than those in most Western European countries. Since Federation, conservative political parties have generally dominated federal government. However, there were reformist post-war Labor governments in the 1941–49 and 1972–75 periods. Labor won again in 1983 and has held federal office since then. The Australian Labor Party (ALP) has been more sympathetic to union interests. Traditionally unions have seen wage bargaining or determination via arbitration as a higher priority than improving social welfare benefits. In the Labor government elected in 1983, prime minister Bob Hawke was a former president of the Australian Council of Trade Unions (ACTU); and several other ministers had also held senior union posts before their entry into parliament. This government, through its Accord with the ACTU, placed more formal emphasis on a range of goals including job creation, improved social welfare and improved standards of living; wage bargaining, then, was only one of its priorities.

The Hawke and subsequent Keating Labor governments have since 1983 sought to reduce tariffs to stimulate competition. The lengths to which government should go to protect particular industries and to encourage competition is subject to much debate in the 1990s. These debates echo some aspects of those of the 1890s.

RELEVANT LAWS

In 1988 the Hawke Labor government replaced the *Conciliation and Arbitration Act 1904* with the *Industrial Relations Act 1988*. In most respects, the new Act was similar to its predecessor, which had been extensively amended since 1904. Federal unions generally registered with the Industrial Registrar to gain access to arbitration and to enjoy full legal status. There were also registration requirements for employers and employers' associations, but registration was more significant for unions since it provided them with an important platform. The Act prescribed that a union should not be registered if there was already another in existence to which employees could 'conveniently belong'. While this helped to reduce inter-union disputes, it also inhibited the development of new unions (for example, specific enterprise unions) and helped preserve some whose traditional membership areas had declined.

The arbitration system includes federal and state industrial commissions. The federal Court of Conciliation and Arbitration used to have arbitral and judicial functions. More recently, the industrial division of the Federal Court administered the judicial provisions of the Act, while the Australian Industrial Relations Commission (the commission) or its predecessors carried out non-judicial functions. These changes of functions were implemented following the 'Boilermakers' Case (1956) in which the High Court ruled that, under the 'separation of powers' doctrine in the Constitution, arbitral and judicial functions could not be carried out by the same tribunal. This requirement does not apply to the state industrial commissions, which administer awards in each state, covering approximately half the workforce; federal awards cover approximately a third of the workforce. In late 1993 amendments to the federal Industrial Relations Act provided for a new Industrial Court to take over the work previously done by the industrial division of the federal court and to undertake some new functions.

THE MAIN ACTORS

Employers' associations

The early apparent strength of unions in Australia encouraged the development of employers' associations and led them to place greater emphasis on employment issues than their counterparts in some other countries (Plowman, 1980). However, there is great variation in the size and complexity of employers' associations from small, single-industry bodies to large organisations that attempt to cover all employers within a particular state. Most employers' associations offer a range of services to their members, so that industrial relations advice may be only one of their priorities. Trade and commercial matters are increasingly to the fore. In 1977, the Confederation of Australian Industry (CAI) was established as the major national employers' body, 50 years after the formation of the ACTU. In 1983, a group of large employers set up the Business Council of Australia (BCA) partly as a result of their dissatisfaction with the apparent inability of the CAI to service the needs of its diverse membership. During the 1980s there were several important departures from the CAI. These included large affiliates such as the Metal Trades Industry Association (1987) and the Australian Chamber of Manufacturers (1989). One repercussion was the airing of differences between employers.

In a bid to coordinate employer policy more effectively, the CAI merged with the Australian Chamber of Commerce to form the Australian Chamber of Commerce and Industry (ACCI) in 1992. The ACCI comprised some 40 employer organisations, which represented around 300 000 individual businesses spread across the economy. None the less, several major employers' associations did not affiliate with the ACCI. The views of Australian employers, then, are still represented in a fragmented way. The ACCI argues that there are many policy and other matters over which employers agree and that their case will be strengthened by coordination and unity. The alternative view is that there are inevitable differences among employers and their associations and that the diversity of employers' associations reflects this. The disunity among employers' organisations can be contrasted with the relatively high level of unity demonstrated by unions under the umbrella of the ACTU.

Unions

The establishment of the legally-based arbitration system in the early twentieth century encouraged the rapid growth of unions. By 1921, approximately 50 per cent of the Australian labour force was unionised. But union density has fluctuated. During the depression of the early 1930s it dropped to little over 40 per cent. In the 1940s there was a steady increase in density with a peak of 65 per cent (according to data collected by unions) in 1953. Union density has also been gauged on the basis of household surveys. This shows a steep decline since the mid-1970s. In 1976, 51 per cent of all employees were in unions (56 per cent males; 43 per cent females). By 1992 this had fallen to 40 per cent (43 per cent males; 35 per cent females) (ABS, 1993b). One projection is that density will fall to 20 per cent by 2004 (Jost, 1994). Contributing factors have been the relative decline in employment in manufacturing (a bastion for unions), and the strong growth in the service sector, which is generally more difficult to unionise. Significant growth in part-time and casual employment has been an additional factor, as these workers are also difficult to unionise.

The profile of unions has been transformed since 1983. The Australian Bureau of Statistics (ABS) recorded that in 1983 there were 319 unions (ABS, 1984a). Membership was spread unevenly with, at one end of the scale, 105 unions each with fewer than 500 members and accounting for less than 1 per cent of total membership. At the other end, nine unions had 80 000 or more members each, accounting for 34 per cent of membership. In 1987 the ACTU urged its affiliates to seek mergers and amalgamations to streamline union operations. The ACTU's rationale was that a smaller number of larger unions would be more effective and deliver higher quality services to members. Also, the government introduced legislation that further encouraged and facilitated union mergers. Subsequently, there has been rapid change. Union leaders at the 1993 ACTU Congress claimed that 98 per cent of union members were by then covered by only 20 unions or union federations.

The ACTU, formed in 1927, is the main confederation for manual and non-manual unions. Few important unions remain outside it. The high inclusiveness of the ACTU follows the decision of two former white-collar union confederations to join forces with the ACTU: the Australian Council of Salaried and Professional Associations (ACSPA) joined the ACTU in 1979 and the Council of Australian Government Employee Organisations (CAGEO) followed in 1981. The ACTU's considerable influence over its affiliates was reflected at ACTU congresses and conferences throughout the 1980s and early 1990s, when nearly all its executive recommendations were endorsed (Davis, 1992). Officers of the ACTU play key roles in the presentation of union cases before the commission and in the conduct and settlement of important industrial disputes.

As in the USA and UK, then, there is now only one main central union confederation. This is in contrast to many Western European countries, which have several confederations (Bamber and Lansbury, 1993: chs 6–7). Nevertheless, in each of the states, trades and labor councils also play a significant role in industrial relations. Although the state trades and labor councils are formally branches of the ACTU, they generally have a much longer history and display some independence and often considerable power in their localities. (This is unlike trades councils in England and Wales, which have a much smaller role.)

The basic unit of organisation for unions is the branch, which may cover an entire state or a large district within a state. Workplace organisation tends to be informal, but shop stewards' (or delegates') committees have developed among key groups of manual workers and, especially in the public sector, among non-manual staff too. In another contrast with the UK, however, the role and power of most workplace union delegates is relatively undeveloped. The centralisation of industrial-relations decision-making has induced a dependence on union full-time officials at state and federal levels. Nevertheless, greater reliance on enterprise bargaining is increasing the role of workplace delegates in the 1990s.

Government

The federal government has used a range of tools that have influenced industrial relations. For instance, monetary and fiscal policies designed to stimulate or depress the economy have inevitably had an impact on the bargaining power of employers and unions. Governments have enacted or amended legislation on a diverse array of matters connected with industrial relations, conciliation and arbitration. Governments have regularly made submissions to the commission on wages and conditions, playing a pivotal role at national wage cases and in major cases determining conditions on workers' rights in the face of redundancy, and maternity and other leave matters.

The Labor government since 1983 has wielded considerable influence over industrial relations through its Accord with the ACTU. This took the form of an agreement (or social contract) that spelt out a shared vision and blueprint for economic, industry and social policy. The original Accord of 1983 has been renegotiated at least seven times. Accord Mark 7 was endorsed by the ALP and the ACTU in 1993.

Federal, state and local governments are also major employers in their own right, employing approximately a quarter of the labour force. Their policies as employers are therefore significant. The 1972–75 Whitlam Labor government sought to establish pace-setting conditions for its employees and to encourage the extension of union coverage. The election of the conservative coalition government in 1975 brought considerable change. The conditions of public servants began to fall behind those prevailing in the private sector, and legislation was introduced that strengthened the ability of the government as an employer to lay off or dismiss workers if it chose. It also cancelled the system of members' dues being deducted directly from their wages. The post-1983 Labor government repealed those laws regarded as least palatable by the unions and restored the automatic payroll deduction of union dues. Public-sector employees failed, however, to regain their status as pace-setters, so there has been a growing disparity in remuneration for public- and private-sector employees.

INDUSTRIAL RELATIONS PROCESSES

The Australian system of industrial relations has federal and state components. Historically, federal awards have taken precedence, but the state systems have also been important. Problems arising from overlapping jurisdiction of the state and federal commissions have been a source of concern to reformers, but changes have often been difficult to achieve. This difficulty is compounded when there is, for instance, a federal Labor government but non-Labor governments in most states, as in the mid-1990s. In effect, there remain seven separate systems of industrial regulation; in addition to the federal system, each of the six states has its own legislation and its own distinctive style.

The federal system has been based on conciliation and arbitration. The federal commission has encouraged employers and unions to discuss, negotiate and settle matters related to pay and conditions. Conciliation has always been the greater part of the day-to-day work of commissioners. The process of arbitration has been compulsory in two senses. First, when activated, it has required the parties to submit to a mandatory procedure for presenting their arguments. Second, commission awards have been binding on the parties. Awards have specified minimum standards of pay and conditions, which an employer must meet or else face legal penalties.

One early argument for introducing compulsory arbitration was to render strikes unnecessary. The 'rule of law' provided under arbitration was supposed to displace the 'rude and barbarous process of strike and lockout'. For many years, the Conciliation and Arbitration Act rendered strikes illegal and subject to penalties. Although this provision was removed in 1930, Australian workers were not granted the formal right to strike until the implementation of a 1993 federal law. Even this right is limited to situations where there is a dispute between an employer and unions with members employed at a single enterprise, who are covered by an award, and are negotiating a certified enterprise agreement (*Industrial Relations Reform Act 1993 (Cwlth)*). Another 'sanction' sometimes used by the commissions has been to deregister a union that strikes in defiance of a commission order to return to work. In practice, however, union deregistration has been difficult and those few unions affected have usually been re-registered after making a suitable apology.

One of the main effects of arbitration has been to shorten the duration of strikes. Although international comparisons of strike statistics are notoriously difficult, the experience of Australia is illuminating. It has often been among those countries with a relatively high number of working days 'lost' per 1000 employees. For instance, in an analysis of industrialised market economies, Australia came eighth with an annual average of around 300 working days lost per 1000 employees between 1980 and 1989 (Figure 6.1). The seven countries with a higher strike propensity were Greece, Spain, Italy, Canada, New Zealand, Finland and the Irish Republic. The UK was close behind Australia (see Bamber and Lansbury, 1993, p.313). A relatively adversarial style of industrial relations has prevailed in Australia, then, in comparison with countries such as Japan, Germany and Austria, which all 'lose' significantly fewer working days.

Industrial disputes have always received a great deal of attention. The media focus on industrial adversarialism. Conflict is news, while industrial peace is not. Therefore, there remains a popular view that Australian workplaces are rife with industrial conflict and mutual antagonism between management and workers. However, a thorough survey of workplaces with more than four employees showed that nearly three-quarters of all workplaces have never experienced any type of industrial action (Callus et al., 1991). As the then Minister for Industrial Relations, Senator Peter Cook, put it when launching the survey results:

> In the year preceding the survey (1988–89), only 12 per cent of workplaces had been involved in some form of industrial action. In most cases, these were stop-work meetings, including information sessions and the like as well as stoppages per se. Moreover, whether one relies on the account of managers or union representatives, management-employee relations are generally perceived as being reasonably harmonious. About three-quarters of general managers and more than half of all union delegates rated industrial relations as being very good. (Cook, 1991, p.4)

Figure 6.1 Working days lost per 1000 employees: all industries and services*

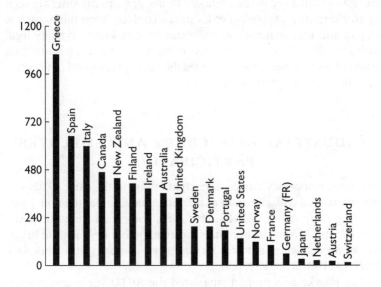

Note: * Annual averages 1980–89 (those for Greece and Portugal are based on incomplete data).
Source: Bamber and Lansbury, 1993, p.313

Since 1983, average working days lost per 1000 employees have been halved. Since then, annual average numbers of working days lost have ranged between 150 and 270 per 1000 employees (ABS, 1994b), whereas in the previous decade they ranged between 336 and 1273 per 1000 employees (ABS, 1993a). Beggs and Chapman (1987) have argued that while changing macroeconomic conditions have played a part in this absolute and relative decline in the impact of industrial stoppages, so too has the ALP–ACTU Accord. Besides industrial stoppages, there are many other expressions of industrial conflict including accidents, absenteeism, labour turnover, working without enthusiasm, working to rule and bans (Hyman, 1989). There is much less comparative data available on such forms of conflict, even though most employers lose more working days through accidents and absenteeism than through formal stoppages. A 'ban' is 'an organised refusal by employees to undertake certain work, to use certain equipment or to work with certain people' (Sheehan and Worland, 1986, p.21). There is some evidence to suggest that there was an increased implementation of bans in the 1980s. As the decline in the incidence of industrial stoppages correlates with a rise in the number of bans, perhaps the latter are seen as an alternative expression of industrial conflict: 'Bans minimise loss of pay and may make it more difficult for employers to apply legal sanctions against unions' (Frenkel, 1990, p.14). But, even more than with strikes, it is difficult to secure reliable data on bans and other manifestations of industrial conflict.

INDUSTRIAL DEMOCRACY AND EMPLOYEE PARTICIPATION

Industrial democracy attracted much attention in the early 1970s, but interest waned with the onset of unemployment under the non-Labor federal government of 1975–83. After 1983, however, there was renewed interest; the Accord stressed that 'consultation is a key factor in bringing about change in industry (at) industry, company and workplace level' (ALP–ACTU, 1983, p.9).

The Hawke government supported the ACTU at the commission in its claim for improved job protection standards to be inserted into workers' awards. This led to the commission's Termination, Change and Redundancy Decision in 1984. Employers were required to consult their employees and unions before introducing major changes to work methods or to organisational structure. Where redundancies were contemplated, the length of notice was increased. Unions welcomed this decision. Many employers were less enthusiastic, seeing the decision as increasing costs and impinging on managerial prerogatives.

Some employers had forged agreements that went beyond the employee and union rights determined by the commission. For example, Telecom made and re-endorsed a Technological Change Agreement, which committed its managers to provide information to unions at the contemplative stage and to seek union participation in the process leading up to a decision. Managers and union officials commented that the agreement facilitated the introduction of new technology in this enterprise during the 1980s (Davis and Lansbury, 1988).

Leaders in government, business and unions agreed apparently on the importance of developing more cooperative workplaces, characterised by higher levels of employee participation. To this end, the parties issued several joint statements and tripartite reports. The most obvious formal support for more employee participation was found in the important National Wage Case decisions since 1987, which stressed that cooperation should underpin the approach of unions and employers to the overhaul of work organisation and productivity. For instance, the 1989 National Wage Case decision pointed to the need for agreement on 'appropriate consultative procedures to deal with the day-to-day matters of concern to employers and workers'. In the 1991 decision the commission stated that enterprises should 'establish a consultative mechanism and procedures appropriate to their size, structure and needs for consultation and negotiation on matters affecting their efficiency and productivity' (Lansbury and Davis, 1992, p.233). Despite such moves, evidence from the Australian Workplace Industrial Relations Survey suggested that employee participation in decision making remained limited (Callus et al., 1991, p.136).

EQUAL OPPORTUNITIES

As female participation in the workforce has increased, there has been more attention paid to women at work by the media as well as the industrial parties. In 1961 women comprised approximately 25 per cent of the workforce; by 1981 this had increased to 37 per cent and by 1993 it reached 42 per cent (Women's Bureau, 1993).

The federal *Affirmative Action (Equal Employment Opportunity for Women) Act 1986* covers all private-sector employers with one hundred or more employees, and obliges employers to take eight specific steps designed to remove discrimination towards women and promote equality in employment. The evidence so far indicates indifferent compliance (Davis and Pratt, 1990). Also, despite award provisions for equal pay for work of equal value, women's earnings on average have remained below male earnings. In large part, this has been because women have remained concentrated in occupations and industries characterised by relatively low pay and poor conditions.

However, such matters as childcare, maternity and paternity leave, equal employment opportunity, affirmative action, and sexual harassment are increasingly seen as being in the industrial relations and human resource management (HRM) arena, rather than exclusively as women's issues. Further, concern for business performance has induced many employers to improve childcare and related conditions in order to attract and retain women workers.

Many Australian employers have also responded to labour shortages by employing migrant workers. Before 1949, most migrants came to Australia from the British Isles. Since then, Mediterranean countries, Eastern Europe and South-East Asia have also been important sources. In relative terms, the Australian workforce is even more multicultural than the American. By 1981, 38 per cent of all those engaged in Australian manufacturing and 30 per cent of those in construction were born overseas (Lever-Tracy and Quinlan, 1988, p.1). This mix of languages and cultures poses a challenge for employers, especially when trying to improve two-way communication on health and safety procedures and hazards, or on new technologies and methods of working (Quinlan & Bohle, 1991).

PAY DETERMINATION

The arbitration system has usually been associated with the centralisation of pay determination. The commission has often exercised considerable influence over key wage issues. Its predecessor, the federal Court of Conciliation and Arbitration, initially became involved in fixing a minimum wage in 1907 when it described the 'basic wage' as intended to meet 'the normal needs of an average employee, regarded as a human being living in a civilised community'. The basic wage was set at a level sufficient to cover the minimum needs of a single income family unit of five and became the accepted wage for unskilled work. A custom of pay differentials (margins) for skills was developed in the 1920s, based largely on traditional differentials in the metal and engineering trades.

The court thus began to regulate wages and differentials through its decisions on the basic wage and margins at the national wage case hearings. These have been a much publicised ritual at approximately annual intervals. Employers, unions and governments made submissions to the commission, which eventually handed down a decision. This then determined a change to pay or conditions for nearly all employees throughout Australia. In 1967, the commission discontinued the custom of basic wage and margins in favour of a 'total' award. It also introduced a national minimum wage, representing the lowest wage permissible for a standard work week by any employee.

During the early 1970s, the commission sought to adjust the relative structure of award wages in different industries and to reduce the scope of 'over-award' increases by attempting to bring formal awards more closely into line with actual earnings. But by 1973–74, the contribution of national wage cases to total wage increases had declined to approximately 20 per cent as unions bargained directly with employers for large over-award payments. Collective bargaining had therefore become the dominant force in wage increases, its leading settlements soon flowing on to most of the economy.

Faced with the dual problem of rapidly rising inflation and unemployment, the Labor government moved to restore the commission's authority. In 1974, the federal government and the ACTU sought the introduction of automatic full cost-of-living indexation of wage increases, against the opposition of non-Labor state governments and private-sector employers. However, between 1975 and 1981, partial rather than full indexation was the norm, and the commission abandoned indexation in 1981 (Dabscheck, 1989). A round of direct negotiations followed. Some unions won large pay increases and these began to flow on to other sectors. At the same time, there was a sharp fall in demand for goods and services, while unemployment rose.

The election of a Labor government in 1983 returned the commission to a powerful role in pay policy. The 1983 Accord agreed between the ALP and the ACTU included a return to centralised wage determination with guidelines based on wage adjustments for price movements and, at longer intervals, for movements in national productivity (Lansbury, 1985). This approach was reflected by the commission in 1983, which reintroduced wage indexation. However, there was a requirement that each union should pledge to make 'no extra claims' in return for receiving indexation. Most unions accepted this requirement, and there was little movement in wages on top of nationally determined pay rates. Those unions seeking to press for wage increases outside the Accord found themselves isolated and their campaigns were usually unsuccessful (for example the domestic airline pilots in 1989).

SOME INNOVATIONS

Although opinion has been divided over the effectiveness of the Accord, two researchers have argued that it was responsible for generating an extra 313 000 jobs between 1983–89 (Chapman and Gruen, 1990). This represented a 4 per cent rise in employment and a 2 per cent reduction in unemployment. On this reasoning, the Accord produced about one-fifth of the 1.6 million new jobs during this period. A major factor was, they estimated, that real wages fell by 10 per cent between 1983 and 1989.

This estimate sparked debate within the union movement, with some arguing that unions should seek to reverse the fall in real wages. ACTU officials contended, however, that the impact of the fall in real wages was more than offset by increased employment (thereby increasing household incomes), tax reform, improved superannuation and a raft of more generous social welfare provisions. They claimed that such innovations had led to an improvement in living standards. Officials also pointed to the greater influence by union representatives over economic, industry and social policies. The Accord included jointly-agreed policies on prices and non-wage incomes, industrial law, social security, occupational health and safety, education, health and Australian government employment. After 1983, the Accord became identified as a regular process of decision-making involving senior ACTU and government officials. It provided the framework for the development of union and government policies on economic, industrial and social matters.

With regard to pay, the original 1983 Accord (which later became known as Accord Mark I) envisaged federal government support for full wage indexation. However, following a 1985–86 economic crisis, the government abandoned this commitment. It also secured the agreement of the ACTU to support a new-style wages policy, linking pay increases to measures designed to improve productivity and efficiency. Most employers and their organisations welcomed the change; the views of the major parties were put before the commission in national wage case hearings in late 1986.

In the 1987 national wage case decision, the commission introduced a dual system of wage adjustments. A first tier provided $10 for all workers following the decision. A further 4 per cent pay increase depended, in the main, on unions and employers agreeing to improve efficiency in their industry or workplaces. The following year, wage increases were conditional on discussion of 'structural efficiency' which resulted in a mixture of industry-by-industry and employer-by-employer productivity negotiations. These national wage case decisions reflected the central role of the commission, while also incorporating moves toward devolved industry and enterprise agreements between employers and unions.

Reaffirming these previous national wage case decisions, in 1989 the commission elaborated on the items that unions and employers might consider in their negotiations to improve efficiency. Among their suggestions were issues such as overtime, penalty rates, flexible hours, part-time and casual employment and changes in staffing. Thus the 1989 decision provided the opportunity for unions and employers to address issues that had long bedevilled performance, but had been widely regarded as immutable.

The early 1990s witnessed considerable turbulence in the politics of wage determination. The Business Council had declared in 1989 that enterprise-based bargaining was the key to improved competitiveness and the route to the constant adjustment of methods and technologies, the development of a sense of common purpose, better dispute settlement and improved pay systems, linking pay and performance (BCA, 1989, pp.8–9). The ACTU stated in 1990 that it wished to see a much greater emphasis on decentralised bargaining rather than on the central determination of wages and conditions. It therefore appeared to endorse the Business Council's call for more enterprise-based bargaining. The Labor government joined in the call for greater reliance on bargaining and a diminished role for the commission. These views were put to the commission in national wage case hearings in late 1990.

In April 1991 the commission rejected such submissions, arguing that a rapid move to much greater decentralisation might see a surge of wage increases not linked to productivity. This would prove inflationary and would reverse the progress made over the previous few years (AIRC, 1991a, p.18). The commission was also concerned that although the government, unions and employers all apparently agreed on the need for more bargaining, there were significant differences in interpretation and approach. For instance, should pay increases be linked to enterprise profitability or productivity? How should either or both be measured? What role, if any, should the commission play? And what would be the nature of bargaining in the large non-unionised sector? (1991a, p.25). The commission concluded that 'the parties to industrial relations have still to develop the maturity necessary for the further shift of emphasis now proposed' (1991a, p.38). The commission wished to see a more receptive environment — one more likely to encourage successful bargaining. It therefore deferred the matter until the parties had resolved significant outstanding matters.

Government and union leaders then rejected the commission's decision and stated that they would pursue more bargaining. Later explaining the reaction of unions, ACTU secretary Bill Kelty said that centralised wage fixing removed the main incentive in getting workers active, interested and involved in their workplace. It also reduced the influence of workers at their workplace. He continued:

> The result of wages being totally controlled by people who have never visited their workplace, and through a process which workers do not understand or have direct input into, had reduced workers' capacity, willingness

and confidence to use their creativity and put forward innovative ideas. The new wage bargaining strategy is a strategy designed to create more interesting and financially rewarding jobs, by stimulating greater worker involvement in all aspects of the way their industry and workplace operates, thereby driving enterprise reform and pushing up productivity levels. (Kelty, 1991, p.1)

In mid-1991 another round of national wage case hearings began. This time no submissions for a wage increase were heard; the focus rather was on the appropriate rules for wage fixing. In late 1991 the commission determined a new enterprise bargaining principle, though it remained concerned about continuing and significant differences between the parties with regard to the implementation of bargaining. It also restated its fears that inadequate bargaining mechanisms would fail to promote higher levels of productivity and that wage outcomes might prove inflationary. Nevertheless, the commission elaborated the framework for bargaining. Key elements included the provision that pay increases must be based on the implementation of efficiency measures designed to effect real gains in productivity and the demonstration of a broad agenda for negotiation. The commission therefore sought to retain an important role as overseer of the new system (AIRC, 1991b).

In 1992 amendments to the Industrial Relations Act undermined the role of the commission. A new division in the amended Act (3A) was designed 'to facilitate the making and certifying of agreements'. The amended legislation meant that the commission must certify agreements, where these agreements involved single enterprises and the appropriate bargaining unit and several tests were met (such as the inclusion of a grievance procedure, specification of the period of operation and employee-union consultation). These amendments therefore diminished the influence of the commission over bargaining.

In 1993 the Labor government embarked on a further round of changes to the Industrial Relations Act. These came into force in early 1994 and were designed to facilitate bargaining in the non-unionised sector while at the same time strengthening awards as 'safety-nets' and setting minimum rates of pay and conditions. Important features of the newly amended Act included the creation of a sanction-free bargaining period in the negotiation of certified agreements and the establishment of a specialist Industrial Relations Court to replace the former industrial division of the federal court.

The Act broke new ground in its reliance on conventions of the International Labour Organisation (an agency of the United Nations). Federal government endorsement of conventions on minimum wages, equal pay for work of equal value, rights to redundancy pay, protection against unfair dismissal and rights to 12 months of unpaid parental leave meant that all employees across Australia were covered. It appeared therefore that the federal government had found a way to spread its influence in industrial relations beyond the federal jurisdiction. (Nonetheless, states governed by non-Labor parties aimed to challenge the constitutionality of the amendments that were implemented in 1994.)

A further intention of the Labor government was to take steps to encourage more bargaining. Prime minister Paul Keating had predicted in 1992 that within a year bargained agreements would cover half the workforce and would be the normal mode. A year later it was probable that only 10 per cent of the workforce were covered (mainly from the metals and the public sectors) and there was concern that many agreements were poorly designed and implemented. Many of the agreements focussed on a very limited range of issues, leaving most conditions as still determined by awards.

At issue is the extent to which legislative changes can lead to more and better agreements. In other words, has it been the centralised system that has deterred bargaining, or has it been a lack of skills and reluctance on the part of managers, employees and union representatives? Whatever the cause, it is probable that the late 1990s will see more bargaining because it will be the main and fastest route to pay increases. It may, however, prove difficult to monitor the number and quality of agreements as many managers, their employees and unions may choose not to register their agreements with the commission.

CONCLUSIONS

There has been much debate on the reform of industrial relations. These debates have taken place against a background of a great deal of economic, organisational and technological change. Further significant changes have included the increasing proportions of women in the workforce and of part-time workers. The debates have canvassed the perceived linkage between industrial relations and economic performance, at the macro and the micro levels. Proponents of greater reliance on enterprise bargaining have asserted that industrial commissions should play a much diminished role, with managers, employees and their unions left to make their own decisions about industrial relations at enterprise and workplace levels. This, it is asserted, would lift efficiency and performance.

It may seem that Australia faces a choice between conciliation and arbitration, or enterprise bargaining. But the Australian system, at federal and state levels, has always involved a mix of centralised regulation and bargaining. Periodically the balance has shifted towards arbitration and then again towards bargaining. At the time of writing, it seems probable that there will be more enterprise bargaining and on an increasingly decentralised basis. Nevertheless, awards remain significant, and the federal and several state commissions will continue to be involved in conciliation and arbitration for the foreseeable future.

FURTHER READING

Deery and Plowman (1991) probably is the most established textbook and Callus et al. provides the most comprehensive set of data on Australian industrial relations. Textbooks that have a slightly more practical orientation include: Dufty and Fells (1989), and Sappey and Winter (1992). The federal Department of Industrial Relations publishes leaflets on various aspects of the federal jurisdiction. It has offices in the capital city of each Australian state (phone 1800 068 690). For an analysis of industrial relations law, see Bennett (1994). Bamber and Lansbury (1993) includes chapters on industrial relations in Australia, Great Britain, the USA, Canada, France, Italy, Germany, Sweden and Japan. It also includes international and comparative data on these countries, including various labour market and more general statistics. Although it refers primarily to Great Britain, Hyman (1989) is a useful analysis of industrial conflict.

REFERENCES

Australian Bureau of Statistics 1993a, *Labour Statistics, Australia, 1991*, Cat. no. 6101.0, ABS, Canberra.
—— 1993b, *Trade Union Members, Australia, August 1992*, Cat. no. 6325.0, ABS, Canberra.
—— 1984a, *Trade Union Statistics, Australia, December 1983*, Cat. no. 6323.0, ABS, Canberra.
—— 1994b, *Industrial disputes, Australia*, Cat. no. 6321.0, ABS, Canberra.
Australian Industrial Relations Commission 1991a, *National Wage Case*, April, Print J7400, AIRC, Melbourne.
—— 1991b, *National Wage Case*, October, Print K0300, AIRC, Melbourne.
—— 1993, *National Wage Case*, October, Print K9700, AIRC, Melbourne.

Australian Labor Party–Australian Council of Trade Unions 1983, 'Statement of accord by ALP and ACTU regarding economic policy', ALP–ACTU, Melbourne.

Business Council of Australia 1989, *Enterprise-based Bargaining Units: A Better Way of Working*, BCA, Melbourne.

Bamber, G. J. and Lansbury, R. D. (eds) 1993, *International and Comparative Industrial Relations*, 2nd edn, Allen and Unwin, Sydney.

Beggs, J. J. and Chapman, B. J. 1987, 'Australian strike activity in an international context: 1964–1985', *Journal of Industrial Relations*, 29(2), pp.137–49.

Bennett, L. 1994, *Making Labour Law in Australia: Industrial Relations, Politics and Law*, The Law Book Company, Sydney.

Callus, R., Morehead, A., Cully, M. and Buchanan, J. 1991, *Industrial Relations at Work: The Australian Workplace Industrial Relations Survey*, AGPS, Canberra.

Chapman, B. J. and Gruen, F. H. 1990, 'An analysis of the Australian consensual incomes policy: the prices and incomes accord', in *Paper*, Australian National University Centre for Economic Policy Research, Canberra, p.221.

Cook, P. 1991, 'Address at the launch of *Industrial Relations at Work*', *Workplace Australia conference*, Department of Industrial Relations, Canberra.

Dabscheck, B. 1989, *Australian Industrial Relations in the 1980s*, Oxford University Press, Melbourne.

Davis, E. M. 1992, 'The 1991 ACTU congress: together for tomorrow', *Journal of Industrial Relations*, 34 (1), pp.87–101.

Davis, E. M. and Lansbury, R. D. 1988, 'Consultative councils in Qantas and Telecom', *Journal of Industrial Relations*, 30 (4), pp.546–65.

Davis, E. M. and Pratt, V. (eds) 1990, *Making the Link: Affirmative Action and Industrial Relations*, AGPS, Canberra.

Deery, S. J. and Plowman, D. H. 1991, *Australian Industrial Relations*, 3rd edn, McGraw Hill, Sydney.

Dufty, N. F. and Fells, R. E. 1989, *Dynamics of Industrial Relations in Australia*, Prentice-Hall, Sydney.

Frenkel, S. 1990, 'Australian trade unionism and the new social structure of accumulation', paper presented to the Asian Regional Congress, International Industrial Relations Research Association, Manila.

Hagan, J. 1981, *The History of the ACTU*, Longman Cheshire, Melbourne.

Hyman, R. (1989), *Strikes*, 4th edn, Macmillan, London.

Jost, J. 1994, 'Time for unions to pay their dues', *Australian Business Monthly*, March, pp.24–8.

Kelty, W. 1991, *Together for Tomorrow*, ACTU, Melbourne.

Lansbury, R. D. 1985, 'The Accord: a new experiment in Australian industrial relations', *Labour and Society*, 10 (2), pp.223–35.

Lansbury, R. D. and Davis, E. M. 1992, 'Employee participation: some Australian cases', *International Labour Review*, 131 (2), pp.231–48.

Lever-Tracy, C. and Quinlan, M. 1988, *A Divided Working Class: Ethnic Segmentation and Industrial Conflict in Australia*, Routledge & Kegan Paul, London.

Plowman, D. H. 1980, 'Employer associations: challenges and responses', in *Australian Labour Relations: Readings*, eds G. W. Ford, J. M. Hearn and R. D. Lansbury, Macmillan, Melbourne.

Quinlan, M. and Bohle, P. 1991, *Managing Occupational Health and Safety in Australia: A Multidisciplinary Approach*, Macmillan, Melbourne.

Sappey, R. B. and Winter, M. 1992, *Australian Industrial Relations Practice*, Longman Cheshire, Melbourne.

Sheehan, B. and Worland, D. 1986, *Glossary of Industrial Relations Terms*, Industrial Relations Society of Victoria, Melbourne.

Women's Bureau 1993, *Women and Work*, Department of Employment, Education and Training, Canberra.

7

AGRICULTURE

··

Colin Brown and John Longworth

Australian agricultural institutions have a certain uniqueness and mystery about them. Yet, when examined from a historical perspective and after taking into account the special socio-economic features of the rural sector, there is always a rationale for their existence and their structure. Of course, in some cases an institution may appear to have outlived its usefulness, at least in its current form. However, it is extremely important not to reach this conclusion without fully understanding the origin and historical development of the entity in question.

This chapter, therefore, begins by outlining some of the key factors moulding agricultural institutions in Australia. Two sets of factors are described. The first involves those special characteristics of the rural sector that explain much of the uniqueness of traditional agricultural institutions. Many of these institutions have contributed to the transformation of Australian agriculture into the modern, internationally competitive and technically advanced sector of Australian society that it is today. The second set of factors are emerging megatrends that have been exerting increasing pressure on agriculture and rural society over the last two decades. These broad macro-developments have challenged many traditional agricultural institutions and, in some cases, major changes have occurred.

Since a plethora of agricultural institutions is to be considered, a logical approach to classifying institutions in general, and these institutions in particular, is then explored. The remainder of the chapter discusses some key features of agricultural institutions drawn from each of the major groupings identified.

SPECIAL FEATURES

Rural communities and agricultural industries in Australia exhibit a number of socio-economic characteristics that differentiate them from the predominantly urban-based society in which the majority of Australians live and work. Campbell (1980) demonstrates many of these differences. Five of the most important are:

1 Large number of small independent businesses (farms) dispersed over a vast geographic area

All individuals in society recognise the need to form social groups to achieve collective goals. However, the geographic isolation faced by most Australian farm families has created the need for formal institutions to represent their collective interests. For example, historically it has been argued that individual farmers lack market power when selling to or buying from the agribusiness sector. While greatly improved access to market information and the general increase in both size and sophistication of farm businesses have substantially weakened this argument for collective action, it remains a major reason for the creation of many institutions concerned with agricultural product marketing. Similarly, the need to develop countervailing power in the industrial relations and political arenas encouraged the formation of industrial and political institutions to represent farm interests.

2 Heterogeneity of farm households and farm production systems

Although farm households throughout Australia face broadly similar problems, they have diverse value systems and lifestyles. The physical production systems under the managerial control of the farmers can also vary enormously, even within the one industry. For example, in the beef industry, operators of large-scale pastoral beef properties in northern Queensland have little in common with small farmers in Victoria running some beef cattle as well as raising sheep and growing crops. Of course, across the rural sector as a whole the differences can be even more obvious.

Despite the diversity of economic interests, beliefs, values and production systems, there are issues of common concern to large groupings of farmers. However, developing and maintaining institutions to accommodate the diversity while at the same time serving the common interests has not been an easy task.

3 Large production and market uncertainties

Farming is often a high-risk business. Drought, floods, pests and diseases can all strike when least expected. Fluctuating commodity prices also greatly increase the level of uncertainty faced by many farmers. Various institutions have emerged to help farmers cope with and adjust to these production and market uncertainties.

4 Rapid structural change

As economies develop and the average level of income rises, people change the pattern of their expenditures. The demand for some goods and services increases while society requires relatively less of the traditional goods such as food and fibre (the basic products of the rural sector). Economic growth and the associated technological change are both the result of and the reason for resources shifting out of one line of production into another. Economic growth means that all industries face pressures to adopt new technology, to keep costs down and to make a better quality product. All industries undergo structural change as some individual businesses that cannot adjust fast enough are forced out of production and new ones start up, perhaps in a new location.

The agricultural sector of Australia, especially since the late 1960s, has been under exceptionally strong pressure to make structural adjustments. In some industries and in some localities, the number of farm businesses has declined sharply as farm families have been forced off the land. Many of the families that remain are living in poverty. The speed of change as been too great to be accommodated by the normal attrition and adjustment processes, resulting in calls for the establishment of institutions not only to ameliorate these burdens on the farming sector but also to ensure an efficient reallocation of resources to more productive uses. Longworth (1979) describes the problem of rapid adjustment in the rural sector.

5 Export orientation of the major rural industries

The major rural industries (wool, beef, wheat, dairy, sugar and cotton) are all heavily dependent on overseas markets. The domestic market for these commodities is small relative to potential production. Furthermore, except for wool (especially fine wool), Australian exports represent a modest proportion of the world market for these commodities. Thus Australian farmers face a very different marketing situation compared with farmers in the USA, the European Community or Japan, where the domestic or home market for agricultural products is so much larger.

In addition, even in the 1990s, export income earned by agricultural industries constitutes a major share of the total Australian export income. The living standards of the nation remain dependent on agricultural exports. Therefore institutions have been developed to promote and facilitate the export of agricultural commodities, not only to help farmers but also to protect the economy from the vagaries of international commodity markets. The export orientation has spawned various statutory marketing authorities to facilitate single-desk selling of the key rural export commodities as well as a major involvement in various international trade organisations and negotiating forums.

Special characteristics of the agricultural sector and its institutions are not unique to Australia. Most countries retain ministries and departments of agriculture with powers seemingly out of line with their relative economic importance in society. Furthermore, agriculture has been subject to special exemptions and considerations in past multilateral trade negotiations and trade rules.

GLOBAL MEGATRENDS

Australian agriculture and rural society are influenced by a number of emerging megatrends. At least some of these also affect other parts of Australian society and other countries as well (Warley, 1990). The three major worldwide trends especially important to Australian rural sector institutions are:

1   Increasing internationalisation and competitiveness

Australian agriculture faces increasing internationalisation and competitiveness. Heavily dependent on export markets, it is greatly affected by developments in global agricultural markets. Because these markets have been highly protected, agricultural trade patterns have been distorted. In general, however, recent developments such as the hard-won GATT agreement have tended to make international agricultural markets more open and to create a trading environment that is more competitive.

A less protectionist trade environment will be welcomed by Australian agriculture since, for the most part, it is less protected and receives less government support than agricultural sectors of other countries. Therefore, Australian farmers tend to be highly competitive in an international sense. Furthermore, Australian agricultural institutions and policy instruments have not been insulated from the general program of microeconomic reform implemented by Australian governments to address fundamental economic problems. Indeed, many would argue that the agricultural sector and its institutions have borne the brunt of these reforms and have been disadvantaged by a relative lack of reforms elsewhere, notably in labour markets.

Despite absorbing major changes, Australian agricultural institutions face substantial, ongoing adjustments as a result of changing economic and social developments in Australia and the rest of the world. For example, import protection for Australian products is changing from more overt quantitative restrictions to more covert anti-dumping arrangements. To compete in an increasingly aggressive trading environment, exporters are being forced to step up the quality assurance, market intelligence and market development aspects of their business activities, aspects that have often been ignored or downgraded in the past. At the farm and community level, households are finding it essential to augment their production skills with business management skills in areas such as finance and marketing. Various schemes such as the Rural Counsellor's program have been implemented by state governments to enhance farmers' skills in these areas.

2   Declining importance of market intervention policies

Many agricultural institutions in the past played a major role in implementing those government policies that depended upon intervention in agricultural product or input markets. However, in line with attitudinal changes both in Australia and overseas, interventionist policies are now becoming much less important. Instead, new policies and institutions are emerging, which more directly target issues such as regional and farm development and the well-being of rural households. Although not necessarily the principal driving factor, the trend away from market intervention policies has been strengthened by the growing public awareness of the political and economic cost of pursuing such policies in a more open and competitive global market environment.

3 Growing global interest in environmental and other social issues

As a prominent user of natural resources, Australian agriculture has been influenced by increasing environmental awareness in society. In general, farmers are acutely aware of the need to value highly the natural resources on which they depend, although short-term considerations may see them take actions seemingly inconsistent with those values. Furthermore, the value farmers place on their natural resources may differ in kind from other groups in the community. Consequently, some interesting new arrangements have emerged. For example, farmers have organised themselves into environmental protection networks such as 'Landcare' groups and some remote area pastoralists have been formally commissioned as 'stewards' of newly acquired national estate land, especially in respect of weed and feral animal management.

Apart from the environmental movement, agriculture is also greatly influenced by other issues such as chemophobia, animal welfare and Aboriginal land rights. In the past, debate over agricultural policies was largely contained within the rural sector itself. Nowadays, the emergence of these broader social issues has forced agricultural institutions and others representing rural sector interests to adopt an increasingly sophisticated and professional approach in order to discuss these issues with the wider community.

TOWARDS A CLASSIFICATION OF AGRICULTURAL INSTITUTIONS

Some would argue that the family farm is the central institution in the Australian agricultural sector and that virtually all other agricultural institutions serve to nurture and preserve this form of agricultural organisation. The role of the family farm has been central to the development of modern democratic societies. In the second half of the eighteenth century, the family farm was enshrined in the Constitution of the USA. Highly developed modern societies in Europe and Japan as well as in the USA all have extremely protectionist agricultural policies in place in the name of preserving the family farm. Since 1979, the People's Republic of China has disbanded its massive agricultural communes and created a system of family farms, which support 800 million people. The family farm is an institution of immense economic and political importance not only in Australia but also world-wide.

This is not the place to debate the merits of family farms as the basic production unit in agriculture. Nevertheless, anyone concerned about agricultural institutions needs to be aware of the pivotal role of the family farm concept. Many of the institutions described in the remainder of this chapter are collective organisations created to meet the needs of farmers (and their families), be they family farmers or otherwise. In regions other than those immediately adjacent to large urban centres, the fortunes of rural communities still wax and wane with those of the farm sector and farm households. Close institutional links exist, therefore, between farm households and the rest of the rural community.

At the local level, there are a significant number of self-help organisations such as bush fire brigades, country women's associations, and show societies. These local organisations, which are often branches of state-level and even national institutions, play a major socio-cultural role as well as creating specific material benefits. Local media outlets, for obvious reasons, usually provide a comprehensive coverage of the activities of these institutions. In recent times, and partly as a result of some of the megatrends outlined previously, an increasing proportion of government assistance to the rural sector is being channelled through these self-help organisations.

At the regional and state level, rural institutions often begin to take on a semi-governmental appearance. That is, government support for and control over their operations becomes more obvious and important. Indeed, at the state and national level, the rural institutions that attract the most media attention are usually those established by government legislation. There are two major theories about the establishment of these institutions, namely, the 'public interest theory' and the 'distributive theory' (Sieper, 1982).

The public interest theory postulates that governments act altruistically to promote the public interest. That is, the public sector (or the state) provides goods and services that are needed by society in greater quantities and perhaps in different forms to those provided by private firms responding to market signals. For example, agricultural research is not something in which individual farmers are likely to invest, even though they need a steady stream of new technology to help them remain competitive. Agricultural research is also usually undertaken on a scale beyond the financial means of most farmers. In addition, it is difficult to capture the benefits (profits) from the results and hence recover the original investment outlays. Thus the private market would tend to under-invest in agricultural research. This situation is termed a 'market failure' in the economics literature. The public interest theory assumes that market failures can be corrected by public sector or state intervention. Intervention often involves legislating to create an institution.

Supporters of the distributive theory argue that the state has the power to redistribute economic benefits from one group to another. There are many ways in which this redistributive process may operate. Some are obvious, such as direct taxation and the payment of pensions. Others are more obscure and their effects more difficult to ascertain. Governments have the power to use or create redistributive mechanisms and various interest groups demand them for their own benefit. Thus, a political market exists in parallel with the private sector, price-driven marketplace. The same individuals and groups function in both marketplaces. However, while their self-interested behaviour is open for all to see in the private sector market, that same behaviour in the political market often occurs behind closed doors. Not surprisingly, therefore, 'political failure' may be just as common as market failure. That is, when a situation exists in which market failure could be expected, it is highly likely that political failure will also occur. The solution, according to the distributive theory, is to improve economic market mechanisms (for example, by redefining property rights and obligations) rather than initiating political solutions such as institutional intervention in the hope that it will act in the public interest.

The two alternative theories suggest that it is possible to classify formal institutions into two groups — institutions created in the public interest and institutions concerned with the redistribution of income. Furthermore, as shown in Table 7.1, it is instructive to sub-divide these two major categories further. A glance at the rural industry directories in the National Farmers Federation (NFF) (1993, pp.392–433) and the Department of Primary Industries and Energy (DPIE) (1990) will confirm that the institutions cited as examples comprise only a small fraction of the formal organisations associated with the Australian agricultural sector.

It is also important to note that the groupings in Table 7.1 are not mutually exclusive. That is, rural institutions will often have characteristics and functions that indicate that they belong in more than one of the categories shown. For example, a marketing board may have the exclusive right to market a commodity, such as fresh milk, in the public interest. For this purpose it belongs to category A(ii) in Table 7.1. However, the board may also practise price discrimination aimed

Table 7.1 A classification and some examples of agricultural institutions

A *Institutions concerned with correcting 'market failures' and acting in the public interest*
  i *Private market augmenting institutions*
  - Rural credit agencies (Commonwealth Development Bank)
  - Marketing boards/corporations (Australian Meat and Livestock Corporation)
  - Co-operatives (GRAINCO Cooperative Association Ltd.)
  - Conservation agencies (National Soil Conservation Program and Landcare groups)
  - Trade facilitators (Austrade)
  ii *Private market replacing institutions*
  - Research and development corporations (Rural Industries Research and Development Corporation)
  - Marketing boards/corporations (Queensland Dairy Authority)
  - Economic information providers (Australian Bureau of Agricultural and Resource Economics)
  - Commonwealth, state and local government departments (Extension and adult education agencies)
  - Agricultural education (Universities)
  - Testing and quality guaranteeing services (Australian Wool Testing Authority)

B *Institutions concerned with redistribution of income and wealth*
  i *Benefits seeking institutions*
  - Farm organisations (National Farmers' Federation)
  - Agribusiness associations (Australian Council of Wool Exporters)
  - Trade unions (Australian Meat Industry Employees Union)
  - Trade associations (Meat and Allied Trades' Federation of Australia)
  ii *Benefit providing institutions*
  - Political parties (Country/National Parties)
  - Commonwealth government departments (Department of Primary Industries and Energy)
  - State government departments (NSW Agriculture)
  - Local governments
  iii *Benefit facilitating institutions*
  - Marketing boards/corporations (Australian Wheat Board)
  - Commonwealth, state and local government agencies (Queensland Fish Management Authority)
  - Inter-governmental agencies (Australian Agricultural Council and Standing Committee)
  iv *Benefit reviewing institutions*
  - Industries (Assistance) Commission
  - Senate and other parliamentary committees
  - Universities and other independent bodies (Centre for Independent Studies)

at increasing the incomes of farmers. In this case, it would also belong to category B(iii).

This example raises an important point. The distributive theory suggests that even when a government institution is initially established 'in the public interest', it will eventually be 'captured' by interest groups who want to use its powers for their own benefit. Of course, both the self-interest groups and the government will always claim that the institution in question is operating in the public interest. This will be true for all groups and institutions, not just farm groups and agricultural institutions.

CORRECTING MARKET FAILURES

The special characteristics of agriculture result in many market failures. That is, the collective actions of individuals do not lead to an efficient use of resources or equitable distribution of income. Various institutions seek, in the public interest, to address these failures either by augmenting private markets or by replacing them entirely (see Table 7.1).

One key area where the government has augmented private markets in attempts to correct a perceived market failure is the Australian rural credit market. Standen (1982) describes how shortfalls in privately sourced credit to the agricultural sector after World War II led to increasing government provision of credit through specially created institutions, such as the Commonwealth Development Bank and the Primary Industry Bank of Australia. Essentially, these organisations sought to augment medium and long-term loans through existing rural lenders such as the trading banks, with some concessionary interest rates applying to long-term loans.

Deregulation of the Australian financial system in 1983 seriously affected these rural credit institutions. However, they continue to exist despite deregulation, albeit in a different form. For instance, the Primary Industry Bank of Australia was privatised in 1987, and the Commonwealth Development Bank has been restructured throughout the 1980s and 1990s and now competes more directly with trading banks for rural loans. For farmers, the deregulated financial system greatly increased the range of financial services, though at the expense of some of the interest rate concessions. Various schemes and institutions have emerged to help farmers adjust to the new financial and business environment.

Although deregulation removed the need for public augmentation of private rural credit markets, the government continues to intervene on public interest grounds, namely, to help farmers cope with the rapid structural adjustment in the industry. Originating in a major crisis in the wool industry in the early 1970s, the Rural Adjustment Scheme (RAS) not only was one of the first of its type for agriculture among developed countries, it was also one of the first industry adjustment schemes in Australia. The RAS has undergone significant changes since its inception, but it gained increasing momentum in the late 1980s and early 1990s as declining rural commodity markets and adverse production conditions increased the adjustment pressure on farmers (Musgrave, 1990; Gerritsen, 1992).

The current RAS provides concessional finance for enhancing productivity (adoption of new technologies, sustainable farming methods, farm development, increasing resource intensity, debt/capital restructuring) as well as for relief in exceptional circumstances (such as drought in Queensland and low commodity prices). In addition, the scheme provides for training grants to upgrade farm business and property management skills as well as re-establishment grants for those leaving the sector.

In addition to access to adequate finance, Australian farmers also require an ongoing flow of new technology if they are to survive and remain competitive. Rural research and development (R&D) has played a key role in maintaining the international competitiveness of Australian agriculture. In the past, expenditure on rural R&D in Australia has compared favourably with other countries both as a proportion of Gross Domestic Product and relative to other R&D expenditure. As explained earlier, governments are likely to become involved in rural R&D both because most agricultural research entails investments too large for an individual farmer and the results of that research are generally freely available to all producers. In Australia, various independent institutions undertake rural R&D activities, although state governments, CSIRO and universities account for most of the expenditure (Williams and Evans, 1989).

Significant changes have occurred in the funding of agricultural R&D. In the belief that it can promote new industries and exports, diversify our industrial base and have a favourable impact on our trade balance, the government has changed its R&D emphasis from traditional sectors such as agriculture to rapidly growing, high technology, or so-called 'sunrise', industries (Jarrett, 1990; Richardson, 1990). However Hooke (1989), Richardson (1990), Lloyd (1988) and others have expressed serious doubts about whether agriculture can be considered a 'sunset' industry. These authors have queried the wisdom of reallocating R&D

resources away from the agricultural industries in which Australia has a comparative advantage.

As the government funds around three-quarters of rural research in Australia (Bartos, 1990), a change in its R&D emphasis will have serious consequences for rural research. Partly in an attempt to address this problem, the government changed the administrative arrangements for the funding of rural research during the mid-1980s. The old system of having industry 'trust funds' for research was replaced by a series of research councils linked to statutory marketing authorities or administered by separate R&D organisations. The fourteen research councils created in 1985 were 'corporatised' by 1989 and reorganised to constitute research corporations (Gerritsen, 1992). The two major reasons for these changes were a desire on the part of the government to increase the amount contributed by producers for R&D and to make the administrators of these research funds more accountable both to the industry and to the government.

Some key aspects distinguish the new research corporations from earlier industry research funds. First, apart from funding research, the corporations disseminate information, host seminars and provide post-graduate research scholarships. Second, they not only accept applications for the funding of research projects, they also commission research programs. Third, approved projects are typically funded under legal contracts that require that project objectives, timetable and budget be agreed to before funding, which 'protect the Corporation's and industry's interests in any results generated during the life of the project' (AMLRDC, 1990). Fourth, research directions have tended to move away from direct production to new products and markets. These changes will impact not only on other rural R&D funding agencies but also on the institutions undertaking research funded by these agencies. Furthermore, while the changes will lead to more accountability of researchers to the industry, such industry-commissioned or industry-approved research may not necessarily be consistent with the public interests of society at large.

REDISTRIBUTION OF INCOME AND WEALTH

The shearers' strikes of the 1890s spawned some of Australia's major industrial relations and political institutions. They also led to the formation of some key rural institutions. To counter the emerging organised labour movement among shearers, pastoralists formed the Pastoralists' Federal

Council. This fledgling farm organisation soon developed into a forum for promoting the private interests of farmers and pastoralists. Yet the history of Australian farm organisations since the emergence of the Pastoralists' Federal Council has been bedevilled by the formation of new splinter groups to accommodate the divergent interests and beliefs among farmers. This has led to the emergence of a diverse array of commodity-based groups, a structure reinforced by the commodity orientation of other agricultural institutions, notably state departments of agriculture and marketing boards. Trebeck (1990) and NFF (1991) provide an outline of the various farm organisations and their history.

The formation of splinter groups is well illustrated by the creation of the Cattlemen's Union in 1976. Two years earlier, the Australian National Cattle Council had emerged from the Australian Woolgrowers' and Graziers' Council as a policy forum for specialist cattle producers. However, specialist beef farmers in northern and central Queensland produce heavy carcasses from mature cattle primarily for export, whereas their southern colleagues produce lighter carcasses from younger animals for the higher priced domestic market. Hence, views within the beef cattle industry on marketing issues and responses to overseas and domestic market developments can differ widely. These differences were exacerbated by the collapse of the beef markets in 1974 and 1975. The final result was the formation of the independent Cattlemen's Union. The split in the beef industry was also a reflection of grass roots disenchantment with the long hierarchical channels of communication that exist in the federally-structured traditional producer organisations.

Despite the tendency for farm groups to disintegrate, in 1979 all the major farm organisations agreed to unite in the form of an umbrella organisation known as the National Farmers' Federation (NFF). The NFF, a federation of national commodity councils, is now the key Australian farm organisation. It has state member organisations and some associate members (Trebeck, 1990). The NFF Council works through a number of executive committees to review policies and make recommendations on broad issues affecting the rural sector, such as interest rates, exchange rates, trade policies and industrial relations matters. Specific commodity issues are left to the autonomous commodity councils. Representation on the NFF comes from these commodity councils and state organisations with voting rights based on the value of production of each commodity in each state.

Given the long history of disunity in relation to farmer groups, the successful formation of the NFF in 1979 may seem paradoxical.

However, it occurred because the perceived benefits of amalgamation and unity increased in the late 1970s. Farm groups recognised that the need for an organisation capable of tackling the emerging issues of broad concern to the rural sector such as interest rate policies, exchange rate policies and industrial relations and wages policy, was intensifying. The increasing sophistication of both policy debates and the process by which industry assistance was reviewed forced many farm organisations to adopt more professional lobbying activities (AFFF, 1993) and appoint appropriately trained personnel.

The formation of a pinnacle body such as the NFF was seen as a means of spreading the considerable costs of providing these services. It is possible that further rationalisation could occur in the future as farm organisations are forced to respond not only to new government agencies but also to other emerging pressure groups such as conservationists and animal welfare lobbyists. Nevertheless, the NFF remains a loose association of state and commodity organisations and embodies the inherent conflicts that exist between these groups.

While farm organisations seek regulation yielding economic benefits, it is governments and their agencies who supply that regulation. In most industrialised countries, rural interests have been served by influential farm organisations who have lobbied governments of all persuasions for assistance. Australia is almost alone, however, in retaining a major political party at the national government level with its roots in the rural sector, namely the National Party (formerly the Country Party until 1975). There are also similar but more or less independent rural-based political parties in all states.

The Country/National parties arose from farm organisations that were first formed in the late nineteenth century. The antecedents of the present federal National Party emerged as a political force as a result of the change to preferential voting and the general weakness of the established political order during and after the First World War. Graham (1966) and Ellis (1963) present a detailed history of these agrarian parties while their structure is described in Costar and Woodward (1985). The federal National Party emerged as a sectional party with few specific policies, but a broad philosophy of conservatism and 'country-mindedness' (Verrall et al., 1985). The policies they developed have been described as 'agrarian socialism' aimed at the nationalisation of the losses incurred by farmers and a privatisation of the gains. Despite the apparent lack of broadly-based policy initiatives outside agriculture, the federal party has had a marked impact on many rural institutions and agricultural policies at the Commonwealth level since the early 1920s.

Historically, the Country/National Parties received most of their electoral and financial support from the rural sector. However, structural adjustments in Australian agriculture since the 1950s have caused a significant decline in the number of farms and in the rural labour force. A series of influential leaders (Page, Fadden, McEwen, Anthony), therefore, have sought to broaden the party's narrow sectional base in order to maintain their political influence in non-Labor coalition governments. In order to arrest its declining electoral fortunes, the federal party was forced to adopt new measures including name changes in 1975 and 1982 and an expanded policy agenda to include the interests of other groups, notably in the mining sector. At the same time, farm organisations have also sought to broaden their political ties. With the advent of Labor governments in the 1980s and 1990s, farm organisations have increasingly lobbied parties of all political persuasions and have openly criticised coalition policies and actions deemed to be against their interests (such as the federal Opposition's approach to the Mabo legislation in 1993).

One major legacy of the Country/National Party at the federal level has been in relation to trade and resource policies. For example, one of the most influential Country Party leaders, 'Black Jack' McEwen, achieved a remarkable feat of statesmanship in 1957 when he negotiated the bilateral trade agreement with Japan. This agreement made it possible for Australia to redirect its exports away from Britain during the 1960s as Britain prepared to join the European Economic Community and for Australia to participate in the post-war economic boom in Japan. However, perhaps the most important legacy of the Country/National Parties at both national and state levels was the establishment of agricultural marketing boards.

Traditionally, marketing boards have provided most of the assistance to the Australian farm sector through home price schemes, production and marketing quotas, stabilisation schemes and other related measures. Although their introduction was strongly defended on 'public interest' grounds, such as the provision of regular and safe supplies of food, the principal purpose of their establishment was to raise farm incomes. During the 1920s, levels of protection for the manufacturing industries were increasing rapidly and the leaders of the then Country Party understood the serious negative impact this would have on the rural sector. But they also recognised that fiscal limitations and the relatively large size of the agricultural sector compared with the rest of the economy precluded major policy initiatives involving direct budgetary support for the Australian agricultural sector. Their response was to call for the establishment of monopoly marketing boards. These boards, under certain conditions, could practise discriminatory pricing policies (the so-called home consumption pricing policies or two-price schemes) to maximise their sales revenue from both domestic and overseas markets.

Marketing boards (or corporations or authorities, as many of the boards are now termed) exist at the state and Commonwealth level. At the state level, they have been enacted either under specific Acts of parliament or under blanket enabling legislation. They have performed a variety of mostly private interest activities including: fixing prices and practising price discrimination, pooling producer returns, storing commodities, instituting production or marketing quotas, devising grading schemes, undertaking research and advisory services, and advertising and promotion. Most of the Commonwealth statutory marketing authorities (SMAs), as federal marketing boards are often called, were enacted under specific legislation (Vinning, 1980; Commonwealth of Australia 1990). Commonwealth SMAs are mainly involved with export marketing and with research, promotion, and product development activities.

Designed to advance the private interests of farmers, marketing boards and their two-price schemes were seen as a quid pro quo for tariff protection provided for the manufacturing sector. In an attempt to broaden the narrow sectional base of the Country Party in the 1950s and 1960s, McEwen advocated an industry policy of 'protection all around'. As Minister for Trade and with responsibility for the Tariff Board, he was well placed to ensure the implementation of such a policy. In recent years, however, many of the discriminatory pricing schemes in the rural sector have been abolished or significantly modified and there has been a substantial reduction in the general level of tariffs on many manufactured goods (Gruen, 1990; Piggott, 1990; Mauldon, 1990). These changes have largely been aimed at advancing the public interest over the private interests of special groups by reducing the large, often obscure, costs to Australian society of the high levels of industry protection. Much of the impetus for these changes can be attributed to the activities of the Tariff Board's successor, the Industries Assistance Commission (IAC).

Although not specifically a rural institution, the IAC had a remarkable impact on the agricultural sector and policies affecting agriculture after it replaced the Tariff Board in 1973. As an independent authority reviewing industry assistance, the IAC raised public awareness of the costs imposed on rural export industries in particular and on the economy as a whole, by the high levels of protection granted to some industries. The IAC quickly began to have a major impact on public policy debates because it was given the resources necessary to do the job properly, because it extended the scope of its analysis to include non-tariff forms of assistance, and because it had the ability to initiate inquiries without a ministerial request. It identified which industries in both the manufacturing and the agricultural sectors were heavily assisted.

The IAC forced farm organisations to present more professional submissions when seeking or debating industry assistance. This development was a major factor in the creation of the NFF. As an independent review body, the IAC had no means of ensuring that its 'public interest' recommendations were implemented as government policy. Indeed, the influence of the IAC in the past may be attributed more to the influence of three key individuals associated with it (Crawford, Rattigan and Carmichael) than to its organisational structure. Nevertheless, it raised public awareness and encouraged more informed debates about industry assistance in Australia. In 1989 the IAC was combined with the Business Regulation Review Unit and the Interstate Commission to form the Industry Commission, essentially to extend the scope of the assistance review process to include state policies (Industry Commission, 1990).

The creating of benefit-reviewing institutions and the growing political strength of those concerned with the public interest have led to fundamental changes in the structure and roles of both Commonwealth SMAs and state marketing boards since the 1970s. Various reviews have been conducted in the areas of accountability (Commonwealth of Australia, 1990) and efficiency (Industry Commission, 1991). Both Commonwealth SMAs and state marketing boards were considered to be inefficient in the provision of marketing services because historically they were controlled by producer representatives with little commercial experience in marketing; constrained in their financial and staff dealings; and required to operate pooling and other administered pricing schemes (Royal Commission, 1988). Reforms to Commonwealth SMAs in the 1970s and 1980s, mirrored by reforms to state marketing boards since the mid-1980s, sought to select board directors according to experience and expertise and on corporate rather than representational bases; to assign the policy, marketing and research roles of the Commonwealth SMAs to separate bodies; and to introduce more accountability to the industry and to the government.

The speed and nature of the reform has varied across industry groups. Crisis situations led to the virtual overnight deregulation of the New

South Wales Egg Board in 1989 and the dropping of the Reserve Price Scheme operated by the Australian Wool Corporation in 1991. Other Commonwealth SMAs, such as the Australian Wheat Board, have undergone gradual though almost complete deregulation of their activities. In addition, the nature of the reforms has varied across institutions. Some have been completely privatised (activities transferred to a private cooperative or company) and others corporatised (restructured as government-owned companies), while the degree to which the remaining boards have lost statutory powers varies greatly.

The extent to which private and public interests mould rural institutions is well illustrated by recent changes to the sugar industry and in particular by its opposition to tariff cuts in 1992. The Industry Commission and other review bodies advocated substantial deregulation of the sugar industry, including removal of the tariff, on public interest grounds (Industry Commission, 1992). However, with six very marginal federal electorates and an even larger number of state electorates in the principal sugar growing areas located in a coastal strip along the North Queensland coast, neither the Australian nor the Queensland government was going to pursue a path strongly opposed by the cane growers.

This was especially the case when the losses from tariff reductions are concentrated among a relatively small number of cane growers whereas the benefits, which in total are greater, are highly obscure and minimal when dispersed over the much larger number of individual consumers in the Australian population. Although the Australian and Queensland governments did submit to private interests in the areas of tariffs and compulsory acquisition powers, concessions were made to the public interest by measures designed to expand and promote flexibility in the industry, which is considered vital to overall industry efficiency.

The sugar industry also reflects the inter-relationship of industry changes across states. Edwards (1993) argues that the main beneficiaries of the tariff and other regulations will be the small minority of sugar cane growers located in New South Wales who will retain access to higher domestic prices yet be unconstrained in their production or marketing channels. Conversely, regulatory changes in the egg and dairy industries in New South Wales and Victoria, which are much larger than these industries are in Queensland, have forced changes to the respective Queensland marketing boards.

While benefit-reviewing bodies have brought increasing awareness about public interest issues, they have also starkly revealed the extent to which private interests have been served or not served by the SMAs and their statutory powers. Consequently, some producers have pushed for deregulation because they have come to recognise that the inefficiencies of marketing boards in marketing their commodities can outweigh any potential economic benefits that can be extracted from the regulated markets. Their concerns have been fuelled by some spectacular and highly visible 'disasters', for example, in the wool industry. In order to survive, marketing boards will need to develop their commercial expertise, demonstrate particular niche roles and establish their bona fides in servicing the private interests of their farmer clientele.

CONCLUSIONS

Australian rural institutions are many and varied. This chapter concentrates on the economically and politically important rural institutions that operate at the state and national level. It emphasises that most important rural institutions have a relatively long and complex history, and an appreciation of this background is a prerequisite to understanding their current structure and function.

Remarkable changes have occurred in many rural institutions since the early 1970s in response to changing community developments and emerging megatrends in agriculture. The surviving institutions are much leaner and more sophisticated than their counterparts two decades ago. In general, the rural community supported a restructuring of its institutions in line with community-wide microeconomic reform, as they perceived it to be not only in the public interest but, more importantly, in their own interests. However, a stalling of economic reforms in some other areas of the economy (such as labour markets), a loss in the momentum of the community-wide support for lower protection and deregulation, and a severe downturn in the economic fortunes of the rural sector at the start of the 1990s have seen some rural institutions attempt to turn the clock back. Nevertheless, the fundamental changes to rural institutions and the vastly different global and Australian environments in which they must now operate mitigate against any major reversal of the changes that have occurred in the last two decades.

FURTHER READING

Campbell (1980), Cribb (1982) and Warley (1990) each provide overviews, from very different perspectives, of agricultural society and the factors moulding agricultural institutions. Longworth & Riethmuller

(1993) highlight features of rural Australia often misunderstood by urban Australians and foreigners. The yearbooks published by the National Farmers' Federation (for example, NFF, 1993) contain detailed information about Australian agriculture and the many agricultural organisations. Similarly, Williams (1990) provides useful reference material on most aspects of Australian agriculture and its institutions, including history, policy developments and links with other parts of Australian society.

REFERENCES

Australian Farmers' Fighting Fund 1993, 'Fighting Fund projects 1985–1993', *Farmers Voice*, 9, pp.4–5.

Australian Meat and Livestock Research and Development Corporation 1990, *Annual Report*, AMLRDC, Sydney.

Bartos, S. 1990, 'Competing demands for Commonwealth funding — the effect on rural research and development' in Standing Committee on Agriculture Workshop on Research Priorities and Resource Allocation for Rural R&D, *Bureau of Rural Resources Proceedings*, no. 7, AGPS, Canberra.

Campbell, K. O. 1980, *Australian Agriculture: Reconciling Change and Tradition*, Longman Cheshire, Melbourne.

Commonwealth of Australia 1990, *Review of the Commonwealth Industry Statutory Marketing Authorities*, AGPS, Canberra.

Costar, B. and Woodward, D. 1985, 'The national party of Australia — future? or no future?', *Current Affairs Bulletin*, 62 (3), pp.24–31.

Cribb, J. 1982, *The Forgotten Country*, Australasian Farm Publications, Canberra.

Department of Primary Industries and Energy 1990, *Rural Industry Directory 1990*, AGPS, Canberra.

Ellis, U. 1963, *A History of the Australian Country Party*, Melbourne University Press, Melbourne.

Edwards, G. 1993, 'Two government failures? a tale of sugar and wool', *Review of Marketing and Agricultural Economics*, 61 (2), pp.97–112.

Gerritsen, R. 1992, 'Labor's final "rural crisis"? Australian rural policy in 1990 and 1991', *Review of Marketing and Agricultural Economics*, 60 (2), pp.95–113.

Graham, B. D. 1966, *The Formation of the Australian Country Parties*, Australian National University Press, Canberra.

Gruen, F. 1990, 'Economic development and agriculture since 1945' in *Agriculture in the Australian Economy*, 3rd edn, ed. D. B. Williams, Sydney University Press, Sydney.

Hooke, G. 1989, 'The real price of agricultural products', *Agricultural Science*, 2 (4), pp.62–5.

Industry Commission 1990, *Annual Report 1989–90*, AGPS, Canberra.

Industry Commission 1991, *Statutory Marketing Arrangements for Primary Products*, Report no. 10, AGPS, Canberra.

Industry Commission 1992, *The Australian sugar industry*, Report no. 19, AGPS, Canberra.

Jarrett, F. G. 1990, 'Rural research, organisation and policies', in *Agriculture in the Australian Economy*, 3rd edn, ed. D. B. Williams, Sydney University Press, Sydney.

Lloyd, A. G. 1988, 'The importance of agriculture: what hope for agriculture, and what needs doing?', *Review of Marketing and Agricultural Economics*, 56 (1), pp.129–34.

Longworth, J. W. 1979, 'Agriculture's changing prospects', *Current Affairs Bulletin*, 55 (10), pp.4–17.

Longworth, J. W. and Riethmuller, P. C. 1993, 'Sorting the wheat from the chaff: exploding some myths about the rural sector in Australia', *Current Affairs Bulletin*, 70 (1), pp.13–21.

Mauldon, R. 1990, 'Price policy', in *Agriculture in the Australian Economy*, 3rd edn, ed. D. B. Williams, Sydney University Press, Sydney.

Musgrave, W. 1990, 'Rural adjustment', in *Agriculture in the Australian Economy*, 3rd edn, ed. D. B. Williams, Sydney University Press, Sydney.

National Farmers Federation 1991, *Australian Agriculture*, Morescope Pty Ltd, Melbourne.

National Farmers Federation 1993, *Australian Agriculture*, 4th edn, Morescope Pty Ltd, Melbourne.

Piggott, R. 1990, 'Agricultural marketing', in *Agriculture in the Australian Economy*, 3rd edn, ed. D. B. Williams, Sydney University Press, Sydney.

Richardson, B. 1990, 'Rural commodity research policies' in Standing Committee on Agriculture Workshop on Research Priorities and Resource Allocation for Rural R&D, *Bureau of Rural Resources Proceedings*, no. 7, AGPS, Canberra.

Royal Commission 1988, *Royal Commission into Grain Storage, Handling and Transport*, (vol. 1: 'Report'), AGPS, Canberra.

Sieper, E. 1982, 'Rationalising rustic regulation', in Centre for Independent Studies, *Research Studies in Government Regulation*, vol. 2,

Standen, B. J. 1982, 'Credit and agriculture' in *Agriculture in the Australian Economy*, 2nd edn, ed. D. B. Williams, Sydney University Press, Sydney.

Trebeck, D. B. 1990, 'Farmer organisations' in *Agriculture in the Australian Economy*, 3rd edn, ed. D. B. Williams, Sydney University Press, Sydney.

Verrall, D., Ward, I. and Hay, P. 1985, 'Community, Country Party: roots of rural conservatism', in *Country to National: Australian Rural Politics and Beyond*, eds B. Costar and D. Woodward, Allen & Unwin, Sydney.

Vinning, G. S. 1980, *Statutory Agricultural Marketing Authorities of Australia: A Compendium, Standing Committee on Agriculture*, Technical Report Series, no. 9, CSIRO, Melbourne.

Warley, T. K. 1990, 'Megatrends affecting agrifood and rural society', *Canadian Journal of Agricultural Economics*, 38 (4), pp.717–25.

Williams, D. B. (ed.) 1990, *Agriculture in the Australian Economy*, 3rd edn, Sydney University Press, Sydney.

Williams, R. and Evans, G. 1989, 'Commonwealth policy for rural research past and present: a review', in Workshop on the Organisation and Funding of Research for the Rural Industries, *Bureau of Rural Resources Proceedings* no. 4, AGPS, Canberra.

8

EDUCATION

Russell Cowie

The word 'education' is derived from two Latin roots, which, when combined as 'educare' mean 'to lead out' or 'bring out' the potential within an individual. We accept, in modern society, that it means the process by which individuals are provided with systematic training and a variety of learning experiences to equip them for adult life and the responsibilities of citizenship. However, there is much disagreement and debate about how best to achieve this.

Systematic school-based, government-funded education is a very recent phenomenon in world history. Less than 200 years ago it was almost impossible to imagine that elected politicians could, at some time in the future, persuade taxpayers to bear the cost of providing free education to all-comers at publicly-funded schools. In a sense, that this situation now exists is something of a miracle.

All through the Middle Ages, and until only about a century ago, the matter of educating or training the young was a private family concern. A child was educated at home, or in a Church school, or apprenticed to a craftsman to learn a trade. Children of the privileged classes received an education to equip them to maintain their status and function. Most of the children of the poor were assigned to be the next generation of poor by their lack of education. Many were illiterate; most of them could manage only the most rudimentary of reading and writing skills. A few children of the poor might, by entering a monastery, acquire literacy, but only in the service of the Church. The State assumed no responsibility for the advancement of its citizens; in fact the sheer difficulty of a member of the lower classes receiving a purposeful education was the major safeguard of the rigidity of the class system.

A review of the enormous changes that have occurred in education during the last century can be conducted in response to three questions:

1 Why did national governments assume the responsibility for the education of youth, and what have been the consequences?
2 Has the purpose of 'education' altered over the last century, and to what effect?
3 What is the relationship between democracy and education?

THE EUROPEAN HERITAGE

Contemporary Australian educational practice has been largely derived from European precedents, with particular Australian variations evolving during the latter half of the nineteenth century. For most of the Middle Ages the Christian church dominated learning in Europe. The learned and literate clergy, fluent in Latin as well as their own language, were regarded by even the landed gentry with awe and wonder. The priests held the means of communication between humanity and its creator; their power over both nobility and peasantry was based on their educational attainment and status.

In the Renaissance period, learning ceased to be a monopoly of the clergy. A new secular, educated group emerged, but it was confined to the newly-wealthy, urban-merchant classes. They demanded for their children a new type of education, freed from the strict control of the Church. Even with this development, however, only a tiny proportion of the people of Europe received a formal education.

THE ENLIGHTENMENT

The eighteenth century in Europe was a period of intellectual ferment, often referred to as 'the Enlightenment'. From the fourth to the seventeenth century educational practice in Europe had been characterised by unity and conformity, dominated by the two great traditions of Christianity and classical culture. In this system the individual was expected to accept revelation as provided by the Church, and was denied the opportunity to seek rational solutions to the problems of society. The Enlightenment, on the other hand, stressed the release of the individual from his or her bondage; the desirability of an attitude of critical and original thought; and the development of a willingness to seek new scientific explanations for phenomena. It encouraged the individual to trust his or her own intellectual abilities and reject imposed interpretations.

The function of schools

Schools maintained by either the Church or the wealthy middle classes of the cities had one significant feature in common — they were agents of socialisation, that is, institutions that ensured that young people were instructed in the skills necessary for earning a living, and initiated into the values, attitudes and mores indispensable for a well-adjusted entry into adult society.

Schools thus became instruments for indoctrination in conformity, and the acceptance of existing relationships. In Victorian England, for example, it was accepted that if a child attended school, the educational experience was to be seen as a means of preparing the child to fulfil his or her station in life, and not as a pathway to a standard or style of living different from that of the child's parents. The working-class child was expected to learn only as much as was necessary for him or her to perform the menial tasks expected from a person of the same class.

The first edition of the *Encyclopedia Britannica*, for example, defined education as: 'the instructing of children, and youth in general, in such branches of knowledge and polite exercises, as are suitable to their genius and station.' (*Encyclopaedia Britannica*, vol. II, 1771, p.467).

Such inculcation into the acceptance of one's 'station in life' was widespread. It was brought to Australia along with other English attitudes and practices. A school reader used in Queensland primary schools in the 1880s contained this message:

> When you see a rich man who is proud and selfish, perhaps you are tempted to think how much better a use you would make of wealth if you were as rich as he. I hope you would; but the best proof that you can give that you would behave well if you were in another's place, is by behaving well in your own. God has appointed to each his own trials, and his own duties, and He will judge you, not according to what you think you would have done in some different station, but according to what you have done, in that station in which He has placed you.

Education for moral standards

Thus, despite the questioning spirit fostered by the Enlightenment and the new secular interest-groups, up to the middle of the nineteenth century education was still predominantly geared to social control and social stability. Its primary function was to hold people in their appointed class, and to inculcate the basic moral and community standards deemed necessary. Before the twentieth century most members of society could not imagine an education system independent of church influence or religious content. The inculcation of Christian and moral standards was the paramount purpose of education.

THE ENTRY OF THE STATE INTO EDUCATION

By the middle of the nineteenth century these attitudes were undergoing modification. In most European nations the centralised State entered the field of education both from a sense of responsibility and from self-interest. The concept of education as an investment in the national interest was begun by Napoleon, who founded the secular, government-controlled University of France in 1808, not as a university in the twentieth century sense, but as an administrating body to supervise all secondary and tertiary education in France. Napoleonic France, the first of the modern totalitarian states, recognised that the control of education was the key to national unity and strength.

In Prussia and the German Empire this attitude received even greater stress. Prominent German philosophers felt it was the duty of the state to develop the full potential of its own power by bringing out the natural abilities of its people through education. Teacher-training in Germany was part of the national effort; the prime value to the nation of a body of well-trained secular teachers was realised early and acted upon. Germany's remarkable progress industrially, despite its relatively late entry into the Industrial Revolution, was also largely a result of the government's sponsorship of technical colleges for the training of technologists.

Education in Great Britain

Great Britain was remarkably, almost ludicrously, backward in educational progress. The British were content in the early nineteenth century to leave education in the hands of churches and charitable organisations. As a result, only the children of wealthy parents received anything remotely like an adequate education. For the working-class child, Sunday Schools provided a few fleeting moments of educational experience once a week. From 1798, newly-formed organisations provided a rudimentary education service based on the monitor system, in which a teacher trained a few older children as monitors, and they in turn drilled the younger children in the mechanical repetition of a few basic mental skills.

Parents usually paid a small fee for the privilege of having their children 'educated' at such schools; the British government still did not advance funds for this social function. It was content, it seems, to watch with satisfaction the growth of the monitor schools, which catered for 200 000 children by 1820.

The 1832 *Reform Act*, by placing political power in the hands of the middle classes, enabled a more rapid implementation of the principle of governmental responsibility for education, an attitude that had slowly been developing in the public conscience. It was felt by many that the government had a definite responsibility to educate its poorer classes; that an educated working class would be more stable than an ignorant mass; and that there was a growing commercial need for educated workers. The humanitarian movements stressed the desirability of a literate working class for the reception of religious instruction, and argued that the more fortunate members of society had a social responsibility to enrich the lives of the poor. Accordingly, in 1833 the first government grant for education passed the House of Commons — it was for £20 000 (the grant for the Royal Stables was £50 000 in the same year), and was to be divided between the organisations providing the monitor schools. It was, however, merely a small subsidy. The British government had still not built any schools.

The 1870 *Education Act*

The 1870 *Education Act* made provision, for the first time, for the erection of elementary schools with public funds, together with their management by school boards elected within the local area. The stress was still on elementary education — a basic minimum education, at primary school level only, for the children of the poor. The Act was widely acknowledged as necessary after the enfranchisement of a significant proportion of the wage-earning classes in the 1867 *Reform Act*. If the working classes were to make responsible use of their newly-won voting rights, they needed an education.

It could be claimed that the 1870 *Education Act* (called the Forster Act after its sponsor, W. E. Forster) was the most significant reform Act of the nineteenth century because, while the Reform Acts of 1832 and 1867 had given some members of the middle and working classes an increasing share in the political life of the nation, and while the factory reforms protected their physical safety, this Education Act was the first measure that recognised them as human beings with intelligence that might be developed in order to lead them to more fruitful, happier and more purposeful lives.

The Act did not make schooling free. It decreed the continuance of the existing voluntary schools, but provided also or the erection of board schools, to be administered by a local school board, for which the necessary funds would be raised from fees paid by parents, local rates, and a government grant — each providing one-third of the cost. Thus a nation-wide system of primary education was established gradually, though not without some bitterness, because the nonconformists (protestants other than Anglicans) opposed the religious instruction given in board schools as Anglican-biased. In 1880 attendance was made compulsory; in 1891 schooling was provided free. It was not until 1902 that a restricted system of secondary education was established, and not until 1944, in the form of the Butler Act, did the government of Britain take steps to allow all children the opportunity to attend secondary school. The tardiness of the British government in developing a national education system for all children makes a sad contrast to the relatively vigorous promotion of such schemes in France and Germany.

AUSTRALIAN PRACTICES AND COMPROMISES

In the early years of the settlement of the colony of New South Wales, it was assumed by almost all those in authority that the Church of England, being the established church (in effect almost a government department), would be responsible for whatever educational institutions might be warranted. Governor Macquarie wrote a despatch to the British Colonial Secretary (15 May 1818) stressing the desirability of 'all persons sent hither for the purposes of disseminating the principles of education, being of the Established Church, untainted with Methodism or other sectarian opinions'.

To this end, the Anglican Archdeacon, Thomas Hobbes Scott, established the Church and Schools Corporation for New South Wales in

1825 — part of a plan to entrust education in the colony to the supervision of the Church of England, and to set up land grants for this purpose. This decision generated much controversy and debate. Almost half the population belonged to denominations other than the Church of England and protested with such effect that the charter for the corporation was revoked.

The Church of England and the other churches then each set out to obtain land grants and establish schools, with the result that there was much duplication of resources and the establishment of competing schools in areas of small population. The particular circumstances prevailing in New South Wales — a sparse population and a mixture of religious denominations with the Church of England not necessarily in preponderance — led the colonial administration to adopt the 'national system' that had been applied to a similar situation in Ireland, at this time still under British rule.

The Irish National System was based on the belief that it was both possible and desirable to bring children of all denominations together for a general, literary education. It was to be a system of secular schools, with religious instruction entrusted to representatives of the various denominations on a visiting basis.

The churches' insistence that they be permitted to operate their own schools resulted in the establishment, in 1848, of a dual system for New South Wales. Two school boards were set up: a Denominational Board that was to distribute government funds to church schools (without actually exercising control over them), and a National Board, to supervise the national schools and to grant funds for the building of schools, provided that at least a third of the expenditure was to be met by local initiative.

Small communities, partly suspicious of state-managed schooling, but anxious nevertheless to gain the government subsidy offered, often took some persuading to agree to the National school policy. Many churchmen opposed the National system, as they argued that all education was concerned with moral training and should be conducted by the Church. However, by 1849 four National schools had been established and a year later the number had grown to 25.

Even in the National schools, fees were charged. The amount was decided by local committees, with the result that wealthy districts could charge high fees and consequently could also attract the best qualified teachers by offering incentives. Naturally, as fees were charged, attendance could not be compulsory. Many children of the poor still received no schooling.

The first National school in Victoria opened at Bacchus Marsh in 1850. By 1851 seven National Schools were operating in the Port Phillip district. By contrast there were 27 church schools already functioning in the same district. A similar pattern of development was observed in Queensland, which by the 1860s was well on the way towards establishing a state-wide system of primary education. In 1870, Queensland became the first of the Australian colonies to introduce free primary education, and indeed achieved this milestone ahead of Great Britain.

The grammar schools

It was inevitable that pressure would arise for the provision of secondary education. In some of the National Schools the opportunity was created for selected pupils to 'run on' to what were described as 'superior grades', thus acquiring a modified form of secondary education. The absence in Australia of a leisured upper class, and the small numbers of middle-class people, delayed the demand for fully established secondary schools.

As with the primary schools, the churches took the initiative. The Roman Catholic Church opened St Patrick's College in Melbourne in 1854. The Church of England opened Geelong Grammar School in 1857 and the Melbourne Church of England Grammar School in 1858. The Presbyterians opened the Melbourne Academy in 1851, later changing its name to Scotch College.

In New South Wales church schools similarly made their beginnings — often tentatively. Some secondary schools, including King's School Parramatta, actually declined in enrolments after their first year. In Sydney a new model for secondary schooling was established. Legislation in 1854 established Sydney Grammar School as an autonomous non-denominational school with an annual government endowment. The school opened in 1857 with 110 pupils.

In the second year of its existence as a separate colonial parliament, the Queensland Legislative Assembly passed the *Grammar Schools Act* 1860, which, in an arrangement similar to that which established Sydney Grammar, provided that where £1000 was raised by a community for the establishment of a secondary grammar school, the government would then also contribute to the building of the school, and to its maintenance. The first of the grammar schools established under the Act was Ipswich Grammar in 1863. Brisbane Grammar School opened in 1869, and others were founded at regional centres.

Emphasis in the early decades of the grammar schools was upon the study of the classical languages. It was believed that this was important in the disciplining of the mind. Recognition of the importance of science teaching took many decades to develop.

Free, compulsory and secular education

By the 1890s most Australian colonies had established a system offering free and compulsory primary education. Because adherents to the churches paid their taxes as rigorously as anybody else, they were insistent in demanding that state funds should be used to support the church schools. However, in many districts, particularly small rural towns, the churches did not establish schools. They tended to compete with one another in city suburbs.

In New South Wales the interdenominational disputes produced a radical solution. By the 1880 Public Instruction Bill, all state aid to church primary schools was withdrawn. The Public Schools (as the former National Schools had been called since 1866) were declared to be 'free, compulsory and secular'. But they were not truly secular. Rather, they were non-denominational. Religious instruction that was 'neutral' (not biased towards any denomination) was given by the teachers, and visiting clergymen could still visit to give parent-requested instruction to selected groups during school hours. As with earlier developments, similar arrangements were made in the other colonies. One of the major social effects of this prescription of compulsory primary school education was that it served as a type of 'factory Act'. Children, being required to attend school, were legally not available as labour. The incidence of sweated labour was diminished, and more opportunities for adult employment emerged.

The move towards compulsory primary-school education was supported by the voting public — something of a transformation from the relative reluctance to do so in earlier decades. Some of the arguments touched on new sentiments. Frequent appeals were made to support the legislation by references to 'national efficiency', 'national progress', 'industrial progress' and 'social justice'. Comparisons were often drawn with other nations, implying that the Australian communities would fall behind in social standards unless universal education was attained. Another prominent argument was the connection between democracy and literacy. If democracy was to be attained, then an educated electorate was needed (as had been stressed in earlier years in England).

The struggle to establish and maintain universities

A cause–effect link also occurred in founding the colonial universities. When Great Britain conceded to the colonies the right to function under the system of responsible government (with the executive answerable to the legislature), public opinion in the educated classes of the colonies generated a demand for universities — as training institutions for society's leaders. The University of Sydney began classes in 1852, offering a classical curriculum, together with mathematics. Victoria, having obtained separate-colony status in 1851, hastened to match the Sydney initiative. Lectures began at the University of Melbourne in 1855.

Although the desire for a university was shared by most of the privileged segments of society, the universities attracted little support in their early years. By 1867 the University of Sydney catered for only 47 students, with a staff of eleven. By 1880 the student body had expanded to 76, but the staff had decreased in number to six. The University of Melbourne awarded only five degrees in 1860, ten in 1870, and nine in 1878.

Other colonies resisted the trend. The University of Adelaide did not open until 1876. In Queensland, people with university aspirations tended to travel to Sydney or to Britain for their tertiary studies. It was not until 1911 that the University of Queensland began to conduct classes.

The usual explanation for the slow and modest growth of the Australian universities is that colonial society was extremely utilitarian in emphasis, and that the British-style universities, heavily dedicated to classical and theoretical mathematical studies, did not appeal to many. Further, Australian colonies lacked the leisured upper class that traditionally supported universities. Indeed, many of the small number of families who could be so described tended to send their sons to English universities for their prestige value.

Nevertheless, the universities quickly established a significant influence upon Australian educational practice, as they became the examining authorities for school-exit examinations. Very quickly the major academic schools discovered the veracity of the maxim, 'whoever examines, controls'. Schools adjusted their curricula to meet the demands of the universities.

Free state high schools and technical colleges

In Victoria the *Education Act* of 1910 authorised the state to provide secondary education: twelve state high schools had opened by June 1911.

In New South Wales the year 1912 witnessed a similar introduction of free secondary education. In Queensland, the long-awaited extension of free education to secondary school level was also achieved in 1912.

Technical education also received government sponsorship in all states. In several of the states non-academic schools functioned in specifically defined roles — as technical, commercial, or industrial schools. The emphasis was on practical vocation-directed education, with little concern for broad education in the humanities or in social studies.

Secondary education for all

Until World War II and beyond, the low official school leaving age in most states of Australia acted as an incentive for many pupils to leave school at the elementary level and move into employment. Many thousands of pupils reached the school leaving age while still in primary school, and did not enter secondary school at all. Secondary schooling was regarded as either academic in emphasis (as a preparation for university and the professions) or technical and vocational. During the Great Depression of the 1930s the number of pupils in secondary schools diminished.

During World War II the struggle for survival awakened community conscience on such matters as social justice and equality of opportunity. One result was a concerted move to raise the school leaving age to ensure that after the war all young people would proceed to secondary school. In New South Wales the leaving age was raised from 14 to 15. In Tasmania it was decreed that after the war the leaving age would be 16. In Victoria the decision was to raise the leaving age to 15 at the end of the war. South Australia and Western Australia took similar action. In Queensland it was not until 1960 that it was decided that the school leaving age would be raised from 14 to 15. These decisions were applied in the period 1962–64, causing a great upsurge in the number of pupils in secondary schools, which now catered for all pupils.

Federal government intervention

When the Federation of Australia was formed in 1901, education was designated as the responsibility of the states. Gradually — stimulated by some of the major events of the century — the Commonwealth government has acquired greater financial power than the founding fathers intended. The 'power of the purse' has led to federal intrusion into educational policies.

The first Commonwealth government involvement in education was in its sponsorship (significantly through the Ministry of Health) of Lady Gowrie Child Care Centres. During World War II Commonwealth financial supremacy was greatly enhanced by the introduction of uniform income tax — a wartime measure to equalise the war effort among all Australians, which permanently increased the power of the Commonwealth government. In 1942 the Commonwealth Universities Commission was established to direct the work of the universities towards the war effort. This was followed by the 1945 *Education Act*: 'An Act to establish a Commonwealth Office of Education and a Universities Commission to provide for the University Training of Discharged Members of the Forces, to provide for Financial Assistance to University students, and for other purposes'. Using this formula the Commonwealth government has extended its influence to numerous facets of educational practice.

In the 1960s the federal government directed tax-collected funds to provide science laboratories and libraries for schools. Then in 1965 a nationwide chain of Colleges of Advanced Education (CAEs) was funded by the Commonwealth. Many of the former state-provided technical colleges and teachers' colleges were absorbed into the CAE system, which was intended to provide vocation-directed education in contrast to the more academic courses offered by the universities.

The term of office of John Dawkins as education minister in the latter years of the Hawke Labor government (1987–91) marked a further massive intervention into the education system. Dawkins and his advisers sought to rationalise public expenditure on tertiary education in the search for greater efficiency and effectiveness.

In a sweeping series of decrees the federal government forced a series of amalgamations upon the education industry. All of the previously independent CAEs had to accept amalgamation with neighbouring universities. The former 'binary' system was reversed in the interests of administrative rationalisation. The restrengthened utilitarian emphasis on public expenditure on education was made manifest in the creation of the federal 'mega-department' of Employment, Education and Training (DEET).

The Dawkins-driven federal interventions were characterised by a call for 'multi-skilled', highly competent workers, who were destined to add to the productive capacities of what the Labor government optimistically called 'the clever country'. There was a stated preference for 'vocational' rather than 'general' education. Promotion of the

Technical and Further Education (TAFE) sector was complementary to this approach. A corollary to this intervention was the drive for national approaches to curriculum emphases (see 'Curriculum Concerns' below).

In the 1990s, in a further example of the influence of Commonwealth funds in educational policy, 'Austudy' payments were introduced to subsidise the use of educational services by people from lower-income families, while at the same time applying a 'user-pays' principle. The latter was achieved through the Higher Education Contribution Scheme (HECS), whereby graduates repay some of the costs of their tertiary education when their income level permits.

Through these measures, the Commonwealth government extended its management of tertiary education right down to individual participants.

CURRICULUM CONCERNS

The term 'curriculum' is widely used in educational discourse. It has several levels of meaning. The word is derived from the Latin '*currere*', 'to run', and refers to a course that is 'covered' in terms of both time and subject matter and/or skills studied. A 'curriculum' can refer to the total learning offered within a school system, or the set of learning experiences of one class-group or, indeed, of one individual in the class.

The search for a national 'core curriculum'

In the Australian federal system, within which the states have maintained control over education, there have been frequent calls for a national curriculum to eliminate, or at least diminish, differences in approaches to learning and in choice of subject matter between the states.

In 'Core Curriculum for Australian Schools', published by the Curriculum Development Centre, Canberra (1980), it was stressed that Australian educational institutions needed to respond to changes and developments in our society. The document declared that defining a core curriculum was not simply a matter of defining bodies of subject content:

> Since it is the students' learning experiences that concern us — the curriculum as experienced by students — we must also give attention both to how students learn and the resources and situations they need.

Figure 8.1 The core learning environment

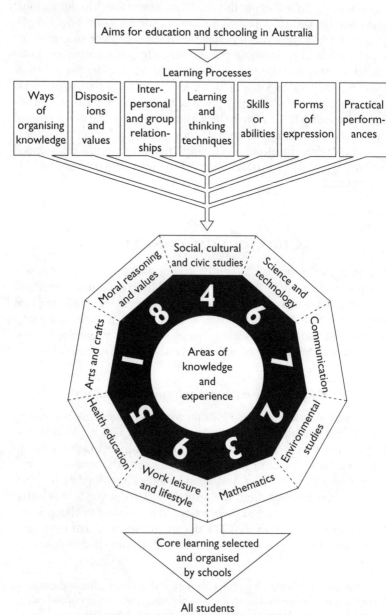

Accordingly the Curriculum Development Centre defined a Core Curriculum in terms of both learning processes and areas of knowledge and experience (represented in Figure 8.1).

The Finn, Mayer and Carmichael Reports

The principle of defining and pursuing national goals has received further emphasis in the 1990s. The Finn, Mayer and Carmichael Reports are a linked set of national reports that deal with national goals for post-compulsory education and training, in both the secondary school and Technical and Further Education settings.

The Finn Report made recommendations on participation rates and work-related key competencies. In simple terms it recommended that all young people should complete post-compulsory education to year 12 in schools or the equivalent level in TAFE, and that about 50 per cent of these should proceed to tertiary education.

The Mayer Report defined competencies required for effective participation in employment, and stressed that its definition of competence involved both the ability to perform in a given context and the capacity to transfer knowledge and skills to new tasks and situations. While this definition was not substantially different from that espoused in many school work programs, the report stressed that key competencies should not just be developed and demonstrated, they should be applied in an integrated manner in new work situations.

The Carmichael Committee, whose chairman, Laurie Carmichael, was also a member of the Finn and Mayer Committees, issued a Report in March 1992, entitled 'The Australian Vocational Certificate Training System'. Its major concern was to seek a nationwide system by which young people could acquire a competency-based qualification (rather than a 'time-served' type apprenticeship) to aid them in their search for employment. A natural corollary to this objective is the greater provision in schools and TAFE colleges of vocationally focussed courses.

THE PUBLIC AND 'PRIVATE' SCHOOLS DEBATE

A perennial topic of debate in Australian society concerns the funding of public and 'independent' schools. Supporters of free public or state schools argue that all or most of public educational funds should be deployed to state schools. They claim that if some parents choose to send their children to church or private schools they should bear the expense of that choice, as they are, in effect, buying a privilege.

Under the present system, all private or 'independent' schools receive a scaled per-capita grant from both the state and the Commonwealth governments to supplement the income they gather from fees. State school supporters claim that this ensures that the private schools are not truly independent, and that, as a result of their combined sources of income, their facilities are generally superior to those of the state schools. The assertion is also sometimes made that the private schools are a divisive influence in what is supposed to be an egalitarian society.

The counter-argument advanced by the supporters of private schools usually runs as follows: all education is inevitably concerned with questions of value. Because of this, the state should not itself be an agent of education as there is no state-espoused set of values in a democratic society. The state should ensure that basic educational facilities are available for all, but otherwise should be involved in education as little as possible. Rather than having a divisive effect, independent schools ensure diversity of approach and parental choice in religious emphasis — both essential elements in a multicultural and heterogeneous society. The difference in emotional overtones between the words divisive and diversity illustrates the effect of prejudice in this debate.

An economic justice argument is also used by advocates of private schools. It is a parental right, they argue, to choose to pay fees for an education of their choice. Many of the parents who do so are not wealthy and are in fact making extreme sacrifices to send their children to a fee-charging school. However, having paid their taxes like everybody else, they claim that it is only just and fair that some reasonable proportion of what could be regarded as their educational tax be allocated to support the school of their choice, and thus hold the fees down. The pupils in an independent school are saving the state system, and thus the general taxpayer, a considerable sum of money. If they were all redirected to state schools, the system would collapse.

This latter argument is particularly effective. None of the major political parties in Australia could risk going to the electorate with a policy of drastically discontinuing aid to church and independent schools. They would simply lose too much voter support.

PARTICIPATION, EQUITY, AND RETENTION RATES

The Australian governments of the 1980s focussed on the need to encourage all young people to complete a full secondary education or some other appropriate education or training. In December 1983 the federal Minister for Education, Senator Susan Ryan, announced the allocation of $74 million for the Participation and Equity Program (PEP), which subsumed the earlier School-to-Work Transition Program.

The relatively low percentage of young Australians proceeding beyond year 10 in their schooling was widely regarded as being related to the fact that most senior school subjects were academic, suiting only the talented minority. The PEP program provided funds for state and non-government secondary schools to reduce significantly the numbers of students leaving full-time education prematurely and to foster equal educational outcomes.

In pursuing the principle of equity of access to education, the PEP program sought to develop courses through which the less advantaged groups in the community could benefit. The official statement specifically stressed that the position of women and girls and other under-represented groups such as Aborigines and ethnic groups should be given particular attention. The statistics published by the Schools Commission to highlight the relatively low retention rates are shown in Table 8.1.

The overall retention rate for the period 1975–86 revealed a major change in emphasis. In 1975 the retention rate for males was higher than for females, but from 1976 the position was reversed. From that year there was a steady growth in the female retention rate, exceeding that for males, possibly because unskilled labouring positions for males were still generally more widely available than for females (Table 8.2).

The Schools Commission report stressed that the differences in retention rates might be closely related to the socio-economic composition of the student population. Government secondary schools may have appeared to have a low overall retention rate, but there were wide variations among them. Data for one state published in 1983 showed

Table 8.1   Percentages of pupils who carried through from first to final year (prior to PEP)

Year	Government schools	Non-government schools
1979	28.9	55.4
1980	28.4	56.1
1981	28.5	56.9
1982	29.6	58.5

Source: Commonwealth Schools Commission, 1984, p.8

Table 8.2 Percentages of apparent retention rates to final year, all schools, Australia, 1975–86

Year	Males	Females	Total
1975	34.6	33.6	34.1
1976	34.6	35.3	34.9
1977	34.0	36.6	35.3
1978	33.1	37.3	35.1
1979	32.4	37.2	34.7
1980	31.9	37.3	34.5
1981	32.0	37.8	34.8
1982	32.9	39.9	36.3
1983	37.5	43.9	40.6
1984	42.1	48.0	45.0
1985	43.5	49.5	46.4
1986	45.6	52.1	48.7

Source: Commonwealth Schools Commission, 1987, p.57

that retention to the final year of school varied between 15 per cent and 70 per cent for government schools serving communities of quite different socio-economic character. There were also indications that rates varied for government schools serving areas of similar socio-economic character, suggesting that the nature of the schools themselves can affect retention through the school climate they create and the courses they offer. One of the objectives of PEP was to reduce these large variations.

While the new initiatives were expected to result in the emergence of some new school subjects, the Schools Commission did not suggest the abandonment of the traditional disciplines. It stated that 'one of the central tasks of schools is to introduce students to the traditional intellectual disciplines and to give them the opportunity to enjoy and master them' (p.15). This might entail serious reconsideration of the teaching methods used, with a consequent move towards more experience-based learning and active research.

The prospects are that, in the 1990s, the percentage of young Australians proceeding to the end of secondary schooling will increase substantially beyond all previous levels. The challenge to the schools and the teachers is to ensure that the students benefit, and that parents will have faith in the likelihood of their children gaining tangible personal qualities and vocational aptitudes from the additional years in school.

Figure 8.2 Apparent year 12 school retention rates, all schools 1972–1990

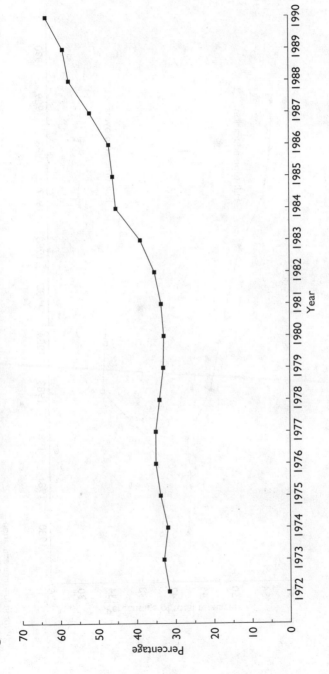

Source: Australian Education Council, 1991, *Young People's Participation in Post Compulsory Education and Training* (The Finn Report), Canberra, p.39.

Figure 8.3 Full-time education and full-time employment* participation rates for 15–19 year olds 1980–1990

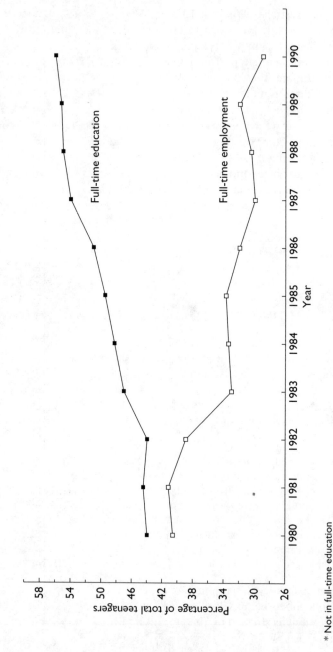

* Not in full-time education

Source: Australian Education Council, 1991, *Young People's Participation in Post Compulsory Education and Training* (The Finn Report), Canberra, p.16.

The Australia-wide year 12 retention rates for the period 1971–91 reveal not only an upward trend, but an accelerating upward trend (see Figure 8.2 on p.171).

Government support initiatives, such as the Family Support Supplement, and the combined effects of granting 'Austudy' allowances to children from disadvantaged families while simultaneously discontinuing the dole allowance for early school-leavers, have contributed to an increase in the retention rate. However, the rate of full-time employment for young Australians has declined in the same period that the school retention rates have increased — partly because jobs are more difficult to obtain and because young people believe they need higher qualifications to obtain employment later in life (Figure 8.3).

Retention rates vary significantly from state to state, for reasons both diverse and numerous. Employment opportunities and aspirations combine to affect the trends. By 1992 in all states more girls than boys were staying on to complete year 12.

THE NATURE OF MODERN EDUCATION

If education was seen in the late eighteenth century to be the instruction of youth to fit their various stations in life, the modern emphasis is quite the opposite. The objective now is to fully realise the potential of individuals and liberate them from restrictions imposed by their status at birth or the poverty of their parents. These objectives can be found in most contemporary statements on the purposes of education:

> An educational programme is concerned with the individual, his/her society and his/her environment. It is designed for the survival of the individual, for the survival of some form of social order, and for the survival of a tolerable physical and cultural environment . . . Each individual must be allowed as much freedom as possible for development and self-expression. There is a great diversity among people, differences in aptitudes and interests; there are also, within each individual, differences which are not static but changing and developing, particularly during adolescence. (Board of Secondary School Studies, 1974)

Accompanying the emphasis on individual differences is the notion of individuals being self-directive. One of the objectives of secondary education, as stressed by the Queensland Board of Secondary School Studies is:

To help individuals when they assume an adult role to live in the complete sense, to be socially dependable and morally self-directive, and to help individuals to be economically self-supportive.

Contradictions and problems

Despite the new emphasis on self-managed learning and the liberation of the individual, many schools today still place a high priority on conformity, with an emphasis on every student dressing the same way, and doing the same work at the same time. Many of the subjects taught are still examined in a manner that demands the acceptance of the principle that there is a 'right' answer to every question. A large percentage of school administrators still seem to be dedicated to the production of a body of unquestioningly obedient workers, conditioned by paramilitary organisational experiences to follow stereotyped behavioural patterns.

All the predictions of the future, however, indicate the need to educate a new type of functioning adult, one who has 'learned how to learn' rather than how to regurgitate material temporarily committed to memory; one who has developed a capacity to make decisions rather than simply obey orders; and one who is ready to ask questions, experiment with innovations, and assume responsibilities.

In a pluralist democratic society, value will have to be placed on the preservation of the rights of minorities and the survival of differing viewpoints. Schooling systems that encourage independent and innovative thinking have to cope with the associated problem of establishing social values. If students are geared to an extreme predilection for criticism of existing practices, they may become agents of social destruction, undermining both useful and moribund institutions without discrimination. The educational experience may still need to foster a high degree of sensitivity to the values and priorities of subcultures, minority groups and alien societies.

Expanded educational opportunities contribute to another modern problem — the difficulty of finding a sufficient number of satisfying and meaningful jobs for the graduates of schools and tertiary institutions. Even as increased mechanisation and automation reduce the amount of labour applied to production, educational systems produce more highly trained people searching for jobs. Expanded leisure-time is not necessarily the answer, as for vast numbers of people a meaning in life, is most tangibly fulfilled in their occupations. Because the age of automation has reduced the employment opportunities for those with a general education, there has also been in recent years a return to emphasis on practical, vocation-directed education focussed on the attainment of key competencies (see the reference to the Finn, Mayer and Carmichael Reports).

Effects of mass education

The extension of education to the masses has enriched the lives of those who have participated by making it possible for them to enjoy literature, music and arts, and by opening up new opportunities in both vocations and leisure. It enabled the Industrial Revolution to accelerate by providing an educated working class capable of performing more intricate tasks, and has helped to raise the standard of living. In politics, it has forced politicians to consider those issues important to people as education has made voters more discerning in their voting behaviour.

Yet the great educational reforms have also brought their attendant vices. Politicians often resort to the arts of the demagogue in order to win votes: they can work to win popularity rather than to pursue responsible, if unpopular, policies. The power of the popular press, while also a possible force for good in the community, can be used to inflame public opinion and to pressurise governments; for although education may teach a person how to read, it may not necessarily develop the ability to discriminate between what is worth reading and what is not.

The role of formal education in modern society is a matter of continuous debate. In the context of the materialist emphasis on the modern industrial state, many educationists are deeply concerned. They believe that schools should not be simply factories for producing employees. The expansion of modern educational facilities may have enhanced social mobility, but the process may not necessarily have expanded human happiness.

FURTHER READING

Barcan (1980) offers a memorable attempt to survey the history of Australian education: a difficult task because the process was not uniform over the various colonies and states. Students should seek specific state histories of education for information on local developments.

Both Foster and Harman (1992) and King and Young (1986) offer profound insights into the relationships between Australian societal practices and the expectations placed upon the education system by both proponents of ideologies and advocates of competencies for productivity. The centralist, rationalist approach to education promoted by federal government agencies in recent times can be reviewed through consulting the Finn (1991), Mayer (1992) and Carmichael (1992) Reports. Lingard, Knight and Porter (1993) address the likely effects of federal government rationalisation policies upon schooling.

REFERENCES

Australian Education Council 1991, *Young People's Participation in Post Compulsory Education and Training* (The Finn Report), AEC, Canberra.

Australian Education Council 1992, *Employment-Related Key Competencies: A Proposal for Consolidation* (The Mayer Report), AEC, Canberra.

Barcan, A. 1980, *A History of Australian Education*, Oxford University Press, Melbourne.

Board of Secondary School Studies 1974, *Aims and Objectives of Secondary Education*, Board of Secondary School Studies, Brisbane.

Commonwealth Schools Commission 1984, *Participation and Equity in Australian Schools*, AGPS, Canberra.

Commonwealth Schools Commission 1987, *In the National Interest*, AGPS, Canberra.

Curriculum Development Centre 1980, *Core Curriculum for Australian Schools*, AGPS, Canberra.

Employment and Skills Formation Council 1992, *The Australian Vocational Certificate Training System* (The Carmichael Report), AGPS, Canberra.

Foster, L. and Harman, K. 1992, *Australian Education: a Sociological Perspective*, Prentice Hall, Sydney.

King, R. J. R. and Young, R. E. 1986, *A Systematic Sociology of Australian Education*, Allen & Unwin, Sydney.

Lingard, R., Knight, J. and Porter, P. 1993, *Schooling Reform in Hard Times*, Falmer Press, London.

9

MEDICINE

....

Adrian Bower and John Biggs

Medicine refers to medical practitioners, the treatment they provide and the administrative systems supporting the delivery of medical care. This chapter also covers the education of doctors before and after graduation, the interface of medical practitioners with allied heath care professionals, and the challenge of the changing needs of society.

The aim of medicine is to provide the best quality of health for the whole community. However medicine is only one profession among many needed to ensure a healthy society: doctors, nurses, physiotherapists, occupational therapists, dentists, pharmacists, psychologists, speech pathologists and others work to improve the physical and mental well-being of patients. In addition, there is some demand for alternative forms of medicine. How to combine alternative medicine with the present health care system so that patients can be sure that the alternative practitioner they see is safe and competent is a continuing challenge.

In the early days of European settlement in Australia, with harsh living conditions and the 'tyranny of distance', medicine played an important role in ensuring the survival and growth of the colonies. Inadequate care in childbirth, the prevalence of fatal childhood infections such as measles, scarlet fever and diphtheria and the large number of injuries in rural Australia (Australian Institute of Health [AIH], 1988, pp.2–5) meant that most families suffered bereavement.

In the nineteenth and early twentieth centuries medicine in Australia was mostly delivered by private practitioners, church-based hospitals and public hospitals. In the late twentieth century there has been increasing government involvement, both at state and Commonwealth levels, largely as a result of the increasing cost of care and the realisation that not all can afford the premiums for private health insurance. Public expectations about the standards of treatment have meant an increasing awareness of the need to regulate expenditure on health care. For example, one heart transplant equals several hip replacements, but with health education programs the same amount of money could reach even more people, thereby reducing the demand for high cost, high technology medicine. Limited resources mean that choices must be made about which areas of health care will receive financial support.

The standard of health care in Australia is high and Australian medicine has pioneered new developments that have been adopted worldwide. However, health care delivery has failed to meet the needs and expectations of the Aboriginal community. Aborigines have higher levels of infant mortality, lower standards of health and a lower life expectancy than the non-Aboriginal population and these have become matters of significant government intervention.

There is a recognition that medical education needs to change in order to maintain the highest standards of medical care for the community (Dornhorst, 1981; Thompson, 1981; Doherty, 1988); these forces for change are not confined to Australia. Following reports published in New Zealand and the United States (NZ Ministry of Health, 1985; Association of American Medical Colleges, 1984) the First World Conference on Medical Education was held in Edinburgh in 1988. The conference agreed upon a declaration of principles to ensure the highest quality of medical graduates (World Federation for Medical Education, 1988), and this was adopted by the World Health Assembly in 1989. A Second World Conference in Medical Education was held in Edinburgh in 1993. In that year the British government made funds available to medical schools to appoint facilitators of curriculum change. Medical education in Australia has to change in order to produce graduates who are competent in an Australian context and also capable of working in medical settings anywhere in the world.

MEDICAL EDUCATION IN AUSTRALIA

The first Australian medical schools were opened in Melbourne in 1862, Sydney in 1883, and Adelaide in 1884. The University of Queensland medical school was opened in 1936. The most recently formed medical schools have been those at Newcastle in New South Wales and Flinders University of South Australia, both of which opened in the mid-1970s. There are moves to open more medical schools, prompted less by a perception of a need for more medical graduates than by a recognition of the changing centres of population.

With the exceptions of the newer schools, the Australian medical schools were founded on British models. Given the demography of the immigrant population, this was inevitable. Changes in British medical schools were generally adopted by Australian medical schools. Thus the curricula tend to have a pre-clinical and clinical divide, where the pre-clinical years are spent learning the basic sciences of anatomy, physiology and biochemistry and the clinical years are spent almost entirely in hospital settings. Models from Great Britain were also important in founding the Australian (and Australasian) specialist colleges. In previous years these colleges encouraged trainees to have periods of training in centres away from Australia, especially in Great Britain. Until recently, undergraduate medical schools in Australia were accredited by the General Medical Council of Great Britain. This task is now undertaken by the Australian Medical Council (AMC), which was founded in 1985.

INFLUENCES ON MEDICAL CARE
The Australian population

At least four aspects of the Australian population have an influence on medical care. The first is the rapid growth of the population: five million people in 1918, ten million in 1959 and 18 million in 1994. Regular reviews of projected needs of medical practitioners are required.

The second aspect is the changing ethnic mix of the immigrant population, with an increasing percentage coming from the Asia-Pacific region. Western medical traditions will be strange to many; it may be unacceptable for male doctors to examine female patients.

The third aspect is the isolated nature of many rural settlements. Although 30 per cent of the population is in rural and remote areas (Federal Department of Health, 1993), there are relatively few medical practitioners for that population, perhaps because most medical students come from a metropolitan background, and are therefore reluctant to move to rural areas. The question of rural health is complicated and needs fuller treatment.

A fourth aspect is the significant increase in life expectancy due to improvements in housing, diet, immunisation programs and health education. Since 1929, life expectancy at birth has risen by 14 years to 73 years for males, and by 16 years to 79 years for females. At the age of sixty, the expectation of life has risen in the same period by three years to 18 years for males (that is, to 78 years) and by six years to 23 years (that is, to 83 years) for females (AIH, 1988, p.13). This leads to a new challenge for health care delivery and indeed for society at large — how to cope with an increasing population of people over the age of 65. The increasing cost of pensions and the increased use of health care systems by the aged, have led the Commonwealth government to introduce compulsory saving schemes in the form of superannuation contributions.

The number and distribution of medical practitioners

In absolute terms, Australia has enough medical practitioners. In 1988 there were about 30 000 to 33 000 doctors in Australia (Doherty, 1988, pp.365–71). The majority graduated in Australia (83 per cent), with the next largest sources being Great Britain, Ireland and New Zealand. Graduation and registration from one state is now recognised by all other states with the exception of Western Australia. A recent change is that recognition of qualifications from other countries, particularly Great Britain and Ireland, has now ceased. Medical practitioners who wish to practise permanently in Australia, except those who have qualified in New Zealand, must sit and pass a clinical examination in order to be accredited by the AMC. There is a quota of 200 successful candidates in any year. Specialists may, however, apply to the relevant specialist college in Australia, which will then recommend to the AMC whether or not registration for limited practice should be given. Medical practitioners wishing to undertake short-term employment can still obtain provisional registration without the necessity of sitting an examination.

In Australia there are 1.95 general practitioners (GPs) per 1000 people in capital cities and 1.08 per 1000 elsewhere. However, the figures vary from place to place. In Brisbane, for example, the ratio is 1.75 per 1000 (571 people per GP), while in the central west region of Queensland it is 0.59 per 1000 (1698 people per GP) (Veitch, 1989). The maldistribution of specialists is even more marked, with 93 per cent practising in metropolitan or major urban areas (Craig, 1992). There is difficulty in getting practitioners into rural and remote areas and in keeping them there, stemming from feelings of professional isolation, difficulties in getting relief for weekends and evening work, and family pressures.

There are now several schemes to improve the delivery of rural health care. The Commonwealth government has put in place the Rural Health Support, Education and Training (RHSET) program with the broad aim of improving the health status of rural and remote communities through provision of increased support, education and training for rural health workers. The Rural Doctors Training Program in Queensland gives potential rural doctors the training needed for the special demands of rural practice, and provides support mechanisms for families, especially the spouses, of rural practitioners. There is a Rural Incentives Program (RIP) with funds for specific rural training projects at undergraduate and postgraduate level. Recent developments include financial incentives to medical schools to increase the number of graduates undertaking rural training programs. There is evidence from North America that such affirmative action programs do increase the number of practitioners opting for rural practice (Adkins, Cullen and Newman, 1987).

In some metropolitan areas overseas doctors have to be recruited on short-term contract to meet staff shortages. This leads to problems of continuity of health care because of the lack of long term commitment to the hospital by its junior staff.

Training of health care professionals

The training of health care practitioners has an important impact on health care. Policies are needed that ensure the right number of practitioners, with the right kind of training are located in places where they are needed.

Medical practitioners

There are ten medical schools in Australia. Courses are six years long (except Newcastle, where it is five years). As in most other countries, Australian graduates must complete a supervised year, called internship, before being fully registered to practise medicine. There follows a period of formal postgraduate training before the graduate is allowed to practise as a GP or specialist. The period of post-registration training can vary, from three to four years for general practice, to seven to ten years for specialties. A recent change in specialist training in Australia is the introduction of re-accreditation. Specialist colleges are insisting that every five or ten years, specialists undertake re-accreditation through a program of approved continuing medical education. Changes in all areas of medical practice are so rapid that a conscious effort must be made to keep abreast of the latest developments.

It is in the field of undergraduate medical education that some of the most far reaching changes are being made. After 1997, the medical schools of Sydney University, Queensland University and the Flinders University of South Australia will have graduate entry programs of four years duration. There will be radical changes to the nature of medical education with the introduction of problem-based learning and vertical integration to remove the pre-clinical/clinical split. Such changes are not unique; North America has a history of graduate entry medical schools, and places like Harvard, McMaster and Maastricht, in Holland, as well as Newcastle (New South Wales) have what are called 'innovative' curricula. In Australia 40 per cent of graduates will be following such curricula. The changes in Australian medical schools have received Commonwealth government funding to develop the curricula. Part of the changes will serve to decentralise clinical training so that a greater role is played by institutions other than metropolitan teaching hospitals. Some of the incentive for this is the move to increase exposure of students to rural practice, and part is in response to the trend for more patient care to be provided outside hospitals.

Nurses

Nurse education has largely been transferred from hospitals to tertiary institutions offering degrees in nursing care. Nurses holding earlier diploma qualifications are being encouraged to update their skills by enrolling in degree programs. Promotion to some of the senior nursing grades will probably require a tertiary qualification. The move to degree-based nursing is supported by the nursing profession and follows similar trends in North America and Great Britain. However, it is not without its problems. One is the difficulty of recruiting suitably qualified teaching staff. A more profound problem is the precise role of nurses with a degree, many of whom see their contribution as being different from the traditional nursing role and believe that they ought to have a greater say in the management of patients. As medicine has become more specialised, so too has nursing. Many areas of nursing now require specialist post-registration training, for example, in paediatrics, intensive care and obstetrics.

Allied health professionals

At the University of Queensland, training in physiotherapy, occupational therapy, speech pathology and in pharmacy has been at degree level for many years. These courses come under the umbrella of the Faculty of Medicine. In many universities a separate Faculty of Health Sciences incorporates these professions together with, for example, nursing and radiography.

The role of allied health professionals is expanding. Because of the emphasis on increasing public awareness of disease prevention, physiotherapists now join forces with human movement graduates in programs aimed at improving the level of fitness in the population and thus reducing the incidence of heart disease, the biggest cause of death in the western world.

THE USE OF HEALTH CARE FACILITIES

Health care is provided at primary, secondary and tertiary levels. Primary health care refers to the local family practitioner; secondary refers to a hospital with a wide range of facilities, with specialists on the hospital staff; tertiary refers to hospitals with very specialised facilities, such as transplant units, or specialists with skills in a so-called 'sub-specialty' area. Referral to a tertiary centre can be either directly from the GP, or from a secondary centre. Broadly speaking, the choice offered to a patient is to go to a general practitioner or to hospital. The expectation is that, except in cases of an emergency, a patient will first visit a local doctor who will then decide if referral to a specialist is necessary. In some cases the visit will be to an alternative medicine practitioner, such as a chiropractor, naturopath or acupuncturist.

In 1989–90, 57 000 people in Australia were interviewed about illness and injuries they had experienced in the previous two weeks, actions they had taken with regard to their health (visit to a doctor, chemist, etc.), and lifestyle characteristics that might affect their health. The results were published (Australian Bureau of Statistics [ABS], 1991). Many of the statistics below are taken from that Health Survey document. A similar survey was carried out in 1983 (ABS, 1986) and comparison of the results shows trends in illness, health care and education.

General practitioners

In 1989–90, 72.9 per cent of the population reported an illness in the previous two weeks; the figure was 63 per cent in 1983. The reasons for the increase are still being identified. There has also been a large increase in the use of medications (excluding the use of vitamin and mineral supplements), from 47 per cent to 64 per cent of respondents.

Complaints about the cardiovascular, respiratory, digestive and nervous systems made up 48 per cent of the total number of complaints. In the two weeks before the interview, 20 per cent of people reported visiting a doctor; of those consulting a doctor, 85.9 per cent visited a general practitioner and 13.9 per cent a specialist.

The most common reason for visiting a doctor in 1989–90 was some form of respiratory system disease (22 per cent of patients). This may reflect the high incidence of asthma in Australia. The next most common illness was musculoskeletal problems (13 per cent). Headache, which accounted for 8 per cent of visits, presents problems for GPs because causes vary from potentially fatal conditions to non-specific stress. Cardiovascular illness accounted for 10 per cent of complaints and the digestive system 5.8 per cent. It is noticeable that many of the complaints were preventable or reducible through health education. Table 9.1 shows the reasons for visiting the doctor in the 1989–90 survey and figures for the same complaints in the 1983 survey.

Of people employed, 8.9 per cent reported taking one or more days off work in the fortnight before the survey, the average number of days was three.

Table 9.1 Illnesses experienced in two-week period

Condition	Percentage of people with condition	
	1989–90	1983
Endocrine, nutritional and metabolic disease	3.4	2.6
Mental disorders	3.7	3.6
Diseases of nervous system and sense organs	7.8	5.0
Circulatory system diseases	10.8	10.2
Respiratory system diseases	21.7	18.1
Digestive system diseases	5.8	11.1
Genito-urinary system diseases	3.9	3.0
Diseases of skin and subcutaneous tissue	6.0	9.1
Musculo-skeletal problems	11.5	9.6
Neoplasms	0.21	0.9
Injuries and poisoning	7.3	3.9
Infectious and parasitic disease	3.0	–
Total experiencing illness	72	63

Note: In absolute numbers the numbers of people consulting a doctor in the two weeks before the interview was 3 400 200.

Source: Australian Bureau of Statistics, *Australian Health Survey*, 1991.

Hospital use

In 1987–88, Australia had 5.1 hospital beds per 1000 of population, which is high by world standards. The use of hospital beds is changing, the length of stay getting shorter, with averages of 10.3 days in 1965–66 and 6.2 days in 1987–88. This reduction in length of stay does not automatically bring a reduction in the cost of hospital care; short stay patients tend to have more intensive medical and nursing care, and surveys in Great Britain have shown that the readmission rate rises when patients are discharged from hospital early.

The rate of admission to hospital in 1989–90 was 137 per 1000 population (ABS, 1991), which represents a considerable fall in the Australian figure since 1983 when the rate was 206 per 1000 population

Table 9.2 People who were in hospital in the twelve months before interview.

Age and sex	Per 1000
Male	
less than 5	78.1
5–14	104.1
15–24	127.5
25–34	106.1
35–44	114.2
45–54	104.1
55–64	117.1
65–74	128.4
more than 75	71.2
Female	
less than 5	63.3
5–14	76.9
15–24	208.8
25–34	339.3
35–44	191.6
45–54	129.5
55–64	106.6
65–74	116.2
more than 75	105.6

Source: Australian Bureau of Statistics, *Australian Health Survey*, 1991.

(ABS, 1986). Table 9.2 (p.185) shows the differences that age and sex made to the hospitalisation rate in the earlier year. Note that between the ages of 15 and 49 years the rate in females was higher than in males because of admissions for pregnancy and childbirth. Hospital use may also be expressed as 13.7 per cent of the population reporting a hospital episode in the year before the survey, of whom 41.9 per cent were males and 58.1 per cent were females.

The cause of hospital admission varies with age and sex. Between the ages of one and five years the commonest cause in both males and females is respiratory disease (34 per 1000). In the age group 5–14 years, respiratory problems are still the most common cause (20 per 1000), followed by accidents, including poisoning (13 per 1000). This cause rises to 23 per 1000 in the 15–24 year age group. In the age group 15–44 years the commonest cause of admission is childbirth (56 per 1000). For those aged over 65 years, the causes of hospital admission are diseases of the circulatory system (42 per 1000), the digestive system (35 per 1000) and the genitourinary system (23 per 1000).

Statistics like these allow decisions to be made about the future needs of the population, and about developments to meet them.

In addition to information about the causes of admission to hospital, the distribution of the population needs to be known so that hospitals can be built in the right places. The movement of people away from inner cities where most of the major tertiary centres are located means that patients have to travel long distances to hospital. This problem exists in many parts of the world, including Great Britain, where some of the most prestigious teaching hospitals face amalgamation or closure because of population movement.

HEALTH EDUCATION

The greatest potential for change in the health of a population lies not in medical intervention, but in prevention of diseases. In common with other developed nations, the increasing cost of medical care has persuaded the Australian government to fund campaigns for illness prevention. However, many diseases and deaths have multiple causes and it can be difficult to decide what should be the focus of a campaign. A problem that causes confusion in the general population is that medical debates tend to be carried out in public, with both electronic and printed media reporting on the issues. For example, there have been many media-conducted discussions on the role of cholesterol in heart disease; when even research workers cannot agree it is not surprising that the public treat some campaigns with cynicism.

Death rates

In 1987 the crude death rate was 7 per 1000 for males and 6.6 per 1000 for females (AIH, 1990, pp.13–19). The major causes of death for both males and females are circulatory disease and cancer. There is a general trend for the death rate from circulatory disease to be falling and that from cancer to be rising. In terms of health education, death rates often fail to have an impact upon the general population; there are other, more meaningful ways of expressing the death rate. One of these is to consider any death between the ages of one and 70 years to be

Figure 9.1   Major causes of death, ACT, 1981–85

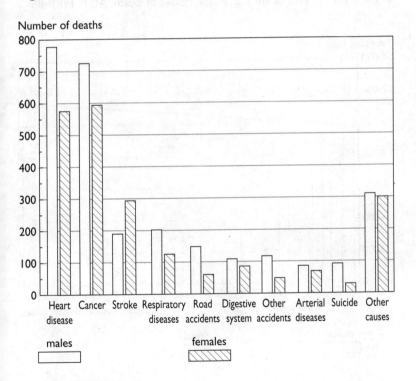

Source: ABS, unpublished data.

premature, and then to count the years of life lost. A person dying at age 50 years would be considered to have lost 20 years of life. As an example, Figures 9.1 (p.187) and 9.2 show the major causes of death for the Australian Capital Territory and the years of life lost. Between 1981 and 1985, 67 000 potential years of life were lost by Canberra residents (ACT Community and Health Service, 1988). The calculations would be similar for any large city in Australia. Although the years of life lost give the same information as the death rate, the figures are likely to make a greater public impression.

Improving health

Instead of campaigning against specific health hazards, the trend is to educate about total lifestyle, in which fitness, diet, non-smoking, stress

Figure 9.2   Years of life lost, major causes of death, ACT, 1981–85

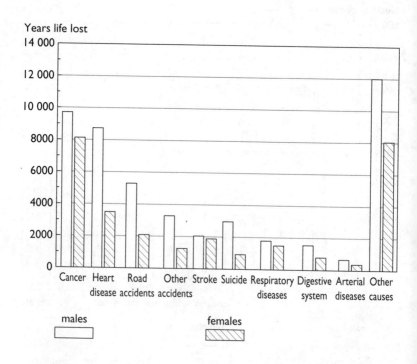

Source: ABS, unpublished data.

management and moderation in alcohol intake all play their part. A mixture of media information and government legislation is used in an effort to improve the health of the population.

Smoking

The link between smoking and ill health has been apparent since the early 1960s. There is a strong correlation between smoking and cancer of the mouth, larynx, lung and stomach, and smoking is a significant factor in cardiovascular disease, including heart attacks and strokes. It has been estimated that in 1984 more than half the deaths of people aged between 15 and 64 years were attributable to smoking-related diseases. Fewer males and females now smoke, although the incidence of cancer in females due to smoking is still rising because of the increase in female smoking that took place after about 1950. While 28 per cent of the adult population smoke, 23 per cent reported they were ex-smokers. There has been a marked decline since 1977 when 37 per cent of the adult population were smokers.

There is probably more government intervention about smoking than any other cause of ill health. Smoking is now banned during domestic air travel; workplaces with shared air conditioning have to be smoke-free and restaurants are encouraged to have large smoke-free areas. There is heightened sensitivity about smoke-free areas following the success of lawsuits in some countries where a non-smoker has worked in a smoking environment and contends that disease has resulted from inhaling the smoke from other people's cigarettes. Legislation regarding smoking (including advertising and sports sponsorship by tobacco companies) has produced heated debates over the issue of personal freedom versus the health of society.

Alcohol

Alcohol-related disease is responsible for about 5 per cent of all deaths in Australia and one in five hospital beds is occupied by a patient affected by alcohol. There is an acceptance that people wish to drink alcohol and recent campaigns have been about its sensible use. Particular messages have been about safe levels of drinking for males and females and about not driving after drinking alcohol, as one-third of all drivers killed in 1988 had a blood alcohol level above the legal limit. The consumption of alcohol fell by about 10 per cent between 1980 and 1990 and the pattern of consumption has changed, with an increase in the amount of wine drunk and a relative reduction in the amount of beer consumed (AIH, 1990 pp.71–3). The average amount of alcohol consumed per day is 23.6 mL, which is equivalent to 285 mL of full strength beer or two 30 mL measures of spirits (ABS, National Health Survey, 1991).

Diet

In world terms, malnutrition and under-nutrition are the greatest hazards to health. However, in Australian society and in many other affluent western nations, excess or unbalanced food intake are responsible for much ill health. Obesity, defined as a weight of more than 20 per cent above a desirable standard (Tortora and Grabowski, 1993) has become common and poses a major threat to health. In 1989–90, 27 per cent of males and 16 per cent of females were classed as overweight and 5.8 per cent of males and 7.1 per cent of females were classified as being obese (ABS, 1991). Heart disease, diabetes, arthritis, strokes, liver and gall bladder disease are all increased in obese people. Major education campaigns have made the public aware of the dangers of diets high in animal fat and low in natural fibre. Many foods now carry symbols to indicate that they meet National Heart Foundation standards.

Two aspects of health education and diet are of note. One is that it is possible to be obese because of overeating, but malnourished because of the lack of vitamin and mineral intake. The other is that the campaign about animal fat has resulted in some children being malnourished because of parents' failure to realise that the dietary requirements of growing children are different from those of adults. A low cholesterol, low fat diet taken to extremes is not good for children.

Over recent years the importance of exercise in reducing the incidence of cardiovascular disease has been frequently reported. Despite this, 35 per cent of Australians in a recent survey said they had not undertaken any exercise in the previous two weeks. This has raised questions about the effectiveness of health education campaigns.

Human immunodeficiency virus (HIV) and AIDS

There is wide awareness in Australia of the impact of HIV and Acquired Immune Deficiency Syndrome (AIDS). To have HIV means that AIDS will develop at some time; and to get AIDS means that one will die prematurely. HIV is spread through sexual intercourse, both homosexual and heterosexual, although, in Australia, the largest concentration of infected people is in the homosexual community. The disease is also spread through the sharing of contaminated needles by users of intravenous drugs. At a time when knowledge about the infection was still being gained, some patients acquired the disease through contaminated blood transfusions. The fatal nature of the disease and the nature of its spread have led to an aggressive education campaign. The graphic and frank nature of some of the images seen on television has created controversy, but the rate of new diagnosis of AIDS in Australia does appear to be falling.

Skin cancer

Australia has the highest incidence of skin cancer in the world. In Queensland, where the incidence of malignant melanoma is a particular problem, the government has campaigned to increase use of cancer prevention measures. There is a conflict between the public's desire to make the maximum use of Queensland's climate and sunshine and the prevention of malignant melanoma. Anecdotal evidence has indicated that the campaign may have the opposite effect to the one intended: people feeling that, because they had taken the recommended measures, they were now safe from malignant melanoma. They thus exposed themselves to dangerous levels of sunshine, which meant that the incidence of the disease was, at best, unaffected. However, a recent report suggests that the campaign has helped, with the skin cancer rate now being close to the national average (Queensland Health, 1994).

MEDICINE AND POLITICS

Medicine and health care are firmly in the political arena. The reason for this is simple: money. Modern health care is extremely expensive and decisions about the use of limited resources are in the hands of politicians and government officials; medical practitioners have relatively little input.

In 1984 the Medicare system was established in Australia and a 1.4 per cent levy upon all taxpayers generates funds for the public health care system. When seeing a medical practitioner, patients either pay the doctor directly and then claim a refund from Medicare, or the doctor bills Medicare directly. Difficulties arise when the schedule of fees approved by the government does not match the fees suggested by the Australian Medical Association (AMA). The AMA-suggested fees are generally higher, and the fee level is a continuing source of conflict between the medical profession and government. A patient may be charged the AMA fees, but is refunded only the government schedule fee and thus pays a proportion of the fee.

One effect of the introduction of the Medicare levy has been to reduce the number of people in private health care schemes. The demands on the public system have thus increased and waiting lists for non-urgent treatment have lengthened. More money is needed to ensure an adequate standard of care for all. In the private sector, the cost of treatment is fully recovered from the patient, usually with the aid of a private health insurance scheme. There have been various proposals to reduce the demands on the public health care system. One is the suggestion that people above a certain income level should pay an increased Medicare levy if they do not have private insurance. A difficulty with this is that private health care insurance in Australia may not refund the full cost of medical treatment and patients undergoing treatment may have large bills to pay. For example, a heart by-pass operation can cost a privately insured patient $3000–$5000 on top of the money paid by the insurance company, but is free if carried out under Medicare.

A limited budget combined with increasing costs of medical treatment forces the government to look for ways by which the impact of treatment can be measured, as an aid to decisions about how health service money should be distributed. One of the more recent concepts is that of 'quality of life years remaining' (QUALYRS). An assessment is made about how many years of good quality of life is achieved for the patient by a particular treatment, and this is compared to assessments of the QUALYRS generated by other forms of treatment. Thus a kidney transplant may generate x QUALYRS and a heart transplant y QUALYRS. If y is greater than x, then that is where the money goes. It should be stressed that this is a statistical and policy decision, not a medical one, and is not based on the needs of an individual patient. It is simply an attempt to decide which areas of public medical treatment should receive funding. These decisions do not apply to the private sector, where costs are recovered from the patient and the health insurance organisations.

The medical profession has to come to terms with the increasing role of government in medical planning. It must work in cooperation with governments to achieve the best quality health care for society.

THE FUTURE

Developments in medical knowledge and technology are occurring at such a rapid rate, and have the possibility of having such a profound impact, that planning for the future is essential.

Medical education

Medical students cannot be taught everything that they need to know in order to practise medicine. New educational methods will help students prepare for a lifetime of medical education, much of which will be self-directed. As described above, changes occurring in the medical curriculum, using new programs and educational techniques should equip medical graduates with the skills necessary to cope with medicine in the twenty-first century.

New technology and ethics

Advances in knowledge and technology have meant that new medical treatments have become available. In-vitro fertilisation (IVF) has transformed the treatment of infertility; it is now possible for a couple to choose the sex of their child. However, the technology has run ahead of the legal and ethical developments necessary to cope with these advances. For example, IVF has resulted in viable fetuses being held, deep frozen. One question is the ownership of fetuses in the event of a breakdown in the marriage. In many countries, legislation is now in place regulating the use of such embryos for research, giving clear guidelines about how they may be used. Another question concerns the rights of the offspring; if the sperm are from a donor, what should the children be told about their genetic parents? There is also concern that offering parents the means to choose the sex of their child may lead to a change in the sex-ratio in the population.

Improvements in suppression of the immune response have led to the use of organ transplantation in treating disease. Kidney transplants now have good success rates and long survival times, however, a system of ethics and legislation is needed to protect potential donors. Strict definitions of brain death have been devised to allow ethical removal of organs for subsequent transplantation.

Since almost all new medical advances are expensive, mechanisms are needed to ensure that the treatments are as widely available as possible. It is also important that other less fashionable areas of medicine continue to receive adequate funding. One very expensive advance is the survival of very premature babies, weighing as little as five hundred grams (normal birth weight is about 3400 grams). Care of these newborn may run into hundreds of thousands of dollars, and many of these babies grow up with permanent disabilities. There is debate about the ethics of this treatment and how to decide whether very premature babies should be resuscitated.

Advances in medical technology have the potential to raise profound ethical issues. In order for doctors to be able to debate these in an informed and logical manner, medical schools have now introduced courses in ethical issues.

Litigation in medicine

Although the level of litigation in Australia has not reached that in the USA, the incidence is rising, and bringing with it increasing costs of medical defence insurance. The fear of litigation is believed to be reducing recruitment rates into some specialties, for example, obstetrics. In accident and emergency centres, some investigations and treatments are carried out as a protection against future litigation. This is another instance of forces outside medicine having an impact on medical treatment.

Genetic engineering

Genetic engineering will have a profound effect on medical treatment. Genetically engineered viruses are already being used on a trial basis in the treatment of cystic fibrosis. The technology may eventually allow manipulation of the fetus to either remove unwanted defects or to add desirable characteristics. The question will be whether this should be allowed to happen, and under what circumstances. This question is perhaps too important to leave to either politicians or medical practitioners.

CONCLUSION

In this review, the institution of medicine in Australia has been described. It is clear that many groups of people need to be involved if the health care of the nation is to continue to improve. There has to be input from medical and other practitioners, politicians and the community at large. The effect of future developments in medical treatment is going to be too profound to leave decisions about their use in the hands of any one group.

FURTHER READING

There is no single volume that deals with the institution of health care. For an introduction to changes in medical education, Doherty (1988) is essential. Another influential review was published by the Association of American Medical Colleges (1984): the GPEP report. A wealth of information about the use of health care facilities is to be found in the Australian Bureau of Statistics Australian Health Reports; the 1983 and the 1989–90 surveys should be compared. The best place to start is with the summary sections — otherwise the information is overwhelming.

REFERENCES

Adkins, R. J., Cullen, T. J. and Newman, F. S. 1987, 'Geographic and speciality distributions of WAMI program participants and nonparticipants', *Journal of Medical Education*, 62, pp.810–17.

Association of American Medical Colleges 1984, 'Physicians for the twenty-first century – the GPEP Report', *Journal of Medical Education*, 59, pp.591–608.

Australian Bureau of Statistics 1986, *Australian Health Survey 1983*, ABS, Canberra.

Australian Bureau of Statistics 1991, *Australian Health Survey 1988–1989*, ABS, Canberra.

ACT Community and Health Service 1988, *Canberra's Health*, AGPS, Canberra.

Australian Institute of Health 1988, *Australia's Health 1988*, AGPS, Canberra.

Australian Institute of Health 1990, *Australia's Health 1990*, AGPS, Canberra.

Craig, M. 1992, 'Are between 2.5 and 4.5 million Australians disadvantaged by our medical education system', Report to the Faculty of Medicine, University of Queensland.

Doherty, R. 1988, *Australian Medical Workforce into the 21st Century: Committee of Inquiry Report*, AGPS, Canberra.

Dornhorst, A. C. 1981, 'Information overload: why medical education needs a shake-up', *The Lancet*, 2, pp.513–14.

Federal Department of Health, Housing, Local Government and Community Services 1993, '*Discussion paper from the Rural Undergraduate Steering Committee*'. AGPS, Canberra.

New Zealand Ministry of Health 1985, *The Role of the Doctor in New Zealand: Implications for Medical Education*, Ministry of Health, Wellington.

Queensland Health 1994, *Queensland's Progress in Achieving National Health Goals and Targets for Preventable Mortality and Morbidity*, Queensland Government Press, Brisbane.

Thompson, E. 1981, *Future Needs for Medical Education in Queensland*, Queensland Government Press, Brisbane.

Tortora, G. J. and Grabowski, S. R. 1993, *Principles of Anatomy and Physiology*, 7th edn, Harper Collins, New York.

Veitch, P. C. 1989, *Regional Characteristics of General Medical Practitioners in Australia, June 1986*, Royal Australian College of General Practitioners, Family Medicine Program (Research Division), Sydney.

World Federation for Medical Education 1988, 'The Edinburgh Declaration', *Medical Education*, 22, pp.481–2.

10

SOCIAL WELFARE

··

John May

Any consideration of welfare as an institution in Australian society requires an appreciation not only of how much things change, but also how much they remain the same. From the first days of European colonisation Australia was a penal colony run by the British army, a total institution in which the governing authorities had control over every aspect of life, including life itself. As colonisation proceeded and civil institutions began to develop, responsibility for welfare began to be passed over to various charitable organisations.

The officers, soldiers, convicts and settlers brought with them the laws, institutions, attitudes and habits of eighteenth century British society. Early welfare organisations were based upon those the colonists had experienced in the 'old country'. This resulted in the establishment of 'charitable societies', which administered relief in cash or kind to the poor. In addition, Benevolent Asylums were set up for the destitute, the aged and the sick, which had many of the hallmarks of the 'workhouse' (Dickey, 1980; Kewley, 1977).

Enshrined in this system were the principles of the British Poor Law, a legal system begun in 1601 and revised in 1834. Before the introduction of modern-day income security programs it was very hard for those who had insufficient income to support themselves. Those who designed the poor laws were concerned to devise ways of separating the 'deserving' poor from the 'non-deserving' poor.

The deserving poor were considered to be those who were not able-bodied and who were not perceived as being responsible for their own condition — the aged, the sick, children and orphans, and lunatics. The non-deserving were those who were able-bodied and able to work. Idleness, gambling and thriftlessness were all grounds for exclusion from the Benevolent Asylum (Connolly, 1989, p.41). These types of moral distinctions informed the decision of government and charitable organisations about whether they would grant assistance. Such moral distinctions still inform much of the debate about welfare in this country today.

The charitable organisations received considerable government funding to undertake their tasks. This 'partnership', in which government depends on non-government welfare organisations to deliver services, while they in turn rely on the government to deliver funds, continues to be a major feature of the welfare system. The inadequacy of government assistance or that provided by non-government welfare organisations to meet either the needs of the poor, or the organisations trying to help them, is another recurrent contemporary aspect of this history.

A major economic recession in 1890 led to enormous economic and social hardship. This experience, together with the development of a strong labour movement, gave rise to reformist ideas concerning welfare provision. In some cases, institutions for older people and needy children were taken over by governments, beginning a shift way from the 'volunteer' based institutionalised charity model (Lyons, 1990). Increased government involvement in turn led to the development of other welfare related institutions. For example, children's courts were established to deal with matters of child protection, care and control. The previously private area of family behaviour found itself drawn into the public realm of the justice system.

In 1907, the Commonwealth Arbitration Court brought down the Harvester Judgment, which established the baseline of a 'family wage' for employed men. The assumption that underpinned the judgment was that a man had to support a wife and family. Women's wages were subsequently set at just over half to three-quarters of the male rate (Booth and Rubenstein, 1990). The social values underpinning this differential ensured that women would most likely be economically dependent upon men. Implications for women in terms of their capacity to maintain economically independent lives would be a central issue in the future development of welfare institutions and practices.

Around the time of federation, ideas concerning the need for some form of basic income support for the poor and the need to de-institutionalise and provide support for families gained some ground. However, the theme of the deserving versus the non-deserving still predominated.

BASIC INCOME SUPPORT — THE OLD AGE PENSION

Australia was the second country in the world to provide an old age pension for its citizens. (New Zealand was first.) Victoria introduced the pension in January 1901, New South Wales later the same year, and Queensland in 1908. But the old age pension was introduced for reasons other than altruistic concern with the plight of the aged. The Depression of the 1890s had shown without any doubt that a voluntary-based charity system was simply unable to cope with the growing number of distressed and destitute aged people in institutions. Increased political tensions and concern over rising public expenditures were more important.

The Commonwealth government, acting on the powers granted under section 51 of the Constitution, introduced the first national Old Age Pension Scheme in 1909. In 1910 it introduced invalid pensions. However, as Jordan (1989) points out, being old and destitute was by no means a simple qualification for the pension. Exclusions from eligibility on moral and racial grounds pervade the legislation. Provision required recipients to be of 'good behaviour'. Drunkards, past prisoners, deserting husbands, Asiatics, Chinese, Maoris, and Aboriginal natives of any state of the Commonwealth of Australia or New Zealand were all excluded.

ABORIGINES AND WELFARE

This chapter cannot deal in detail with the history and experiences of Aboriginal people in the welfare system. Suffice it to note that, in relation to welfare, the treatment of the indigenous population of Australia, the Aboriginal people, will remain a stain upon Australian history forever. It is estimated that at the time of colonisation in 1788 there were approximately 750 000 Aborigines (Mulvaney and White, 1987). By 1900 this population had been reduced to approximately 100 000. Many Aborigines, lacking immunity and health supports, died from diseases introduced by the colonists, including chickenpox and measles. Others were shot and poisoned. Their culture and their very means of existence and way of life were destroyed by the European settlers.

The subsequent sad history of the continuing relationship of the Aboriginal people to the European-based welfare systems is still to be written in detail. It is a history better characterised by the term warfare than welfare. For the Aboriginal people, the expropriation of their traditional lands meant either a life of forced labour, or forced resettlement in church-based missions or government reserves.

Aboriginal Protection Boards, set up from 1883, had the power to forcibly remove children from their families under the guise of 'protection' (Van Krieken, 1991). While offically concerned with 'assimilating' these children into white society by resocialisation, the reality was that they were a source of cheap labour, destined to become jackaroos and servants. Sometimes children were removed and offered for adoption to white families as part of a policy of assimilation. This history and related factors continue to underpin many of the social problems faced by the Aboriginal people today.

WAR AND WELFARE

Welfare history across the world shows the important role war has played in expanding the availability of government-provided welfare provision. In part, these developments have been a response to the type of rhetoric that underpins the urge to go to war. To fight and die for a 'land fit for heroes' requires actions to address the needs of those heroes on their return. In Australia, the First World War played a major role in the expansion of federal government involvement in welfare services. In 1918 the Commonwealth moved to provide repatriation benefits for returning soldiers and their dependants. As Jones notes,

> By 1922, official figures showed that of 329 883 serving Australians, 59 342 had died of wounds or disease in the First World War and total casualties were 314 336 — 6.3% of the population. Many soldiers had wives or dependants, so nearly 10% of the population were eligible for benefits. (Jones, 1990, p.29)

The consequences of the war were enormous. The government had to care for those who were wounded and maimed as well as care for the dependants of the thousands who died in the war. Repatriation assistance was famous for its generosity in comparison to the punitive and grudging assistance provided through the old age and invalid pension scheme. It has been argued that the high costs of the repatriation scheme was a significant factor in retarding the development of an extensive welfare state before the Whitlam government of 1972.

BETWEEN THE WARS

While those with repatriation pensions might have coped reasonably well with the conditions prevailing during the Great Depression, the unemployed had a much harder time. The advent of large-scale structural unemployment in Australia in the 1930s again illustrated the inadequacies of a welfare system still based essentially on charitable and voluntary organisations. State governments provided charitable organisations with funding to provide 'sustenance relief', and also devised 'work for the dole' schemes. The old models of distinguishing the 'morally deserving' from the 'undeserving' in many cases still prevailed.

Documentary films of this period place symbolic images firmly in the mind: long, winding queues of unemployed men; soup kitchens dishing out food; people begging in the streets. That reality was out on the streets for all people to see and identify with. Today, the public experience of unemployment is somewhat more sanitised; individuals are buried within the deep recesses of computer tapes as another statistic. Governments have learnt how to manage structural unemployment, using the administrative apparatus to hide the human impact of its everyday reality away. There can be little doubt that the 1930s Depression reiterated the experience of the 1890s. It was finally clear that market forces could not be relied upon to provide employment or security for all citizens.

WORLD WAR II

One constant aspect of history is that governments are always able to find resources to wage war on another country or an enemy, but never for the purposes of waging war on social and economic conditions that debilitate and destroy humanity just as effectively.

However, World War II saw a number of initiatives of the utmost importance in post-war Australia. Arguably, the most important was the introduction of uniform taxation legislation in 1942: it is this power over revenue raising that gives the Commonwealth financial dominance within the Australian federal system.

The period saw a rapid expansion of allowances, pensions and benefits offered by the Commonwealth: child endowment, widows' pensions, funeral benefit, unemployment benefit. The years 1944 to 1945 also saw the Commonwealth government introduce a pharmaceutical, hospital and tuberculosis benefits scheme, but constitutional impediments prevented a broader program of reform. The old age pension was renamed the age pension, and grouped with invalid and widows' pensions as well as maternity allowances, child endowment, unemployment and sickness benefits into a single statute (Kewley, 1972, p.186). Legislation was introduced in 1948 to establish what would become the Commonwealth Rehabilitation Service, which provided support and vocational training for people with disabilities.

Just as importantly the Commonwealth Department of Social Services was now decentralised, having regional offices outside the capital cities. For the first time there existed a national income security system dependent on taxation contributions and administered by government.

Some writers on welfare hold that the Australian welfare state was founded during this period, arguing that the Australian Labor party should be given most of the credit for creating the national welfare state (Watts, 1987). Others hold that significant advance towards a modern welfare state was not made until the early 1970s (Jones, 1990).

THE POST-WAR PERIOD

After this brief flowering of activity, the next twenty years saw the Commonwealth government introduce no real new social initiatives. In some ways this is not surprising. The defeat of the Labor Party in 1949 ushered in a period of Conservative government that would last unbroken until 1972. The expansion of welfare services hardly fitted the prevailing conservative ideology. Also, apart from the 1961 credit squeeze, the Australian economy was quite healthy. Low inflation, low levels of unemployment, and high levels of migration and population growth predominated. Work rather than welfare was a dominating theme. At a state level during this period government welfare departments focussed essentially on 'child welfare': 'Officials and Children's Courts administered interventions designed to control 'uncontrollable' children and to protect 'neglected' children, frequently involving ongoing supervision or the removal of children from their families for varying periods'. (Australian Institute of Health and Welfare, 1993, p.6)

One aspect of welfare provision at this time, about which many writers are silent, is the role that the non-government sector played. Organisations in the non-government sector, some of them church or charity based, others community based, provided many of the residual services. In particular, they offered basic services like food, emergency relief and shelter directed towards the poor, the marginalised, the homeless and others whose needs were not being met by the market or the State.

Welfare organisations in the government and non-government sector had to cope with the issues and difficulties brought about by 25 years of economic, social and demographic change. In the post-war period Australia had become a multicultural society, but few institutions or social or cultural arrangements had recognised or responded to this reality. The appalling impacts of the colonisation process and the conditions in which Aboriginal people were living began to gain public and international attention. Until 1967 the original inhabitants of Australia were not citizens of Australia. The 1967 referendum changed this and provided the Commonwealth with the constitutional power to make laws for Aboriginal people. This gave the Commonwealth the responsibility and power to initiate national programs to improve health, housing and education for the indigenous population.

THE WHITLAM GOVERNMENT, 1972–75

The first Labor government for 23 years was ushered into office in 1972 with the slogan 'It's time'. The slogan characterised for many the need for radical change in many of Australia's social institutions. The impetus given by the findings of the first survey into poverty in Australia published in 1970 raised questions about just how lucky the poor of the 'lucky country' actually were. In 1975 the first national inquiry into poverty documented clearly the economic and social costs of 20 years of neglect. Utilising an austere measurement of poverty, the Henderson Inquiry found that more than 10 per cent of income units (individuals and families) in Australia were living in poverty.

The Whitlam government's social policies marked a movement away from a welfare system that focussed predominantly on cash benefits, to a system that saw welfare linked to the capacity of citizens to access a wide range of social benefits — sometimes called the 'social wage'. The social wage is essentially those services and benefits provided collectively to individuals and families through government spending. The Economic Planning Advisory Council (EPAC, 1987) defines government spending on education, health, community amenities, housing, social security and welfare as the social wage, which contributes to the overall living standard of every citizen.

The Labor government promoted an explosion of social policy activity. A universal health system was created. Fees for tertiary education were abolished and funding increased for tertiary, secondary and primary education. Pre-school education and child care services were expanded. A Supporting Parents Benefit replaced the existing punitive and often stigmatising state-based provisions. The means tests on age pensioners over 70 was removed. The growth rates in social expenditure during the period of the Whitlam government were extraordinary. Social expenditures between 1972 and 1976 increased by 117.5 per cent in real terms (Graycar and Jamrozik, 1993, p.71).

However, the Whitlam government was short-lived. Its period of office coincided with a period of severe structural economic difficulties, which continued throughout the period of the Fraser Coalition government (1975–83) and still continue today. The brief flowering of an expanded view for social policy ended with the defeat of the Labor government in the election of 1975.

Any analysis of welfare policies in this period has to take into account that it was a period of enormous change in economic and labour market policies. International factors, including economic recession, led to greater levels of unemployment. In addition, changes in family formation, cohabitation, marriage and divorce caused a significant increase in the number of sole parent families. Other factors contributing to the growth in dependency on welfare services include demographic factors such as migration, and an ageing population.

THE FRASER GOVERNMENT, 1975–83

The Fraser Liberal-National party coalition government returned to policies based on principles of selectivity. However, the welfare debate was no longer simply about the merits of universalism versus selectivity. The focus now was turned to the size of government and the respective roles of the Commonwealth, the states and the non-government sector.

The proclaimed intentions of the Fraser government were to return the country to economic health primarily through the mechanism of reducing government expenditures. Despite the political rhetoric, the reality was somewhat different. Social expenditures were reduced in community services and amenities. But these cuts were counterbalanced by increasing outlays in the areas of social transfers, as escalating numbers of unemployed people became dependent upon social security (Cass and Whiteford, 1989, p.277).

As Table 10.1 illustrates, income security dependency in the 1970s was quite different from the late 1980s. The Fraser government presided over a huge growth in unemployment rates, a trend only temporarily reversed between 1983–90. As can be seen from Figure 10.1, the trend towards large-scale structural unemployment has persisted from the late 1970s to the 1990s.

The figures on unemployment highlight a significant difference between the earlier provisions for welfare and the situation that countries such as Australia face today. Earlier initiatives in income security were never meant to provide for anything other than temporary situations. The notion that some people would be unemployed for months or years was almost inconceivable. Today this is a common experience for many unemployed people.

Table 10.1 Numbers on social welfare benefits: 1970 and 1988

Benefit type	1970	1988	1988 as multiple of 1970
Unemployment benefit	13 212	502 514	38.0
Sickness benefit	8 572	74 557	8.7
Special benefit	4 445	21 598	4.9
Age pension	779 007	1 328 892	1.7
Invalid pension	133 766	296 913	2.2
Widow's pension	89 921	143 451	1.7
Supporting parent's benefit	26 286*	182 007	6.9*
Total on Social Security benefit	1 052 209	2 549 932	2.4
War pension	584 676	367 680	0.6
Service pension	74 420	403 000	5.4
Total Australian population	12 663 000	16 532 000	1.3

Notes: All figures are for 30 June.
        * 1974 — supporting parent's benefit was introduced in 1974.
Source: Department of Social Security.

Figure 10.1 Unemployment, August 1970 to 1993

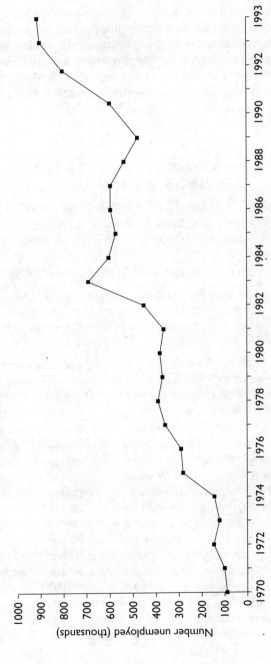

Source: ABS, *Labour Force, Australia,* Cat. no. 6203.0 and unpublished revised data.

In setting about the task of reducing Commonwealth expenditures, the Fraser government challenged the notion of an expanding role for the federal government in social programs. A fundamental question for this government concerned the responsibility for the provision of welfare. The answer was to transfer more responsiblity to the state governments, the non-government sector, the private sector, and the community and the family.

THE HAWKE-KEATING GOVERNMENTS, 1983 TO 1990s

One recent report has described the period of the Labor rule throughout the eighties as, '. . . a deliberate blending of its two predecessors, aiming to deliver a program of social justice in a climate of fiscal restraint'. (AIHW, 1993, p.8)

One commentator, less diplomatic in his assessment states:

> In Australia the experience of the ALP in government between 1983 and 1993 is particularly salutary, the commitment to social justice having effectively been subordinated to the policies of 'economic rationalism' (Stilwell, 1993, p.81).

However, the Hawke/Keating governments have articulated a philosophical approach to 'social justice'. Through a series of strategy statements, successive ALP governments have set out formal policy goals as being concerned with: equity in the distribution of economic resources; equality of civil, legal and industrial rights; fair and equal access to essential services such as housing, health, and education; and the opportunity for participation by all in personal development, community life and decision-making (AIHW, 1993).

Significant initiatives introduced by the Commonwealth under the heading of 'social justice' include: Medicare as a universal health insurance scheme, financed in part from income-related tax contributions; a National Child Care Strategy; the Child Support Scheme to enforce non-custodial parent financial support of their children; reform of the aged care system; labour market training programs for the unemployed; the National Housing strategy; the establishment of the Aboriginal and Torres Strait Islander Commission; the Mabo legislation; the introduction of anti-discrimination legislation and a Multicultural Access and Equity Policy; and a major review of the social security system.

Labor governments of this period have used their relationships with the trade union movement to enter into a series of 'Accords'. These agreements are essentially a negotiated 'trade off' between the union movement and the government over wages policy, fiscal policy, income tax, labour market and welfare measures.

Despite the Hawke government's success in assisting the creation of an estimated 1.5 million jobs during its period of office, unemployment is still the major social policy issue. As the Australian Council of Social Service (ACOSS) notes, 'Only about nine out of every hundred additional jobs created in the period of strong growth from 1983–1989 went to unemployed people' (ACOSS, 1993, p.38).

The unemployment rate, which had fallen to 6 per cent by late 1989, rose to a new high in 1993 with around one million people unemployed — the highest figure since the Great Depression. More than 35 per cent of these had been unemployed for two years or more. These numbers are expected to grow unless policies are put in place to address the problem. Failure to reduce the number of people unemployed after each of the recessionary periods has had the effect of 'ratcheting up' the number of people who have been unemployed for long periods. In May 1993, the Keating government commissioned a Committee on Employment Opportunities, to produce a discussion paper on employment issues. This committee proposed a series of strategies for reducing unemployment to 5 per cent by the year 2000 (Committee on Employment Opportunities, 1993).

SELECTIVITY VERSUS UNIVERSALISM — THE FUNCTIONS OF SOCIAL WELFARE

Australian welfare policy until 1972 was characterised by its residualism and selectivity. Selectivity relies upon the selective provision of cash benefits in the form of emergency cash grants or regular means-tested payments. This approach to the provision of welfare is built upon the argument that scarce resources should be concentrated in the hands of those in most need. Selectivity is often spoken about in terms of a safety net through which those in need should not be allowed to fall. The approach is inherently conservative. It has dominated because those in power believe it to be less wasteful, more equitable and more efficient. It also has political appeal. Means testing of benefits ensures that only those without significant additional resources will receive government assistance. As Jamrozik (1983, p.180) notes,

> The outcome of residualism is legitimation of disadvantage, legitimation of inequality, legitimation of exclusion of the industrial human residue from the mainstream of economic life.

The notion that means testing saves resources needs to be viewed critically. Means tests are themselves a very costly exercise; they have to be administered, assessed and monitored to ensure compliance, and an army of bureaucrats is required to perform the associated tasks. Selectivity is often arbitrary in the manner in which judgments or decisions regarding an individual's needs are made. Essentially, it requires that the population be divided into those who are thought to 'deserve' assistance and those who are thought 'undeserving'. It often depends upon the discretion of the decision-maker and leaves the way open for moralistic judgments, which can stigmatise the recipients.

An alternative approach to selectivity is known as universalism. This conception of welfare informed the policies of the Whitlam Labor government (1972–75). This approach promotes an institutional conception of welfare. Its proponents argue that, by making benefits available to all, a society fosters notions of citizenship and egalitarianism. The stigma and moralistic condemnation often associated with receiving benefits are removed. By viewing collective benefits as the right of all citizens, you are able to remove the disincentives that affect workers on low incomes, who often just fail to pass means tests.

Some research has suggested that the middle class is often the major beneficiary of the welfare state, benefiting by gaining greater access to certain aspects of the social wage, particularly health, housing, transport, urban development and education (Le Grand, 1982). Higher income earners are often able to manipulate the taxation system to their advantage — for example, through taxation deductions for superannuation contributions, dividend imputation on shares, and negative gearing of property investments. They may enjoy occupational benefits such as company provided homes, cars and holidays, interest free or low interest loans, the payment of school fees for children, goods and services at a discount, the issuing of shares at concession prices, etc. To a limited extent, the fringe-benefits tax introduced by the Hawke government has addressed some of these issues.

Critics of the welfare state from the political left tend to reject both universalism and selectivity as approaches to the provision of people's welfare. To these critics, all welfare is essentially a mechanism of social control designed to protect the interests of a ruling class. They argue that the welfare state has done nothing to change the distribution of wealth or income in society. It does nothing to tackle the inequalities generated in the market economy and, at best, it merely compensates for some of the inequalities. Further, it has served to maintain the existing hierarchies of class, power and status. The major function of welfare, they suggest, is to keep the working classes healthy and functioning at a level that allows the capitalist state to continue operating (Offe, 1984, p.154).

Critics from the political right tend to favour a market-based approach to welfare, which emphasises the residual and selective nature of benefits. They seize upon the critique of the political left that the major beneficiaries of the welfare state are the middle classes, not the poor. For proponents of this position, welfare is best provided by participation in the market and the workforce. They point to the growth in public expenditures and taxation in recent years to argue that this growth reflects increased dependency and that the welfare state has created this dependency. Correspondingly the welfare state is perceived as having contributed to the breakdown of the family, because the caring family is replaced by welfare services, and also the breakdown of social and moral values that supposedly predominated in earlier times (Sawer, 1982).

THE STRUCTURE OF WELFARE GOVERNMENTS

The advent of uniform taxation legislation in 1942 saw the Commonwealth gain financial supremacy over the states. Commonwealth expenditures are of four types:

1 Direct expenditures under a clear constitutional power. Pensions and benefits paid to individuals fall under this heading. Payments are not filtered through any other government.
2 Expenditures under section 96 of the Constitution, which provide that the parliament may grant financial assistance to any state on such terms and conditions as the parliament thinks fit.
3 Direct expenditures not within a constitutional power. This includes expenditures and payments that bypass the states. For example, payments to local government, community groups and non-government welfare agencies.

4 Expenditures incurred through the operation of the taxation system, which provides for rebates or concessions. Taxation deductions for superannuation payments or occupational welfare benefits.

Since World War II, Commonwealth government involvement in social security and social wage areas has expanded significantly. The Commonwealth is the major source of revenue for many state-administered programs. Recently, the signing of a Commonwealth State Disability Agreement has allocated responsibility for services between the two tiers of government along functional lines.

Currently 28 per cent of all budget outlays are related to social security. However, if expenditures in health, housing, community services, employment, education and training, and veteran's affairs are added, 59 per cent of Commonwealth outlays are social wage related.

Constitutionally and historically, the responsibility for child and family welfare has belonged to the states. Each state and territory has a department whose functions are concerned primarily with the welfare of children, families and the community. These departments are normally responsible for a wide range of functions, including child protection, care and control of juvenile offenders, adoption, crisis care, fostering of children, emergency accommodation, and family counselling. They also license and regulate services such as foster parents, children's homes and family day care providers.

In the last twenty years state government welfare departments have gradually expanded their brief to incorporate a notion of community welfare. This brief tends to emphasise a movement away from focussing solely upon the welfare of children and towards seeing the family as the major source of welfare. It has correspondingly seen a growth in community-based programs offered by non-government welfare organisations, but funded by Commonwealth and state governments.

In addition, many essential services, such as prisons, community corrections, mental health, child care, family planning, health care, emergency accommodation and domestic violence services, are areas in which state governments play a major role as providers of funds to private and non-government welfare agencies.

Historically, local government has not had an extensive involvement in the provision of health, welfare or educational services. However, they have had a long history in providing sporting and recreational facilities and libraries, as well as providing support to local community organisations, some of which are welfare-oriented.

The movement to smaller community-based services has seen the development of an expanded role for local government in areas such as accommodation for older people and people with disabilities, child care, including family day care, and homeless persons' assistance. However, the extent to which local government has developed in this way has varied considerably from state to state (AIHW, 1993, p.16). The capacity of local government to undertake these roles is constrained by its financial dependence and narrow revenue base.

NON-GOVERNMENT WELFARE ORGANISATIONS (NGWOS)

There has been very little research into the size and scope of non-government welfare organisations. However, Lyons (1993) estimates that more than half of all community services are provided by community organisations. In 1994 the Industry Commission conducted an inquiry into 'charitable organisations'. The Commission's report, due in 1995, is expected to provide a long-needed comprehensive analysis and overview of this sector.

Church-based welfare organisations in the welfare field include the Salvation Army, the Uniting church's Lifeline, the Anglican church's Brotherhood of St Laurence and the Catholic church's St Vincent de Paul. However, it should also be noted that many secular community-based organisations play a central part in delivering Australia's welfare services.

A national survey of NGWOs estimated there were between 25 400 and 48 500 in Australia. They may have up to 600 000 full-time employees (Milligan et al., 1984) and are estimated to have as many as 1.7 million volunteers. These figures may actually be conservative. Statewide surveys undertaken by the Australian Bureau of Statistics in New South Wales (1986), Victoria (1983) and Queensland (1982) report that close to 30 per cent of all people over the age of fifteen volunteer in some form of welfare work.

In Queensland, an ABS survey for the period November 1981 to November 1982, calculated that 483 786 volunteers worked approximately 59.5 million hours. This contribution of labour was valued conservatively at $402 million — the equivalent of over 30 000 full-time jobs at that time (May, 1985).

The range of functions performed by NGWOs is diverse. As Graycar and Jamrozik (1993) note, they provide services to individuals, provide material aid, are involved in social action, provide services that extend the services of the state, act as opponents to the state, provide services that are alternatives to those provided by the state, and act as lobby groups for certain causes or interests.

The national survey (Milligan et al., 1984) classified NGWOs as operating within the following thirteen functional categories: income support, accommodation, education, employment, personal care, therapeutic care, health care, social development, community action, service support, information, and protection. Many NGWOs are multifunctional, covering many of these areas (Graycar and Jamrozik, 1993).

THE INFORMAL SECTOR

There is a danger in assuming that welfare is simply a matter of service provision by government or organisations within the non-government sector. This assumption fails to take account of the importance of families, friends, neighbours and local community networks. While these networks are not part of the formal welfare system, they are nevertheless, a central and important part of welfare provision in society.

An Australian Bureau of Statistics national survey concerned with disability and ageing found that an estimated 322 600 people were providing caring services and assistance to 337 800 people with severe handicaps (ABS, 1990). Of these carers, 64 per cent were female. Half of the carers were caring for their spouse, 31 per cent were caring for a child, and 14 per cent for an adult. Male carers were more likely to be caring for a spouse than a parent or a child. Carers undertook various roles, including meal preparation, housework, and personal care. However, it is interesting to note the segregated roles that emerge, reflecting the gender roles in society. Women were more likely to undertake personal care- and communication-related tasks, while men would assist with transport and mobility needs.

In many respects, this gender-based division of labour represents deeper structural issues regarding the role of men and women in Australian society. Unpaid caring work has traditionally been undertaken by women. To a large extent, both consciously and unconsciously, policy-makers have developed policies and services on the assumption that women will continue to play these roles. Such assumptions are increasingly being questioned by feminist writers on the welfare state (Bryson, 1992). A policy issue that will become increasingly significant in the future will concern the manner in which government policies are able to appropriately support informal caring on a more equitable basis.

WELFARE IN THE 1990S

A major theme in social science in the 1980s was concerned with the 'legitimation crisis' (Habermas, 1976; O'Connor, 1984; Offe, 1984) — the ability of the modern welfare state to satisfy the diverse and extensive demands made of it. There are two essentially contradictory types of demand on the state. The provision of many services, including welfare, acts to legitimise the state by reducing the negative impacts of the market economy on the people, while, at the same time, the functioning of a capitalist market economy requires levels of inequality in order to accumulate capital and generate profits. In Australia, under the Fraser, Hawke and Keating governments, the impact of government expenditures, high taxation and intervention in social and economic life have been presented to the public as a major cause of national economic decline.

During the 1980s, Commonwealth government policy under the direction of the then treasurer, Paul Keating, sought to reduce government expenditures and the size of the public sector dramatically. As a result of these policies, the 1989–90 Commonwealth budget not only contained a surplus of over $8 billion, but, in addition, the Treasurer noted that, 'Commonwealth spending is now at the lowest level as a proportion of Gross Domestic Product since 1974, and in three years will be down to the level of the 1950s' (Budget Speech, 22 August 1990).

The period of the Hawke Labor government was characterised by a commitment to the development of a free or deregulated market economy with little interference from the state. The paradox that underpins this approach is to be found in the government's pledge to create a fairer and more equal society in its 1989–90 Budget statement. Whatever a free market economy might achieve, given its history, it is debatable whether it will produce a more equitable or egalitarian society.

The income security policies of this period moved increasingly towards a selective and residual model, a trend maintained by the Keating government. As a result of the Review of Social Security in the 1980s, many benefits and programs are now tightly linked to labour market programs. This has been done on the basis that many believe poverty alleviation is linked to employment growth and job creation (Cass, 1989). However, one study has raised many questions regarding the presumptions underpinning this link. After a detailed analysis of the experiences of the Hawke government, this study found that the 1.5 million new jobs created had reduced the numbers in poverty by just 39 000 (Saunders, 1990a).

It is difficult to estimate the total number of people in poverty. Some estimates suggest that it may be as high as two million. In 1987, when the then Prime Minister, Bob Hawke, promised that 'by 1990, no child will be living in poverty', it was estimated that approximately 800 000 Australian children lived in poverty. The introduction of the 1987 Family Package is acknowledged by welfare observers to be a significant innovation. It is reputed to have reduced the number of children in poverty to approximately 400 000 (*Impact*, February 1990, p.10).

Research in the area of emergency relief in Victoria and Queensland illustrates clearly how the income security system is failing to meet the basic needs of the poor (VCOSS, 1990). The Queensland study shows that in 1989–90 community welfare agencies responded to approximately 80 000 requests for emergency assistance. These requests involved families caring for approximately 170 000 children. The agencies that were surveyed reported high levels of need among these families, to which they could not respond. Many agencies themselves were found to be in crisis, reporting inadequate budgets, insufficiently trained and overworked staff, and an overdependence on volunteers. Families were being turned away when the agencies ran out of money. It is important to note that 90 per cent of all these applicants were families and individuals in receipt of a social security pension or benefit (Darwin, 1990).

Asset tests and means tests have been introduced on all pensions and benefits and allowances. A new word, 'targeting', has appeared in the vocabulary of welfare administrators and policy-makers. Under the guise of this word, eligibility for services and benefits is being redefined and often narrowed. However, some research does claim that this has not neccessarily had negative impacts, and that more progressive outcomes have been achieved (Harding, 1991).

A trend towards privatisation of many services and the provision of services on a user-pays basis raises many questions about equity in access to services and the role of the profit motive in responding to people's needs. In the area of child care, for example, the availablity of quality, cheap child care, is linked to the capacity of many women to participate in the workforce. Without these services, many women will be forced out of the workforce. One outcome of these policies may well be that caring functions for children, the aged, the sick and the disabled will continue to remain the domestic responsibility of women.

It is often those least able to bear the costs of cost cutting who suffer. In the light of federal government policies, it is important to ask whether there is any justification for these large-scale cuts in public expenditure. This is particularly important when they are occurring at the same time as economic decline, and large scale structural unemployment is creating more people in need of such assistance.

To what extent then is it true to say that public expenditures in Australia have grown out of all proportion, and are too large to be sustained? One way of addressing this question is to ask how other countries deal with these issues.

Making international comparisons is difficult due to different methods of calculating expenditures and the relatively different cultures and institutional mechanisms adopted by other countries. However, Figure 10.2 (p.216) is one of the most recent attempts to draw these international comparisons. Out of the 23 OECD counterparts, only five countries have a lower level of public expenditures per capita of population than Australia.

Of the 22 OECD countries for which there are comparable 1989 data, only three had general government outlays as a percentage of GDP that were lower than Australia — Turkey, New Zealand and Japan. Examination of social welfare expenditures on health, education and income maintenance as a proportion of GDP for 1986–88 shows that only the USA and Japan have less public expenditures in these areas. In health, Australia is similar to most OECD countries, but above the USA. However, if Australia adopted a United States-style private health system, it would leave Australia with the second lowest levels of expenditures in all OECD nations except Turkey.

Unlike other OECD nations, Australia has chosen to fund future retirement incomes by providing tax concessions on contributions to private superannuation funds rather than a contributory pension scheme. In 1992 these concessions amounted to approximately $3 billion in revenue forgone. The Australian Council of Social Service (ACOSS) argues that this system of tax concessions is unfair. The concessions are calculated to be worth only six cents in the dollar to low income earners, while high income earners gain a 32 cents in the dollar tax concession (ACOSS, 1991, p.16). The possible need for a national insurance approach to retirement incomes as used in most other OECD nations, but rejected in 1909, and again in 1937–39, was never even debated in

Figure 10.2   Public expenditure* per capita in PPP†

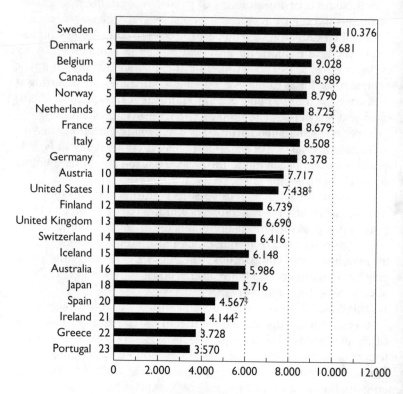

Source: OECD/PUMA Public Sector Database and National Accounts

Notes: * = Total General Government Outlays except for Greece and Switzerland where it is total current disbursements only

† **Purchasing power parities (PPP)** are a special kind of international price index, which express the rate at which a national currency should be converted into another (in this case, US dollars) in order to make it possible to purchase an equivalent 'basket' of goods and services in both countries. Contrary to exchange rates, PPPs take into account differences in price levels and in quantities of goods and services produced in different countries. PPPs can be expressed in various ways, for example PPPs of the gross domestic product, of final consumption expenditure, etc. In the following graphs we have used the PPP of GDP. For example, the PPP (of the GDP) of the yen in 1990 was 195, which means that 195 yen were needed per dollar to buy an equivalent set of goods and services in Japan and the United States.

‡ 1989

the Australian political context of the 1990s. In most other OECD countries these national savings, made for the purpose of providing for retirement income via age pensions, are in the hands of the government. This is another reason why the levels of Australia's public income and expenditures are among the lowest in the OECD.

In the context of the Accord and as part of its wage/tax trade-off with the Australian Council of Trade Unions (ACTU), the government introduced in the 1991 budget a Superannuation Guarantee Levy to be paid by employers. The proposal aims to provide every worker with a nine per cent contribution by the year 2002. Most of this money, which will amount to billions of dollars by the year 2000, is being invested in private superannuation funds. The policy is in effect a compulsory transfer of savings from the public sector to the private sector. The government has chosen a path that has essentially 'privatised' future retirement income policy without any great public policy debate. This is a path distinct from many other nations in the world. The future implications of this decision and the effectiveness, efficiency and equity of these arrangements will only be answered by the passage of time.

Australians, rather than suffering from excessive burdens of taxation, actually have the lowest tax burden of any OECD nation (see Figure 10.3 on p.218).

There exists an urgent need for comprehensive review and reform of taxation and fiscal policy. Such a review is essential to provide a policy framework that will support sustainable economic and employment growth. The revenue base of the Commonwealth has been significantly eroded since the late 1980s. Reductions in levels of taxation have been eroding the Commonwealth revenue base from 27.8 per cent of GDP in 1986–87 to 24.2 per cent of GDP in 1992. The last round of income taxation cuts provided as a result of the 1993 election promise of the Labor government erodes that capacity still further.

It is the erosion of the national revenue base that has seriously curtailed the ability of Commonwealth, state and local governments to finance the necessary investments in public and social infrastructure. This includes the adequate and appropriate funding of community-based services. As the population grows, the need for a wide range of services expands, along with a need for policies that will stimulate job creation in the private and public sector. Australia has actually cut public expenditures from 28.8 per cent of GDP in 1986–87 to 26.7 per cent of GDP in 1991–92.

The Commonwealth currently has the second lowest level of public debt in the OECD nations and proposes to wind back its debt even

Figure 10.3   Total tax revenue as percentage of GDP, 1991

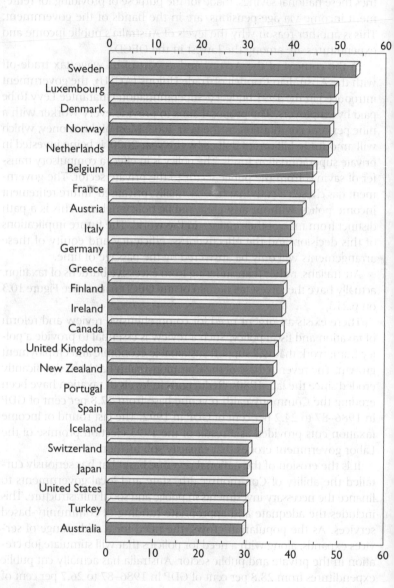

Note: Countries have been ranked by their total tax to GDP ratios.
Source: OECD, 1993, p.14.

further in future years. It has a target of reducing the deficit to 1 per cent of GDP by 1996–97. The likely result of this policy stance will be that state government revenues and expenditures will correspondingly be constrained. The result of these policies has been to exacerbate the impacts of the global recession and increase those trends in Australian society towards increased inequality. Evidence provided by the international Luxembourg Income Study, which provides comparable data for nine nations, demonstrates extensive structural income inequality. As Peter Saunders (1990b) notes;

> Australia is among the most unequal of the countries studied . . . despite claims to the contrary. Australia's wages system, selective income tested social security system, and heavy reliance on progressive tax have not in fact, produced a more equal distribution of income than elsewhere.

Inequalities have increased in the last decade. Lombard (1991) demonstrates that, whereas in 1983 the top 1 per cent of income earners received as much as the bottom 11 per cent, by the end of 1989 they received as much as the bottom 21 per cent. This general trend has since been confirmed by Raskall (1993).

CONCLUSION

This brief and generalised consideration of social welfare indicates a complex and tangled web of relationships. The current policy priorities of government are not to increase social provision, but to limit the economic costs of such provision. The social costs of these policies are evident every day in the human pain and suffering observed by those who work in organisations and agencies in the welfare field. The choices for the future are being framed in the language of economic rationalism. To accept only an economic view of humanity is to adopt only a partial view of the world and human endeavour which ignores the need to make moral, cultural and political choices. In many ways, the history of welfare has been a matter of governments, the non-government sector and the informal sector responding to the failure of the market to be concerned with anything that does not or cannot be turned to a profit.

We need to ask what sort of future is it that we seek to build for ourselves, our children, and future generations. In this context, both the need for welfare services and the positive economic and social contribution that such services make to our society need to be recognised and valued.

FURTHER READING

Dickey (1980) provides a well-documented and interesting assessment of the early history of welfare in Australia. An excellent critical assessment of welfare institutions and practices can be found in Watts (1987). Beilharz, Considine and Watts (1992) give an excellent critical analysis of the Australian welfare state and its origins. Jones (1990) gives an overview of the debates about dependency, while Graycar and Jamrozik (1993) provide a good introduction to a number of areas of social policy, detailed description of welfare institutions and up-to-date tables and charts. The AIHW Report (1993) provides a good overview of housing, children's services, aged care and disability services provision in Australia, while Trethewey (1989) gives a detailed and sad account of the daily reality of ten Australian families living in poverty.

The journal of the Australian Council of Social Services, *Impact*, provides an excellent monthly coverage of welfare related issues. ACOSS also publish a wide range of discussion papers, submissions and books on welfare issues. ABC Radio National programs such as 'Life Matters' often provide detailed coverage of welfare related issues and questions. The publications of the Social Policy Research Centre, University of New South Wales, and the Institute for Family Studies, provide excellent detailed and documented analysis of policies and practices in a wide range of welfare-related fields. Each state and territory has its own Council of Social Service representing non-government organisations that can provide up-to-date commentary and information on welfare related issues.

REFERENCES

Australian Bureau of Statistics 1990, *Carers of the handicapped at home, Australia 1988*, Cat. no 4122.0, ABS, Canberra.

Australian Council of Social Service 1993, *Submission to the Federal Government on Federal Budget Priorities 1993–1994*, ACOSS, Sydney.

—— 1991, 'Speech by Garth Nowland-Foreman', *Impact*, 21 (8), September, p.18.

Australian Institute of Health and Welfare 1993, *Australia's Welfare 1993: Services and Assistance*, AGPS, Canberra.

Beilharz, P., Considine, M. and Watts, R. 1992, *Arguing about the Welfare State*, Allen & Unwin, Sydney.

Booth, A. and Rubenstein, L. 1990, 'Women in trade unions in Australia', in *Playing the State: Australian Feminist Interventions*, ed. S. Watson, Allen & Unwin, Sydney.

Bryson, L. 1992, *Welfare and the State*, Macmillan, Basingstoke.

Cass, B. 1989, 'New directions for work and welfare', *Australian Society*, December.

Cass, B. and Whiteford, P. 1989, 'Social security policies' in *From Fraser to Hawke: Australian Public Policy in the 1980s*, eds B. W. Head and A. Patience, Longman Cheshire, Sydney.

Committee on Employment Opportunities 1993, *Restoring Full Employment: A Discussion Paper*, AGPS, Canberra.

Community Services Victoria 1992, *Welfare as an Industry: A Study of Community Services in Victoria*, Community Services Victoria, Melbourne.

Connolly, A. 1989, 'Introduction of the old-age pension in New South Wales: deserving or undeserving?' *Australian Social Work*, 42 (3), p.41.

Darwin, M. 1990, *Begging Behind Closed Doors*, Queensland Council of Social Service, Brisbane.

Department of Family Services 1990, *Annual Report 1989–1990*, Dept of Family Services, Brisbane.

Dickey, B. 1980, *No Charity There: A Short History of Social Welfare in Australia*, Thomas Nelson, Melbourne.

Economic Planning Advisory Council 1987, *Aspects of the social wage: a review of social expenditures and redistribution*, Paper no. 27, AGPS, Sydney.

Harding, A. 1991, Social security transfers, income taxes and the lifetime distribution of income in Australia, paper presented at the National Social Policy Conference, Social Policy Research Centre, University of NSW.

Henderson, R. 1975, *Australian Government Commission of Inquiry into Poverty in Australia*, First main report, AGPS, Canberra.

Habermas, J. 1976, *Legitimation Crisis*, Heinemann, London.

Jones, M. A. 1990, *The Australian Welfare State: Origins, Control & Choices*, 3rd edn, Allen & Unwin, Sydney.

Indecs Economics 1988, *State of Play 5: The Australian Economy Up to Date*, Allen & Unwin, Sydney.

Jordan, A. 1989, *Of good character and deserving of a pension*, SWRC Reports and Proceedings no. 7, Social Welfare Resesearch Centre, Sydney.

Kewley, T. 1977, *Social Security in Australia 1900–1972*, Sydney University Press, Sydney.

Le Grand, J. 1982, *The Strategy of Equality*, Allen & Unwin, London.

Lombard, M. 1991, 'Income distributed in Australia 1983–1989' in *Economics Papers*, Vol. 10, no. 3.

Lyons, M. 1990, *Government and the non-profit sector in Australia: an overview*, CACOM Working Paper no. 1, UTS, Sydney.

Lyons, M. 1993, 'The structure and dimensions of the community services industry', in *Beyond Swings and Roundabouts*, eds J. Inglis, and B. Rogan, Pluto Press, Sydney.

May, J. T. 1985, Reform of community welfare: the experiences of the states and territories — Queensland, paper presented to Australasian Social Policy and Administration Conference, Melbourne, August.

Milligan, V., Hardwick, J. and Graycar, A. 1984, *Non-government welfare organisations in Australia: a national classification*, SWRC Reports and Proceedings no. 51, Social Welfare Research Centre, Sydney.

Mulvaney, D. J. and White, P. (eds) 1987, *Australians to 1788*, Fairfax, Syme and Weldon, Sydney.

O'Connor, J. 1984, *Accumulation Crisis*, Blackwell, London.

Offe, C. 1984, *Contradictions of the Welfare State*, MIT Press, Cambridge, Mass.

Organisation for Economic Cooperation and Development 1990, *The public sector: issues for the 1990s*, OECD Working Paper no. 90, OECD, Paris.

—— 1993, *Public Management: OECD Country Profiles*, OECD, Paris.

—— 1993, *Revenue Statistics of OECD Member Countries*, OECD, Paris.

Rowley, C. D. 1978, *The Destruction of Aboriginal Society*, Pelican, Sydney.

Raskall, P. 1993, 'Widening income disparities in Australia', in *Beyond the Market: Alternatives to Economic Rationalism*, eds R. Rees, G. Rodley and F. Stilwell, Pluto Press, Sydney.

Sawer, M. 1982, *Australia and the New Right*, Allen & Unwin, Sydney.

Saunders, P. 1990a, *Employment and poverty: an analysis of the Australian experience, 1983–1990*, Discussion Paper no. 75, Social Policy Research Centre, University of NSW, Sydney.

Saunders, P. 1990b, Income inequality in Australia: lessons from the Luxembourg study, Social Policy Research Centre/ ESPG Income Distribution Seminar.

Stilwell, F. 1993, *Economic Inequality: Who Gets What In Australia*, Pluto Press, Sydney.

Trethewey, J. 1989, *Aussie Battlers*, Collins Dove, Melbourne.

Van Krieken, R. 1991, *Children and the State: social control and the formation of child welfare*, Allen & Unwin, Sydney.

Victorian Council of Social Service, 1990, *Off the Street Begging*, VCOSS, Melbourne.

Watts, R. 1987, *The Foundations of the National Welfare State*, Allen & Unwin, Sydney.

11

RELIGION

....

Ian Gillman

Assume for a moment that for your knowledge of religion in Australia you were dependent on the items featured from time to time in the print and electronic media. What are likely to be the impressions left by headlines, news reports or visual images? Perhaps the first to spring to mind would be the reports of the acknowledged failure of certain high-profile religious leaders as well as rank-and-file clergy to maintain the sexual and ethical standards they held to be mandatory for all their members.

On the other hand your impressions may be shaped by images of the pomp and circumstances trappings of a visit from the Pope, or the Archbishop of Canterbury; or the enthronement of an archbishop; or clerical participation in a widely reported wedding or funeral. But you may be more impressed by clashes between the prime minister and an archbishop, or those recurring debates among Anglicans concerning the ordination of women as priests, while recalling also disputes among less well known groups about rights to certain church property.

Outside such appearances by Christians, of one sort or another, you may recall protests from Jews about apparent anti-Semitism, of Palestinian Muslims about Israel, and the debate about the permanent resident status given to the imam of a mosque in suburban Sydney.

All told, you may be left believing that those espousing religion are a contentious lot, and prone to hypocrisy, in that some of them clearly do not practise what they preach. Some of them have a love of spectacular costume, while others have a keen eye for property or for political influence. Very few offer challenges to the status quo in our society that are taken seriously by most Australians.

Impressions formed in this way may well increase scepticism about matters and persons religious. These may not be countered by occasional positive reports about the work of the Salvation Army, the Brotherhood of St Laurence, St Vincent de Paul, Lifeline, or the Blue Nurses. And unless you are much given to Sunday morning ABC television, or to following its national radio programs, you would not be exposed to less sensational religious activities like weekly public worship, international developments, research and scholarly reflection.

To such perceptions, fostered by media reports, you may add your own observations, and those of others you have read, that public observance of religion is very much a minority activity in Australia. And from all this you may have reached the conclusion, along with most news editors, that the impact of religion in Australia is slight to the point of being imperceptible; that outside of a sensation or a gala event, it is neither newsworthy nor significant.

In addition you may find yourself prone to view religion in Australia as if it is a valid sample of religion world-wide; at least as far as the Christian denominational spectrum is concerned. If so, you would be tempted to believe, for example, that Anglicans are as prominent on the world stage as they have been here since they had a government-enforced religious monopoly for the first three decades after 1788.

GROWTH AND DECLINE

So, in a quest for an accurate perspective from which to view religion in Australia let us first step briefly into the realm of religious statistics, both world-wide and local.

On the broadest possible scale, the memberships of the world's leading religions were estimated in the mid-1980s as shown in Table 11.1, while denominational groupings among the 1300 million Christians are shown in Table 11.2. Table 11.3 shows the membership of Christian denominations in Australia.

So perhaps the first corrective we might apply will arise from a new awareness that:

- Catholics, now the largest denomination in Australia, are clearly so also on the world scene.
- Anglicans, while prominent world-wide, are not as predominant as often (in Australia) they are still assumed to be.

Table 11.1 Membership of world religions

Religion	No. of members (millions)
Christians	1833
Muslims	971
Hindus	733
Buddhists	315
Taoists/Confucianists	193
Jews	18

Source: Encyclopedia Britannica, 1993, *Yearbook*

Table 11.2 World membership of Christian denominations

Christian denominations	No. of members (millions)
Roman Catholics	1025
Protestants (in such groups as Lutherans, Reformed, Baptists and Methodists)	374
Orthodox (Russian, Greek etc)	170
Anglicans	75
Pentecostals	35

Source: Encyclopedia Britannica, 1993, *Yearbook*

Table 11.3 Australian membership of Christian denominations

Denomination	Membership (millions)
Anglicans	4.2
Baptists	0.28
Catholics	4.6
Lutherans	0.25
Methodists Uniting	1.4
Orthodox	0.47
Pentecostals	0.15
Reformed Presbyterian	0.73

Source: 1991 Census

- The numbers of Orthodox, Lutherans, Pentecostals and Baptists in Australia in no way reflect their standing world-wide. To a lesser extent, the same may be said for the Uniting Church and the Presbyterians.

To the raw figures for these major groupings we have to add the numbers of others who make up the religious scene here. Among mainline denominations, the Churches of Christ have a membership of 78 000 and the Salvation Army 72 000. Seventh Day Adventists account for some 50 000, while Mormons numbered approximately 38 000 and Jehovah's Witnesses 74 500 in 1991.

To these must be added some 74 000 Jews, who were far exceeded in numbers by some 147 500 Muslims and 140 000 Buddhists. Lesser, in approximate numbers, were some 25 000 Hindus and 10 000 Sikhs.

What these figures indicate clearly is that it is time for us to set aside the assumption that religion in Australia is the preserve of various expressions of Christianity and Judaism. In fact, Muslims far exceed the numbers of Jews, who indeed are less in numbers than are the Buddhists. All this, while the various Christian groups predominate at some 68 per cent of the population, on census figures. Just as much as we have to face the fact that Australia is increasingly a multicultural society, so too it is a multifaith society.

A profile like this, while more detailed than that often encountered, is incomplete without reference to the oldest religious tradition in Australia — that of the Aborigines. While better understood and appreciated over the last few decades, this tradition was dismissed at first, and is still disdained in some quarters. There is not space here to do more than to raise awareness of one key feature. Because of its integration with law and culture, Aboriginal religion cannot, without violence, be separated out for discrete study in the way favoured by Europeans. The very attempt to do so distorts it to the point of destruction — like a plant pulled up by the roots and set aside from the soil in which it was rooted. Coming to grips with this is one of the religious tasks ahead of all Australians, related as it is, for example, to the issue of land rights. The upsurge of interest in Aboriginal culture thus carries with it religious overtones, which have a bearing on the endeavours of Aboriginal Christians to find ways of expressing their 'new faith' in ways consonant with Aboriginal tradition. And it may be that such emerging expressions will have much to teach other Christians about ways of relating religion constructively to the Australian environment.

There remains another factor of which we must be aware in grasping the actual profile of religion in Australia today. There have been

considerable shifts in denominational affiliations shown in census returns this century. In 1901, those claiming to be Anglicans, made up 43
per cent of the population. By 1947 the figure was 39 per cent, but in
1986 it had dropped to 24 per cent. Over the same period the Catholic
percentage moved from 23.6 per cent in 1901 to 27.3 per cent in 1991.
Combined Congregationalist, Methodist and Presbyterian percentages
shifted from 23.4 per cent in 1901 to 12.5 per cent in 1991, while the
Orthodox percentage moved from 1.5 in 1961 to 2.8 in 1991. Variations
in immigration patterns accounted for most of these changes, as Anglo-
Celts ceased to be such an overwhelming majority of the population,
and the simple equation between Catholic and Irish was no longer valid.

But by far the most striking change has been in the numbers of Australians who declare on census forms that they have 'no religion', along
with those who exercise their right not to respond to the question.
Only 6779 (or 0.2 per cent) declared that they had 'no religion' in 1901,
and 37 550 (or 0.4 per cent) in 1961, whereas 2.17 million (or some 12.9
per cent) did so in 1991. Those who declined to answer rose from
56 000 1.5 per cent) in 1901 to 1.7 million (10.2 per cent) in 1991. It
is not appropriate merely to add these two groups together, for some may
have refused to answer the question as a matter of privacy, or as a
protest against even being asked. However, if we regard the two groups
as indicative of a sector of society that refuses to be associated with
religion, the sector comprises the third largest 'religious' grouping in
Australia.

Some may ascribe this growth to the increased secularisation of Australian society. Others incline to the view that there has been less a
growth in secularisation than in the social acceptability of such opinions
about religion in this century — and particularly so after World War
II. The result is something far closer to the reality of what has characterised attitudes towards religion among most Australians since 1788.

It is not that most of them are avowedly anti-religious, although
there was a measure of anti-clericalism among bushmen. It is rather
that they see religion as a private matter and find no necessity to give
public expression to it. Polls have shown that as many as 86 per cent
of Australians identify themselves with one religious group or another
and, for well over half of the population, 'belief in God' was at least of
moderate importance in their lives. But for most of these people, religion is a private concern and remains a matter of traditional identity in
which they may distinguish themselves from others — as in the football team followed in the grand final or political party preference at
elections.

'CIVIL RELIGION'

Hence, religion is predominantly a private matter with no necessary organisational implications recognised or desired, any more than people feel it necessary to join the preferred football club or political party; and it is likely to be expressed in terms of a common religious ethic. This ethic is related to a declared interest in those who do rather than in those who preach and who consider themselves 'better than others' because of their overt religious practice. It may well be that in this attitude among many Australians we find what passes for 'civil religion', or what the poet Les Murray calls 'Strine Shinto'. Almost always tinged with an element of ironic humour, it focusses on the here and now rather than on eternal issues. At its least religious level it may appear today as the demand for a 'fair go' at a cricket or football match. At its most overtly 'religious' it may appear in 'Carols by Candlelight' services in open air auditoriums. In between there is all the mystique associated with Anzac Day observances, with their emphasis on self-sacrifice and mateship as values to be promoted in the community. In such ways, Australians have been adept at treating as if it were sacred that which is essentially secular. This is a tendency made easier by the treatment of Christianity as little more than a high ethical system with so much in common with the ethics of humanism.

Such an approach to Christianity has been apparent since the foundation of the penal colony of Botany Bay. Indeed, the deliberate policy of using religion to promote moral reform and to advance morality was a major concern of the British Government. Governor Philip impressed on the first chaplain, Richard Johnson, before the first fleet left Portsmouth, that he was 'to begin with moral subjects in his preaching'. The governor's own instructions required him to 'enforce a due observance of *religion and good order* among the inhabitants of the new settlement' [my emphasis]. Not only were the few chaplains required to stress morality in their sermons, but they were required to enforce 'good order' by being recruited to sit as magistrates. The irony is that the early chaplains were all evangelical Anglicans. But instead of being perceived as heralds of good tidings of great joy, the chaplains came to be viewed as little more than moral policemen. They were seen as enforcers of a morality that not a few in the 'respectable population' (which was few in number itself) saw as 'the first step' towards 'an equal share in human redemption'. In other words, morality was seen as leading towards salvation, rather than appearing as a consequence of salvation, as was held by the Evangelical Awakening in which the chaplains had been schooled.

That public religious observance did not have priority is clear from the facts that Sunday, 27 January 1788 passed without a public service of worship, and that Richard Johnson was left without an assistant until 1794. No church building for church services was erected until Johnson provided most of the necessary cost for one in 1793, only to have it burnt down by convict arsonists in 1798. While outward forms were observed, it was clear that religion was seen as a handmaid to good order. So apparent was this that even the liberal governor, Richard Bourke, arguing in 1833 for equitable funding of churches, held that through such assistance 'the people of these different persuasions will be united together in one bond of peace, and taught to look up to the Government as their common protector and friend, and that thus there will be secured to the State good subjects and to Society good men'.

Whatever the separation of church and state that was to ensue, the perception was built up of a common cause, to the point of an alliance between churches and governments — all in the interests of morality and law and order, rather than of a gospel of 'free and gracious pardon'.

Over the space of 200 years such an equation of religion with morality has become firmly entrenched among most Australians — among churchgoers as well as non-attenders. A judgment made in 1938 about European Christianity by the Swiss theologian, Karl Barth, is readily applicable (with a slight amendment) to Australia: 'there is nothing much left after the thousand years of the apparent domination of Christianity except a little monotheism, morality and mateship'. [I have substituted 'mateship' for Barth's 'mysticism'.]

Or to consider the views of a journalist closer to home, note what Lawrie Kavanagh wrote in his article in *The Courier-Mail*, 'Here beginneth a lesson for the Church', on 23 July, 1988. Having begun with criticism of the negative attitudes of some in the churches towards the ordination of women, he said:

> I, and many others brought up like me, long ago traded the churches' view of God and its associated mumbo-jumbo for a basic philosophy that honesty and consideration for our fellows is about as close as you can get to God on earth. Churches don't have a monopoly of Him, you know. In fact if basic honesty is not good enough to get you into heaven, even if you've never heard of religion, then it can't be much of a fair dinkum place at all. Besides, honest people wouldn't want to mix with a bunch of religious snobs who spent their days pontificating on who would have landing rights to their particular cloud. Sure! Sure! Hit 'em with all that mumbo-jumbo business, but honesty is a big part of the world's problem. And it pays in the end.

I believe that Kavanagh has reflected pretty accurately the general Australian attitude towards religion: a predominant concern for its outcome in morality and a lack of patience with the esoteric, essential as the latter may be to distinguish religion from moralism. For, without the 'mumbo-jumbo' religion becomes indistinguishable from the ideals espoused by agnostic humanists, service clubs and friendly societies.

Closely related to this overall concern for 'honesty and considera- tion for our fellows' as the desiderata, is the tendency of Australians to judge a religion by its practical expressions. This is shown most widely in attitudes towards the work of such agencies as the Salvation Army, the Brotherhood of St Laurence, St Vincent de Paul, or the Blue Nurses — all of whom have a good public image. Ready acknowledgment is made of the services given to the sick, the needy and those in the midst of tragedy or emergency. But there is little if any interest at all in the dif- ferences in actual religious beliefs that account for the separate exist- ences of the denominations behind these agencies. The majority of Australians could not care less about such doctrinal 'mumbo-jumbo'. They make their judgments on the basis of the adage 'by their fruits you shall know them'. Here again they show the Australian predis- position to focus on actions rather than on those underlying beliefs, without which the admired actions may lose their motivation. The 'Golden Rule' (to treat others as you would wish to be treated yourself) has been conflated with a general acceptance of the opinion that the parable of the Good Samaritan is adequately reflected in the behest that 'come what may you must never let your mate down'. Or, as it was put in *Old Bush Songs* in 1905:

MY RELIGION

Let Romanists all at Confessional kneel,
  Let the Jew with disgust turn from it,
Let the mighty Crown Prelate in Church pander zeal,
  Let the Mussulman worship Mahomet.

From all these I differ — truly wise is my plan,
  With my doctrine, perhaps, you'll agree,
To be upright and downright and act like a man,
  That's the religion for me.

I will go to no Church and to no house of Prayer,
  To see a white shirt on a preacher.
And in no Courthouse on a book will I swear
  To injure a poor fellow-creature.

> For parsons and preachers are all a mere joke,
>   Their hands must be greased by a fee;
> But with the poor toiler to share your last 'toke',
>   That's the religion for me.
>
> Let psalm-singing Churchman and Lutherans sing,
>   They can't deceive God with their blarney;
> They might just as well dance the Highland Fling,
>   Or sing the fair fame of Kate Kearney.
>
> But let man unto like brethren act,
>   My doctrine that suits to a T,
> The heart that can feel for the woes of another,
>   Oh, that's the religion for me.

The historian, Ian Turner, summed up the development of such an approach in the introduction to his collection *The Australian Dream* (1960). In describing the philosophical aspect of the dreams of European Australians he commented:

> Australia was born in the days of the Enlightenment, sired by men of the Enlightenment. Those who first brought Europe to Australia carried with them the ideas of the Enlightenment — and a religion which justified their violence and helped to discipline their charges. There was a punctilious, but empty, observance of the forms of worship among the lower orders.

But even more important than this inauspicious beginning was the unfriendly environment into which religious belief was plunged. As A. G. Stephens (1904, p.153) wrote:

> Our fathers brought with them the religious habit as they brought other habits of elder nations in older lands. And upon religion, as upon everything else, the spirit of Australia . . . has seized; modifying, altering, increasing, or altogether destroying. In the case of religious belief the tendency is clearly to destruction — partly, no doubt, because with the spread of mental enlightenment the tendency is everywhere to decay in faith in outworn creeds; but partly also, it seems, because the Australian environment is unfavourable to the growth of religion, and because there is in the developing Australian character a sceptical and utilitarian spirit that values the present hour and refuses to sacrifice the present for any visionary future lacking a rational guarantee.

While religion as a 'ceremonial for formal occasions' seems to have been retained with respect to funerals, it is apparent that this is less the case with regard to baptisms and weddings. In fact, almost half of the marriages performed in Australia are now conducted by civil celebrants, outside of any religious setting whatsoever. Once it was considered to be socially undesirable to be married anywhere but in a church or synagogue. Clearly it is so regarded no longer. Here we have a ceremonial parallel to the change in attitude that has made acceptable the declaration of 'no religion' on a census form.

RELIGIOUS PARTICIPATION

It should be remembered that, in using data from census forms to assess denominational numbers, we are dealing with very raw evidence indeed. The correlation between what is recorded on such forms and the actual strength of the denomination indicated may be remote. It is certainly likely to be closer with Baptists, Pentecostals and Catholics than it is with Anglicans. In many cases it may indicate no more than a preference for a minister/priest of that denomination to conduct any funeral service required. It may well be nominalism of a high order, and Anglicans in particular are afflicted with this.

So, while Anglicans retain a census strength second only to Catholics, they have a worship attendance record, on a monthly basis, of about 14 per cent. (A mid-1990 census put this as low as 4 per cent.) This is about one half of those who nominate the Uniting Church, one third of Catholics and not much above one quarter of the Churches of Christ and Baptists. In fact, it may well be that on the grounds of the involvement of its members in worship and of its services to those in need, the vitality and effectiveness of the Uniting Church at least matches that of the Anglican Church — and this despite the fact that the former's census numbers are only 40 per cent of the Anglicans.

Now we have begun to use another set of data, frequently cited in attempts to assess the strength of religion in Australia — attendance at public worship. Again we need to be aware of the rawness of such figures, not least because they do not allow us to extrapolate readily from them to the actual vitality of the denomination concerned. Many Australians see no necessity to make such a public display of their declared religion, while nominalism may afflict church attenders as well as census respondents. However, with our consciousness of such in-built traps duly aroused, what do we learn from such statistics?

The first and quite important finding is that, over the more than 100 years for which we have had Australia-wide figures, seldom, if ever, have more than one in three Australians been regular and frequent church-goers. This puts paid to the claim that, whereas church-going was virtually universal at the turn of the century, it has declined markedly since then. For most of the period over which we have had records, church-going has been the custom of between one in four and one in five of the population. In more recent years, figures indicate a drop to between one in five and one in six. That is, it is a practice of between 2.5 and 3.0 million Australians on a regular and frequent basis between Friday (for Muslims), Saturday (for Jews and Seventh Day Adventists), and Sunday (for Christians generally), each week of the year.

Put like that, such figures surprise many people. Not least among the surprised would be the one-time editor of the 'Red Page' in *The Bulletin*, who in 1904 declared confidently that 'every year religion and religious observance have less hold upon Australia' (Turner, 1960). Admittedly such public religious observance is a minority practice; but it is a sizeable minority, and it is instructive to compare it with other societies. In the USA the figures for church attendance are some three times greater than in Australia, while in Great Britain they are less than half those recorded here, whatever that may mean in terms of the influence of religion on the societies concerned.

The two to three million or so involved each week clearly see public worship as a significant activity in their lives. That it is not an activity engaged in by most of their compatriots may be a matter of regret or wonder to such worshippers. But they are not persuaded by the lack of majority support to give it up as outmoded or irrelevant. And attempts to close down sparsely attended churches often lead to strong protests, not least from those whose attendance is spasmodic to say the least.

Of course not all of these regular worshippers go to religious establishments of the same hue, and some abhor the religious practices of others. (This applies not only between faiths, but also within them. 'Denominational' rivalries affect not only Christians, but also Muslims, Buddhists and Jews.) But sectarian antipathies are much reduced from those which prevailed up to 25 years ago. Differences between Christian denominations are still apparent, but what is far clearer is consciousness of what they have in common. In addition, interfaith as well as interdenominational dialogue is not uncommon.

SOCIAL ROLES

While public observance of religion may not be in catastrophic decline in Australia, religion has never exercised much influence on the course of events in the national arena — if we set aside the issue of state aid to church schools. Its marginalisation into moralism drew its teeth as a national motivator, even if it did not prove to be a mortal wound. Increasingly it was privatised, and politicians like Robert Menzies, Joh Bjelke-Petersen and Bob Hawke were adept at reminding church leaders that their roles did not include influencing policy on Australian involvement in Vietnam, street marches, Aboriginal land rights, or child poverty. They were advised, in no uncertain terms, to concentrate on prayers, preaching salvation, and theology — which as it happens were the roles that Mussolini, Hitler and Stalin all saw as appropriate for the churches under their regimes.

This has not prevented churches from criticising policies advanced. The Uniting Church clashed with the Bjelke-Petersen government in Queensland in the late 1970s over government policies related to Aboriginal land rights and to civil rights. The Roman Catholic Church and the Uniting Church each criticised aspects of the federal Opposition's proposed Goods and Services Tax in 1992. One consequence has been a greater readiness on the part of governments to listen to church spokespersons who have done their homework.

But it must be admitted that from the outset of white settlement the role of religion was circumscribed in Australia. It has never had the crucial conditioning and motivating role accorded to evangelical 'puritanism' in the USA. There is no festival in Australia that corresponds with 'Thanksgiving Day'. There has been no nationwide 'Great Awakening', such as that which, in the eighteenth century, gave a national consciousness and conscience to Americans. While some church leaders dreamed of a 'Christian Australia', their dreams and hopes were usurped by the Benthamites and the trade union leaders after the gold rushes had ceased.

The causes with which religion came to be associated in the public mind were temperance and prohibition, condemnation of sexual permissiveness, and Sabbatarianism — not one of which had much appeal to the average Australian. He or she was more likely to be influenced by the advocacy of Charles Dickens than by the appeals of clerics, swiftly dubbed 'wowsers'. John Ritchie (1975, p.83) once described this celebrated novelist's role thus:

> While Dickens brought comfort to the migrants in Australia by making the middling-sort his heroes, and by reducing the stature of their dominators, he also reinforced their predilections for drink and fellowship and fresh air, their attitude toward Christmas and to the teaching of the

man Jesus. In his novels he showed what he thought they would learn from the Galilean fisherman: the lessons of the Prodigal Son, the Good Samaritan, the Magdalen, and the Sermon on the Mount.

In 1850, just as today, many urban-living Australians liked to think of themselves as being opposed to the constricting bureaucracy of system-atisers and to the hidebound prudery of the pious; they saw their pol-iticians as windbags, pot-bellied mouthers of phrases which came to naught. Egalitarian and anti-authoritarian to some extent, the common people in Australia were clear about what they disliked. They also thought they knew what mattered: a full stomach, a roof over their heads, their drink, their mates, the country-side, and a good time for all — particularly at Christmas. Bentham's greatest good for the greatest number had become humanised and less doctrinaire. It all amounted to a kind of secular human-ism, though the masses would never contemplate such a high-flying term.

Whereas for all the vaunted separation of church and state in the USA, religion there is very much a public phenomenon. It is far less so in Australia. That the old 'Dean Martin Show' regularly included a ser-ious, semi-religious item at somewhere near the half-way mark was not surprising, while it would be ridiculous to contemplate it in 'Fast For-ward', or in the case years ago of 'The Naked Vicar Show', the very title of which says much about Australian attitudes to religion.

Likewise, it is as difficult today to imagine an agnostic, let alone an atheistic president of the USA as it is to imagine Australians being unduly worried about the declared agnosticism of Whitlam, Hawke and Hayden. Australians are more likely to be sceptical about those in public office who avow piety.

Although highly unlikely ever to occupy an upfront role in Aus-tralian life, religion is equally unlikely to disappear from our midst. In one form or another, religion is a social phenomenon with the ten-acity of a cockroach. It will not go away even when subjected to ag-gressive countermeasures, as has been found in countries under atheistic Marxism. This is not to say that it will continue to have the institutional expressions with which we are familiar today. For exam-ple, changing age profiles in the population are reflected among the clergy, and it may well be that religions in the future will be more dependent on part-time clergy, who have supporting occupations else-where. Female leadership will become not only more evident than at present, but genuinely and generally valued. House-based commun-ities may well outnumber those that will continue to focus religious life on extensive 'church buildings'.

It will be increasingly clear to those within organised religion that no religion, including Christianity, will be able to expect favoured treatment or financial concessions from a society characterised in the main by its secularity. The marks of a Judaeo-Christian heritage will remain, and the vast majority of Australians will welcome this and resist any attempt to remove those that undergird individual and social rights and freedoms. But they will not be prepared to accept any presumption that the opinions of religious groups have a right to prevail, even assuming that all such groups could reach unanimity on an issue. They will have to win popular support for their concerns from a population not predisposed to give it readily. And this applies even when ecumenical trends have led to a greater consensus among all the major churches on more issues than ever before.

Among those groups who express various forms of Christianity, there will be an increase in the mutual acceptance of ministries and sacraments. Much of this will be rooted in the common theological education of student days. Such openness and acceptance is far more likely to characterise major Christian groups than any outward expression of a 'super church' under one administrative umbrella. This is not to say that denominational or faith distinctions will all be a thing of the past. For a few they will have increased in perceived importance. For most, they will be held with respect against a wider recognition of what is held in common by all Christians and indeed by all people of faith.

Some of these groups will be more charismatic than others, while large-scale charismatic communities will still be in evidence. Other house groups will be characterised by a readiness to call into question, in the name of the claims of a sovereign Lord, the social, economic and political presuppositions of society at large. With less vested interest in the status quo than marks many present congregations, they will exercise a prophetic role in which they may be joined by some from other faiths with similar concerns. For much the same reason, they may also find common cause with artists, writers, composers, and trade unionists who will share their concern for the dehumanising effect of what passed for progress in twenty-first century society.

MULTICULTURAL ISSUES

As we have seen, the religious spectrum in Australia has undergone considerable change in the last 40 years. The majority have come from

Jewish and Christian backgrounds, which have much in common with the general presuppositions of existing Australian society. Consequently, while adjustment has been necessary, it has been a necessity for the newcomer on the whole, rather than for Australian society and its long-term presuppositions.

Those who come from backgrounds in Hinduism, Buddhism, Islam or Sikhism have also had to make adjustments. But challenges to their religious beliefs are unparalleled among those who brought with them Jewish or Christian presuppositions. Some examples may serve to show the traumas that are forced on newcomers.

Cremation itself is quite acceptable to a Hindu, even if the procedure generally adopted here is different from that at Banares. However, deep concerns about the eternal destiny of the dead one are aroused if the family is left uncertain that the ashes provided to be despatched for spreading on the Ganges River are those of the family member. Such fears need to be laid to rest speedily.

It is customary among Muslims to bury their dead in a wrapping that allows some contact with the earth. When public health regulations require the use of a coffin for burial, fears about eternal destiny are raised also. Yet the coffin requirement was reasserted in Victoria in late 1986.

Post-mortems required by law in some cases may equally outrage Hindus and Buddhists, while the forbidding of certain rites for the dead among some Orthodox by the regulations that apply to hospital mortuaries can also arouse fear tinged with bitter resentment.

Ways have been found to overcome many problems associated with the ritual slaughtering of some animals for religious purposes as well as for general consumption (for example among Jews and Muslims). There are also measures taken to allow Aboriginal concepts of justice to be applied in tribal societies. There is a need today to seek solutions to problems that exist for those whose religious presuppositions are different from those of the majority of Australians.

This is not to suggest that the statute book and local health regulations are to be cast aside, and with them certain hard-won guarantees of liberty and safeguards on community health, but perhaps wider consultations should occur on such matters where religious sensitivities may be outraged.

Equally, the time has passed where our religious presuppositions and concerns are set by those of Western Europe and the Americas. Openness to the religious insights and the concerns of Asia and the

Pacific is occurring. Such a redirection will not require the jettisoning of those things we rightly value from our European heritage, but it may enable us to see the values in other systems, and encourage us not to expect them to conform meekly to ours.

CONCLUSION

Whatever the outcomes of these issues, religion will continue to be a factor of significance in our society. For some, it will continue to act as a refuge from the challenges of the world, for others it will continue to offer the certainties of belief and practice within accustomed forms and surroundings. For others again, it will provide a sharpening of insight and a goad to protest against everything that calls into question human worth. For all, it will offer ways of relating personally to what is seen to be of ultimate worth and which gives purpose to living and a sense of harmony with all that is.

FURTHER READING

Gillman (1988), as well as dealing with the history and beliefs of major faiths in Australia, includes an introductory essay on religion in Australia's past and present, with some comments about its likely future. Harris (1982) and Habel (1992) are collections of useful essays, while Mol (1985) contains the mature reflections of a sociologist of religion.

REFERENCES

Breward, I. 1988, *Australia — 'The Most Godless Place under Heaven?'*, Beacon Hill Books, Melbourne.

—— 1993, *A History of the Australian Churches*, Allen & Unwin, Sydney.

Gillman, I. (ed.) 1988, *Many Faiths — One Nation: A Guide to the Major Faiths and Denominations in Australia*, William Collins, Sydney.

Habel, N. C. (ed.) 1992, *Religion and Multiculturalism in Australia*, AASR, Adelaide.

Harris, D. (ed.) 1982, *The Shape of Belief: Christianity in Australia Today*, Lancer Books, Homebush.

Mol, H. 1985, *The Faith of Australians*, Allen & Unwin, Sydney.

Ritchie, J. 1975, *Australia As Once We Were*, Holmes & Meier, Melbourne.

Stephens, A. G. 1904, *The Red Pagan*, Bulletin Newspaper Company, Sydney.

Turner, I. (ed.) 1960, *The Australian Dream*, Sun Books, Melbourne.

Wilson, B. 1983, *Can God Survive in Australia?*, Albatross Books, Sutherland.

12

SPORT

Ian Jobling

Throughout our history many people have considered sport to be a particularly important institution in Australian society. Some observers have gone so far as to call it a national 'religion' or 'obsession'. Certainly, over the last hundred years, many visitors and observers from overseas have commented that sport has had a predominant effect on the culture, value systems and forms of expression of Australians. For example, Richard Twopeny (1883) wrote in *Town Life in Australia* that, 'the principal amusements of the Australians are outdoor sports of one kind or another'. The wife of a former United States ambassador to Australia wrote 'living in Australia is like living in a gymnasium — there's always somebody practising something' (Dunstan, 1973). In the assessment of Donald Horne (1964):

> Sport to many Australians is life and the rest a shadow. Sport has been the one national institution that has had no 'knockers'. To many it is considered a sign of degeneracy not to be interested in it. To play sport, or watch others and to read and talk about it is to uphold the nation and build its character. Australia's success at competitive international sport is considered an important part of its foreign policy.

Following the announcement in September 1993 that Sydney would host the Olympic Games in the year 2000, New South Wales premier, and president of the Sydney 2000 Games Bid, John Fahey, stated:

Holding the Olympics will inspire a generation . . . When the Olympics are on — it is cartwheels around the back garden and across the lounge room floor. The Olympics in Sydney will inspire children to compete. They will be healthier, they will learn the pleasure of victory, the consolation of defeat, and in the end, we can perhaps teach our youth to take on the world and do their best. (*Australian Olympian*, Spring 1993)

To form any opinion about the role and place of sport in Australian society it is necessary to look at several factors. The social, political, economic and technological changes that occurred during the nineteenth and twentieth centuries influenced the development and direction of pastimes, games and sports. This chapter will focus on sport in Australian society from a historical and contemporary perspective by highlighting such factors as race, nationalism, government, gender, commercialism and the media.

SPORT AND NATIONALISM

Australians competed against individuals and teams from other countries sporadically during the latter decades of the nineteenth century. The relationship of these sporting exchanges and an awareness of Australia and Australians can be gleaned from the following selections from an article in *Town Talk* of London, which was reproduced in the *Sydney Morning Herald* of 3 August 1878. The article was entitled 'What her athletes are doing for Australia':

> There was something wonderfully sensational in the victory of the colonials at Lord's . . . Hitherto, it has been the fashion to regard Australia as a kind of place from which everybody sought to escape when sufficiently rich, and the impression has become confirmed by the large number of wealthy squatters and others who have taken up their residence permanently in this country . . . But when the multitude see a man like Trickett come over here, lick our best sculler, and after patiently waiting for another opponent, quietly return to Australia, they begin to think that a country which produces such a man must be worth living in, especially when it can tempt its best children back across the ocean. It is the same with the cricketers. They do not conceal their preference for the land from whence they have arrived, or their eagerness to return when their campaign here has terminated. The result is a great rise of the Australian colonies in popular estimation.

This was 1878 — Australia had beaten England in cricket and Edward Trickett was the world champion in sculling. Australia was then a land still comprised of six colonies. It was also embarking on a plan of federation in 1896 when the first multination and multisport athletic competition — the Olympic Games in Athens — was conducted. The extent of awareness of the significance of such events by Australian sporting organisations and individuals to the 'making of a nation' and to an Australian identity are factors worthy of consideration (Jobling, 1988). The term 'national identity' is simplistically defined as the identification of a distinctive character and assignment of this identification to a collective of people as a whole. Nationalism has been defined by Louis Snyder (1968) in these terms:

> A condition of mind, feeling or sentiment of a group of people living in a well defined geographical area, speaking a common language, attached to common traditions and common customs, venerating its own heroes and, in some cases, having a common religion . . . Nationalism should be considered first and foremost a state of mind, an act of consciousness.

Bearing this in mind, what did the Olympic Games mean to colonial Australians before and following these Athens Olympics in 1896? Australians would have known little and cared less about the revived Olympic Games had they not had a 'representative' competing. He also happened to win two events. Edwin H. Flack was born in London but lived in Australia from infancy. Soon after leaving the Melbourne Church of England Grammar School, where he studied Greek history, Flack became the one mile champion of Australasia in 1892 and 1893 and the two mile champion of New South Wales and Victoria. Flack sailed to England in 1895, where he obtained an appointment with Price, Waterhouse and Company. He wrote:

> Before I left Australia I knew that the Olympic Games were coming off in Athens in 1896 and I decided then that if I could arrange it I would take part in them, or at any rate, go and see them. Well, I went across as a member of the London Athletic Club, but I ran in my old Melbourne colours. (Price Waterhouse & Co. Centenary, 1974).

Flack's presence at the Athens Olympics was a surprise to his family and friends in Australia. He had taken a month's holiday and travelled by train and boat to Greece and, unknowingly, became influential in the promotion of nationalism and national identity in Australia through his achievements. Before 1896 the Olympic Games were 'no more than a line in the newspaper'. Australians were unaware that a fellow countryman was competing until cabled reports of Flack's victories filtered through. Following Flack's victories in the 800 and 1500 metres, his losses in the tennis singles and doubles, and his courageous efforts in the race from Marathon to Athens, the Australian daily and weekly newspapers gave more coverage to Olympic Games items. Richard Coombes reported in his column in *The Referee* that 'Teddy Flack was made an inordinate fuss of, and was quite the Lion of Athens' and, in many cases, *The Referee* included lengthy extracts from Flack's letters to his father.

Flack was the typical modest hero but over the next few years, especially after his return from London, he was frequently interviewed and featured in many publications throughout Australia. It is clear that Edwin Flack, 'The Lion of Athens', fostered nationalism: it was seen that Australian athletes could be successful in sporting competitions with countries other than Great Britain and those of her Empire.

At the 1908 Olympic Games in London *The Australasian* (19 September 1908) published a lengthy account of the marathon race, which vividly depicted the scene and highlighted some aspects of nationalism:

> Aitken got a great reception as he passed along through the crowds. The cheers and clappings have been ringing in my ears ever since. As he came along with 'Australasia' on his vest, ladies standing in their carriages called out. 'Here's Australia!' and there were deafening cheers and cries of 'Buck up, Aitken', 'Buck up, Atkins', 'Stick to it', 'Come on, colonies', 'Good old Melbourne', 'Good old Sydney', 'Good land, Kangaroo', 'Coo-ee' and 'Bravo Australia'. An old grey-haired man waved his hat and yelled, 'Come on, the colonies and Great Britain, we'll down the Yankees yet'. Meantime Aitken was going strongly and well.

Aitken later collapsed and withdrew from the race!

By the 1912 Olympic Games at Stockholm there was considerable evidence that the Olympic movement was taking root in Australia. Australia sent 21 men and two women to Stockholm and followed their efforts with much enthusiasm and optimism. There were several civic farewells for our national representatives.

Some performances by Australian athletes were outstanding: Fanny Durack and Wilhelmina Wiley were first and second, respectively, in the 100 metres swimming; the men's 4 × 200 metres relay team won a gold medal; Cecil Healy won a silver medal in the 100 metres freestyle and the rowing eight were beaten by Leander of Great Britain, which went on to win the gold medal.

Although it was already established that the 1916 Games would be in Berlin, the enthusiasm was so great that it was even mooted that Perth should host the 1916 Olympic Games to coincide with the proposed opening of the Transcontinental Railway. Clearly, the significance of the Olympic Games to national pride was manifest in the 'Perth' notion:

. . . the value to the country of such a gathering can be understood and publicity gained by an influx of athletes and visitors from all parts of the world would be the finest advertisement that Australia could receive. (*Sydney Morning Herald*, 12 June 1912.)

Of course, it was not until 1956 that the Olympic Games were first held in Australia and the arrival of the Olympic Torch at the Melbourne Cricket Ground on 22 November brought with it a fervour of nationalism and a pride in our athletes of which we are still reminded today.

Cricket has also been a major activity that has promoted nationalism. An editorial in the *Australian* after an Australian defeat in 1981 spoke of the 'miserable, gutless, inept performance of our Test team', 'the shame and degradation of Australia's stupid surrender' and 'the display of pig-iron when steel was needed', concluding:

It is, when all is said and done, only a game and our Test players — though we would prefer them otherwise — are not supermen. But it embarrasses to see them flounder so, grates that the green and gold should capitulate so easily and it irks mightily that they should do so to England, the old and arch cricketing enemy.

Mandle (1973) has provided an excellent analysis in his article 'Cricket and Australian nationalism' about how this sport was used as a 'measure' of the development of the colonies in Australia. Colonial Australians in the mid and late nineteenth century were concerned that the convict origin of 'some of the population' had been 'harmful' and also that the Anglo-Saxon qualities had deteriorated in such a hot land.

Against this background, consider the significance of victories in cricket against England from the 1870s. The leading article of *The Australasian* of January 3 1874 provides an example, praising the young colonials whose 'sympathies, hopes, and wishes, in connexion with contests like the present, are with those who represent the land of their birth, and who, to all appearance, has vindicated the ability of the Victorian cricketers to meet their English rivals upon equal terms'.

It should be stated that the Victorian team of that year comprised 22 players against the All England XI. It was not until 1877, in what has become known as the first official 'Test Match', that an Australian XI beat an England XI. That rivalry, and the test of national supremacy in at least one, if not vicariously many domains, continues today. Consider the elation over Alan Border's team regaining 'the Ashes' in 1990, and the reactions in 1983 when Australia wrested the America's Cup from the New York Yacht Club, where it had been for 132 years. Donald

Horne, author of *The Lucky Country*, expressed his feelings of patriotism when watching that final race in which *Australia II* beat *Liberty* across the line at Newport:

> I found myself gripped with a great yearning that it should be 'our' side that would win . . . I don't recall abandoning myself like this since, as a schoolboy in the 1930s, I sat in front of my parents' wireless and hoped that Kingsford Smith would make it to Batavia, or that Bradman would survive the bodyline bowling of the perfidious English. (*National Times*, 30 September 1983)

The significance of the expression of such nationalistic fervour through success in sport is worthy of further consideration. Sociologist Jim McKay has used some of the events surrounding the America's Cup victory by Australia to show how sport can legitimise and reshape hegemonic ideologies. McKay (1991) asserts that no individual or group could have planned the reactions to the *Australia II* victory, 'yet the responses were not as spontaneous as they appear'. His analysis of how politicians, business people and mass media controllers appropriated those aspects of the events that legitimised their values is pertinent to the context of sport and nationalism.

SPORT AND RACISM

The sporting achievement of Aborigines in recent decades has been outstanding. The number of Aborigines currently playing in the various codes of football at the highest representative level might lead one to think that sport has provided upward social mobility and that Australia really does have an egalitarian society. However, this has neither been true of the past nor of the present, and especially where Aboriginal sportswomen are concerned, despite the success internationally of track sprinter, Cathy Freeman, in the 1990s.

In the latter half of the nineteenth century male Aborigines became involved in 'white man's sport', especially cricket, running ('pedestrianism') and boxing. Indeed, the very first cricket team from Australia to tour England comprised thirteen Aborigines. After departing Sydney on 8 February 1868 and a sea journey of more than three months, the team played an exhibition match in Kent the day after their arrival. The London *Sporting Life* of 16 May 1868 reported:

> They are the first Australian natives who have visited this country on such a novel expedition, but it must not be inferred that they are savages;

on the contrary, . . . [t]hey are perfectly civilised, having been brought up in the bush to agricultural pursuits as assistants to Europeans, and the only language of which they have a perfect knowledge is English.

For the record, the team played forty-seven matches resulting in fourteen wins, fourteen losses and nineteen draws; entertaining features of the tour were the exhibitions of boomerang and spear throwing, and other 'native' activities (Mulvaney and Harcourt, 1988).

According to Blades (1982), Aboriginal cricketers' roles were deemed immutably inferior by stereotypes that labelled them as entertainers, comics, and respectable but 'poor blacks'. As the concept of 'amateurism' took a firmer hold in sport, ways of excluding Aborigines from participation became more sinister. The tents in the side-alleys of agricultural shows and galas provided opportunities for Aborigines to earn a living for a few years in the fight-game. Of course, the owners of these boxing tents were white Australians and, as Richard Broome's study of Aboriginal boxers has found, most were exploited and fought up to five bouts a day:

> It is true that many Aboriginal boxers received applause from fans, but it was always ambivalent praise, given on European's terms. They were always a 'credit to their race', still Aboriginals, rarely individuals. Therefore, boxing reinforced the prevailing racial stereotypes rather than challenged them. (Broome, 1980)

Doug Nicholls was a product of Jimmy Sharman's boxing tents; he became a professional footrunner and eventually played Australian Rules football for Fitzroy between 1932 and 1937 after trying out for Carlton and being told that, because of his colour, he smelled. Nicholls later became a pastor of the Churches of Christ, was knighted in 1972, and appointed governor of the state of South Australia in 1976. The various codes of football in Australia have provided an avenue for male Aborigines in numbers quite disproportionate to their population. Tatz (1992) has reported that, by 1991, 14 Aborigines had represented Australia in rugby league and five had amassed 46 rugby union tests between them, with Mark Ella as captain on nine occasions. In the 1970s Harry Williams played 17 matches for the Socceroos and there have been many great Aboriginal Australian Rules players who have won best and fairest medals in their respective states. Two Sandover medallists who ventured east from Western Australia to become immortalised in the annals of the Victorian Football League are Graham 'Polly' Farmer and Barry Cable. The 1993 Brownlow Medallist for the best and fairest player in the Australian Football League was Gavin Wanganeen.

Although many Aboriginal footballers have been and are regarded as 'stars' by their own club supporters, they have also been the subject of racist taunts by opposing players and supporters. In April 1992, St Kilda's Nicky Winmar responded to racial insults during an Australian Football League match against Collingwood by defiantly baring his chest towards the Collingwood cheer squad and declaring 'I'm black — and I'm proud to be black' (*Age*, 18 April 1993). Debates about the extent of racism in sport, especially that involving Aboriginal athletes, raged for several weeks after the Collingwood Football Club president said that Aboriginal players would earn respect 'if they behaved like white people'. Despite a later apology from the president, the 'Winmar incident' has served as a reminder that the claim by some that sport breaks down racial barriers is a hollow one and athletes and sporting administrators need to act aggressively to redress such racism.

Clearly, there have been fewer opportunities for Aboriginal sports-women to participate and excel in sport. Tatz (1987) shows that sport for Aboriginal women did not exist until recently, or 'was a caricature of nineteenth century modestly dressed, modestly-performed callis-thenics'. A remarkable exception was Evonne Cawley (nee Goolagong) who was born in Barellan, New South Wales, of a white father and an Aboriginal mother in 1951. By 1971, under the tutelage and legal guardianship of Vic Edwards, she had won the Wimbledon champion-ship. Marcia Ella, Nicole Cusack and Sharon Finnan have played net-ball for Australia. Cathy Freeman won Commonwealth Games gold medals in the 4×100 metres relay in Auckland in 1990, and the 200 and 400 metres in Victoria, Canada in 1994. She also represented Aus-tralia at the Barcelona Olympic Games.

Although Australian society has become more sensitive to Aborigi-nal culture and the role and place of Aborigines in society in recent years, the extent of representation by Aborigines in sport is not well known. Tatz stated in 1988 that at least one Aborigine had represented Australia in the following sports: basketball, boxing, cricket, football (Australian rules, rugby league, rugby union, soccer), horse-racing, net-ball, tennis, and track and field. Sports in which no Aborigines had rep-resented Australia included archery, auto and motor-cycle racing, bowls, cycling, fencing, golf, gymnastics, polo, rowing, sailing, and swimming.

SPORT, GENDER AND THE MEDIA

According to Anne Summers (1975), 'Australian society has been writ-ten about by men as if it consisted only of men'. This is very true in the sporting domain, and the lack of attention given to women in Australian society has affected what can be gleaned and analysed from historical records; it is difficult to ascertain the extent of female participation in sport and women's involvement as spectators. It is known that a principal element in the formation of the social character of early Australia was the disproportion between the sexes. For example, only about one in ten of the 200 000 convicts transported before 1840 were women (Cumes, 1979). This initial imbalance provided a heritage from which later generations found difficulty in escaping. And, in this context, it is not surprising that men greatly influenced the characteristics of early Australian leisure activities.

The emergence of women's sport in the late nineteenth century has been linked to their social progress. Lawson (1973) suggests that 'the invasion of sport by women represented another in their series of successful assaults on all-male preserves' in the 1890s. Similarly, King (1979) has contended that 'a study of the relationship between the development of sport among women and the rise of feminism may explain the sudden attraction to more robust sports in the 1890s and the emancipation of women'.

Croquet and tennis, although first played in the spacious grounds of the wealthy, soon became a very popular pastime among the middle class. They were considered suitable for women in their elaborate and restrictive clothing because they were played in such a leisurely manner — indeed, the activities were praised because they brought men and women together at play (*Courier*, 20 August 1898). The Brisbane *Courier* reported that some ladies excelled at tennis; however, women were not included in the intercolonial competitions at that time. Women were admitted as associate members of golf clubs throughout the 1890s, but were usually denied access to the clubhouse and allowed to use the links only on week days and not on public holidays (Bushby and Jobling, 1985). Cycling complemented the growing social freedoms many women were seeking by giving them greater physical freedom, but there is little evidence of organised cycling competitions for women. Although some of the activities women played in the late nineteenth century included cricket, hockey, archery, skating and swimming, sport for women was not highly competitive and it was not supposed to intrude upon their household duties (Jobling and Barham, 1990).

In contrast to the absence of competitive women's physical activities, Australian men were competing in highly organised and structured individual and team sports by the turn of the century (Dunstan, 1973;

Jobling, 1980). The masculine characteristics of 'muscular Christianity', which emanated from Britain, had taken a firm grip. Many aspects of Victorian moral principles were evident in sport in Australia: the healthy mind — healthy body concept; manliness, which was evident in displays of courage and strength; and 'gentlemanliness', which advocated 'fair play'. The indigenous 'bush ethos' (Connell and Irving, 1980) and 'tough suntanned Aussie' images, which had been given some credibility through the poetry of Henry Lawson and 'Banjo' Paterson, were also promulgated, along with a fostering of the notion of 'nationalism' through sport (Mandle, 1973). None of these traits were seen to be pertinent to Australian women as they entered the twentieth century.

The influence of the First World War and technological expansion combined to give women a greater role in the work force and, amid the fervour of the 1920s, women's sport bloomed (Bushby and Jobling, 1985). However, warnings against women participating in too much sport were published, such as that in the *Australian Woman's Mirror* of 25 November 1924:

> The woman who goes in for sports generally does it so strenuously or it might be more correct to say stridently, that she becomes too muscular and ungainly to ever attain the grace, ease and smoothness requisite for the ideal of feminine loveliness. Yet moderate sports are the ideal mode for keeping fit and young, provided one eats judiciously, and cares for the skin and hair at the same time.

Notwithstanding such cautions, in the years before World War II there was a considerable increase in both the range of sports available to women and the number of participants. Several of the sports offered competition at both the national and international levels (King, 1979; Bushby and Jobling, 1985). It was during this period that women's sport was recognised by advertisers, who depicted them promoting a host of products (*The Bulletin*, 7 December 1932; 4 December 1935; 10 August 1938).

There was not a willing acceptance of women entering into the male domain of organised competitive sport. Most attention in press reports was given to the physical appearance and dress of female competitors: the wearing of shorts by women tennis and golf players incited both controversy among sporting officials and plentiful comment in the press. The women portrayed in sporting situations in cartoons were usually depicted as lacking sporting ability and knowledge.

The relative success of Australia's female athletes in international competitions since World War II has made both the press and the public slightly more aware of the many injustices and inequalities Australian sportswomen have suffered, and are suffering. Between 1948 and 1992, women have won 25 of the 64 gold medals (39 per cent) gained by Australians at summer Olympic Games. Only 24 per cent of the total number of events were available to women, who comprised only 21 per cent of the total participants in Australian teams. In swimming, women have won 14 of the 24 Olympic gold medals won by Australians in swimming events since 1912. Since 1948 Australian women have won 11 of the 14 Olympic gold medals in track and field events (Table 12.1).

One may be tempted to believe that, because of the international success of Australian women athletes in recent years, they are equally represented in Australian sporting activities. This, of course, is not so. In 1985, the estimated percentages of Australians 14 years and over who participated in organised sport were 24 per cent of males and 16 per cent of females (Recreation and Participation Survey, DASETT, 1985–86). Of the 6.5 million registered participants in sport in Australia in 1990, 1.5 million were female (male 77 per cent; female 23 per cent) (ASC, 1990). The figures changed by only 1 per cent in a similar survey undertaken in 1992, (male 76 per cent; female 24 per cent) (ASC, 1992).

National research on sport for young Australians has confirmed that gender differences in self-perception affects sport participation (ASC, 1991). Boys describe themselves as vigorous and daring; girls are more

Table 12.1: Australian gold medal winners at Olympic Games, 1948–1992

	Men	Women	Mixed	Total
Total participants	1836 (79%)	484 (21%)		2320
Total number of events	1707 (76%)	536 (24%)		2243
Total Gold Medals	38 (59%)	25 (39%)	1	64

Source: WSU, ActiveInfo, ASC, 1993

likely to admit to being nervous, depressed or cautious. Boys perceive sport as their domain and had difficulty with girls participating in 'male' sports.

A survey of junior sport in the Australian Capital Territory found that fewer girls (44 per cent) than boys (53.3 per cent) had represented their school in interschool competition in 1991 and 1992. Similarly, fewer girls (37.4 per cent) than boys (54.1 per cent) had played community interclub competition (Clough and Traill, 1992). These findings have been supported by research on junior sport in South Australia, which showed that girls have a lower involvement in both primary and secondary school sport, and in community sport (*Junior Sport in South Australia*, 1992). The lowest participation of females in organised school sport is at age 15 (40 per cent of Year 10 girls) — a 'drop-out' of 60 per cent.

Following the summer Olympic Games of 1992, Kathy Watt, the first Australian woman to win an Olympic medal in either road or track cycling, said:

> Hopefully, my performances in Barcelona will be an inspiration to other young girls wanting to take up cycling, and will lift the profile of women's cycling in Australia, because it has spent too long in the shadow of men's events. (*Active*, Spring 1992)

Media portrayal of women in sport is also an important issue. The introductory paragraphs of a report to the Australian Government entitled *Women, Sport and the Media* highlights the significance and relationship of sport and the media:

> The media and sport provide two powerful socialising influences in Australian society. They provide evidence of, and an opportunity to emulate, role models on which people, especially young people, base their attitudes and behaviour. The confluence of these two elements — that is, when sport is presented in the media — creates a highly potent socialising influence. (Australian Sports Commission and the Office of the Status of Women, 1985)

Netball champion, Vicki Wilson, commented on the release of the ASC's 1994 report, *Invisible Games: A Report on the Australian Media Coverage of Women's Sport*: 'For too long, the media have socially conditioned people into believing that men's sport is far better and far more interesting than women's sport' (Meade, 1994, p.3). Netball was, however, shown in Stoddart's report to be the success story of women's sport. A commitment to regular television coverage by the ABC resulted in good ratings and an increasing profile for the sport. According to

Stoddart: 'Netball seems to have won the debate about television 'wor-
thiness' . . . and it may be that other women's sports need to look
closely at their model. . . . Netball, and more recently basketball, have
worked hard on their image and appeal to both sexes and the corporate sector' (Meade, 1994, p.3).

The research shows a significant increase in the reporting of shared
sport (Stoddart, 1993) (Table 12.2).

The figures for the coverage of women's sport increases considerably when data from surveys of regional newspapers is included. Regional
newspapers provided better coverage of women's sport (2.6–11.8 per
cent) than metropolitan newspapers (0.7–7.2 per cent) (Stoddart, 1993).
Menzies (1989) has found that women are also under-represented in
media organisations' sports departments.

Stoddart (1993) has compared data from his 1993 survey of television coverage with results in 1988 (Table 12.3).

Clearly, the modest increase for women is outweighed by an increase
for men and a significant decrease in mixed sport.

Table 12.2   Comparative newspaper coverage of men's and women's sport

	1980	1984	1988	1992
Men	96.2	95.9	95.8	83.7
Women	2.0	1.3	2.5	4.2
Shared	1.8	2.8	1.5	12.1

Source: Stoddart, 1994

Table 12.3   Comparative television coverage of men's and women's sport

	1988	1992
Men's Sport	63.4	72.8
Mixed Sport	35.7	26.0
Women's Sport	0.9	1.2

Source: Stoddart, 1994

SPORT AND GOVERNMENT

In anticipation of the 1908 Olympic Games in London, the following
exchange took place in the House of Representatives of the Australian
parliament:

Mr Maloney: . . . Subscriptions are being raised to enable representative Australians to compete in the marathon race in connexion with the revival of the Olympian Games. Since the representation of Australia at the carnival would do as much to advertise the Commonwealth as the visits of Australian cricket teams to the Old Country, does the Prime Minister think it would be possible for the Commonwealth government to subscribe, say, half the amount raised by the public for this purpose?

Mr Deakin: . . . Commencing with an avowal of innocence as to what a 'marathon' race may be, but of full confidence in the capacity of Australians to hold their own in that or any other form of competition, I doubt whether it comes within the power of the Commonwealth, strictly interpreting the constitution, to interfere with the rights of the states in that matter. We shall consider that question. (*Hansard* (1908) House of Representatives, 20 March p.1330)

Two features of this extract — that sport is significant in promoting a national image, and the passing of financial responsibility from the federal to state governments — were to continue to be issues in Australian sports policy throughout the twentieth century.

It was not until 1939 that the federal government established a national fitness movement by providing funds to set up councils in each state. However, financial support was meagre and even in 1968–69 the amount allocated for National Fitness Council purposes was \$416 000 for the six states and the Australian Capital Territory: an allocation of 3.4 cents per head of population (Willee, 1972). But, in the Australian Labor Party policy speech of the 1972 election, Gough Whitlam stated:

There is no greater social problem facing Australia than the good use of leisure. It is the problem of all modern and wealthy communities. It is, above all, the problem of urban societies and thus, in Australia, the most urbanised nation on earth, a problem more pressing for us than for any other nation on earth. For such a nation as ours, this may very well be the problem of the 1980s; so we must prepare now; prepare the generation of the '80s — the children and youth of the '70s — to be able to enjoy and enrich their growing hours of leisure. (Whitlam, 1972)

Elected to office, the Labor government established a Department of Tourism and Recreation, headed by Frank Stewart — effectively Australia's first minister for sport. The government allocated \$1 million in its first budget to assist Australian amateur athletes to participate in national and international teams, giving support to the statement that 'our dedicated amateurs have been ignored long enough and we intend to remedy this situation' (Stewart, quoted in Jobling,

1974). The total allocation to recreation and sport in 1973–74 was approximately 5.2 cents per head. However, in comparison, the federal budget provided for expenditure of $14 million on programs to be developed by the Australian Council for the Arts — an increase of $7.3 million from the previous budget (*Advertiser*, 22 August 1973).

A key factor in the role and influence the federal government would have on the development of recreation and sport was the relationship and extent of cooperation from the states. Commonwealth–state relationships have caused concern in many areas, and recreation and sport are not excluded from these problems — especially in the early stages. All states now have a ministry of sport and recreation but they vary in aims, structure and administration.

In 1974 Dr Allan Coles headed a task force to consider support for the elite athlete. The Australian Sports Institute report (Coles, 1975) was tabled in the House of Representatives in November 1975, but its recommendations were not implemented because, in a unique turn of political events, the Labor government was dismissed by the governor-general and replaced in the subsequent election by a Liberal-Country Party coalition government. In this new administration, sport was allocated to the Ministry of Home Affairs.

The glorious international reputation that Australians had enjoyed in sport seemed to be waning by the mid-1970s. Using Olympic gold medals only as a guide to sporting excellence, Australia's sporting achievements seemed to be on the decline. Concern was aroused by the results shown in Table 12.4, particularly in 1976. At the Montreal Olympics in 1976, Australia failed to win a gold medal and gained only one silver medal (men's hockey). The print and electronic media reacted strongly to this 'failure' — as can be gleaned from the many cartoons about the 'penny-pinching attitude' of the Liberal-National federal government and, in particular, prime minister Malcolm Fraser's visit to the Games Village and exhortations to athletes. John Daly (1985), track and field coach at those Olympics has reported that:

> Australians, shocked by the 'poor showing' of their athletes, demanded to know what had 'gone wrong'. A public inquiry was initiated which ultimately resulted in greater governmental funding of Australian sport to bolster the system. For it was not the system itself at fault. Indeed, the club system of Australian sport still exists but whereas most sports operated on a self-funded, ad hoc basis with volunteer, 'kitchen table' administration and untrained coaches and 'chook raffles' to fund their efforts before the 1970s and early 1980s. It had to!

Table 12.4 Australian Olympic gold medals, 1956–76

Olympic Games	Number of gold medals won by Australia
Melbourne, 1956	13
Rome, 1960	8
Tokyo, 1964	6
Mexico, 1968	5
Munich, 1972	8 (3 won by Shane Gould in swimming)
Montreal, 1976	0

Prime minister Malcolm Fraser officially opened the Australian Institute of Sport (AIS) in Canberra on 26 January 1980. Athletes at the AIS receive scholarships, which may include accommodation, educational allowances, clothing and equipment for training and competition, coaching, domestic and international travel and competition, and the support services provided by sports science and medicine. Specialist training and competition facilities were developed for the 'institute' sports, as well as a sports science and medicine centre, residential accommodation for scholarship holders, as well as accommodation for athletes in residence for short duration, and an administration and information resource centre.

When the Labor Party was returned to government in 1983, the Minister for Sport, Recreation and Tourism, John Brown, while retaining the AIS, proposed that an Australian Sports Commission (ASC) function as a statutory authority. The ASC, established in September 1984, had three main objectives: to sustain and improve Australia's level of achievement in international sporting competition; to increase the level of participation in sport by all Australians; and to increase the level of assistance from the private sector (which led to the establishment of the Sports Aid Foundation).

In late 1987 the ASC, AIS, and elements of the Department of the Arts, Sport, the Environment, Tourism and Territories (DASETT) were amalgamated to form a new commission under a second Australian Sports Commission Act. The chairman, Ted Harris, described the commission's functions as 'promoting sport for the community and increasing the level of sports participation by Australians. Equally, it is seeking to improve the level of performance of Australian athletes nationally and internationally'(Harris, 1990).

It is clear that the ASC has assumed responsibility for sport in Australia and seeks to redress the situation that the first federal sports minister, Frank Stewart, described in the 1970s: 'Australia's sport is among the most unorganised and uncoordinated in the world'. Nine major priorities were identified by the ASC in the development of sport in Australia. They included raising the international performance of Australian athletes at Olympics and other world championships, improving the quality and equity of sporting opportunities and increasing participation in sport for all Australians (Australian Sport's Commission Strategic Plan, 1990).

A recent trend in Australia has been a perceived need to support 'elite' athletes. Indeed, in the foreword of *Going for Gold: the First Report on an Inquiry into Sports Funding and Administration* undertaken by the House of Representatives Standing Committee on Finance and Public Administration and published in March 1989, the chairman, Stephen Martin, wrote:

> Sport today is at the crossroads. The funding . . . does little more than allow Australia's elite athletes to attend residential camps and compete against each other. It implies a withdrawal from international competition. Australians could still be represented at such competitions but it is doubtful if they would be competitive. Such a proposal is not acceptable to those, indeed the majority of Australians, who encourage other Australians in their pursuit of excellence in sport.

The issue of whether governments should promote 'elite sport' as compared to 'sport for all' is a continuing one. In its 1992 budget the federal government announced a four-year funding commitment of $293 million to sport and recreation. In launching the funding program, called 'Maintain the Momentum', the then Minister of Sport, Senator Ros Kelly, highlighted three main elements: 'Pride in our elite Australian sportswomen and men; participation for all Australians, increased professionalism in Australian sporting organisations and programs' (Sport Report, Spring, 1992). This indicates support for both 'elite' and community sport, but a breakdown of the various programs is needed to ascertain how funds are actually allocated. In a summary of the Australian Sports Commission 1992–93 proposed sport funding allocations, comprising approximately 100 sporting groups and a total budget of $32.2 million, the breakdown was: Elite — *$23.578 million; Other — $8.5 million; Unallocated — $1.8 million. In addition, the proposed allocation to the Australian Olympic Committee was $2.5 million.

Further evidence of government support for elite sport may be inferred from the spontaneous action of prime minister Keating who, as guest of honour, and midst the euphoria of the fundraising breakfast for the Sydney 2000 Olympic bid in May 1992, pledged $5 million for the bid. Keating said he would get it through cabinet 'later': he did. In the 1994 Budget the government committed $135 million over six years to help athletes prepare for the Olympic Games, in addition to $150 million already allocated for infrastructure development.

SPORT AND COMMERCIALISM

Commercial sponsorships and the media have changed sport dramatically in recent decades. Australia's greatest horse race, held on the first Tuesday in November, has become known as the *Foster's* Melbourne Cup. Foster's also gained naming rights to the Australian Formula One Grand Prix in Adelaide and the grand final of the Australian Football League in Melbourne. One may think that the Australian Rugby League 'State of Origin' matches are really battles between breweries rather than between players from New South Wales (sponsored by Toohey's) and Queensland (sponsored by XXXX-Castlemaine Perkins). Rothmans and Benson and Hedges, the giant multinational cigarette companies, supported rugby league and cricket respectively, and gained much from the media coverage, especially from exposure through television. However, in 1992, in the face of evidence that sports sponsorship was linked to young people's smoking preferences, the federal government legislated that tobacco sponsorship of sport would be banned totally by 1998. There are, of course, many companies ready to take their place. The state of Victoria assisted, through the establishment in 1987 of the Victorian Health Promotion Foundation, in providing sponsorship for sports that had previously relied upon tobacco sponsorship. 'Quit' logos are now seen at a wide range of sporting venues and on the uniforms of many sportsmen and women (Victorian Health Promotion Foundation, 1991).

As Stoddart (1986) shows, the relationship between sponsors, television and popular sports blossomed throughout the 1980s; If a sport was televised it would attract sponsors through advertising potential. This suited television owners because sport was generally cheaper to produce than drama and other programs, and proved to be good for ratings, which attracted advertisers.

Commercial television was long unable to secure rights to the summer passion of so many Australians: cricket. The Australian Cricket Board traditionally gave the national broadcaster (the ABC) exclusive rights. It did so again in 1976, even though Kerry Packer's Nine Network had submitted a proposed fee far exceeding the ABC's (Haigh, 1993).

Packer then set about establishing his World Series Cricket venture by contracting most of the world's leading cricketers to play in matches that coincided with 'official' Tests staged by the Australian Cricket Board (Stoddart, 1986). The actions and eventual success of Kerry Packer to secure rights to televise what he rightly perceived as a commercially profitable sport were significant in the ongoing relationship between sport, media, marketing and sponsorship. World Series Cricket did much to provide talented athletes in the 'right' sports with an opportunity to gain financial reward for their efforts both on and off the playing fields, courts and arenas.

Media influence on sport is entering a new phase with the introduction of pay television. The federal government allayed fears that prime sporting events would be inaccessible to free-to-air television by declaring in 1994 that pay TV could not have exclusive rights to major events. However, details of the arrangement are yet to be developed, and governments are not renowned for the stability of their media policies. At best, the emergence of new media outlets should mean the availability of a wider range of sport than is currently broadcast — but competition is inevitable for the top rating programs.

CONCLUSION

Over the past few decades numerous books and articles have been written about sport in Australia. Many have been written by journalists or ex-athletes and have highlighted sporting endeavours, others have sought to justify or explain the purported 'sporty' Australian, and, in more recent years, there has been an attempt to place sport more realistically within the context of Australian society. The issues of nationalism, race, government, commercialism, gender and the media as they relate to sport have been used throughout this chapter to consider the role and place of this significant institution in Australian society. As intimated in the overview, it is important to examine many other factors that impinge upon and influence sport in order to gain a broader and more accurate understanding of the role sport plays in Australian society.

FURTHER READING

Stoddart (1986) covers aspects such as the evolution of a sporting culture, class, status and community, politics, media, commercialism, amateurism and professionalism, and sport as sexual stereotyping. McKay

(1991), in his own words, draws on 'a number of critical traditions — feminism, semiotics, radical pedagogy, hermeneutics, Marxist and Weberian sociology'. Vamplew et al. (1992) is useful for students who require a basic background in specific topics and themes or for those who enjoy reading about sport and sportspersons of the past and present.

REFERENCES

Australian Olympic Committee 1993, *Australian Olympian*, Spring.

Australian Sports Commission 1991, *Sport for Young Australians — Widening the Gateways to Participation: A Survey of Market Research Findings*, ASC, Canberra.

Australian Sports Commission and the Office of the Status of Women 1985, *Women, Sport and the Media*, AGPS, Canberra.

Australian Sports Commission 1987, *Sport to the Year 2000*, ASC, Canberra.

—— 1990, *Australian Sports Commission Strategic Plan, 1 January, 1990 to 31 December, 1993*, AGPS, Canberra.

—— 1990, *Australian Sports Dictionary*, ASC, Canberra.

Blades, G. 1982, 'Sport, Aborigines and racism: a case study of cricket and the Deebing Creek Aboriginal Reserve (1892–1916)', in eds M. Howell & J. McKay, *Proceedings of the VII Commonwealth and International Conference on Sport, Physical Education, Recreation and Dance*, vol. 9: Socio-historical perspectives, Department of Human Movement Studies, The University of Queensland, St Lucia, pp.71–7.

Broome, R. 1980, 'Professional Aboriginal boxers in eastern Australia, 1930–1979', *Aboriginal History*, pp.41–2, 49–72.

Bushby, R. and Jobling, I. 1985, 'Decades of sport and the shape of Australian womanhood', *Fit to Play — Women, Sport and Recreation*, New South Wales Women's Advisory Council, Sydney.

Clough, J. R. and Traill, R. D. 1992, *A Mapping of Participation Rates in the Australian Capital Territory*, ASC, Canberra.

Coles, A. 1975, *Report of the Australian Sports' Institute Sydney Group*, AGPS, Canberra.

Connell, R. W. and Irving, T. H. 1980, *Class Structure in Australian History: Documents, Narrative and Argument*, Longman Cheshire, Melbourne.

Cumes, J. W. C. (1979), *Their Chastity Was Not Too Rigid: Leisure Time in Early Australia*, Longman Cheshire, Melbourne.

Daly, John 1972, 'Australia's national sport — winning', *Australian Journal of Physical Education*, 57, pp.5–14.

Daly, A. 1985, 'Structure', in *Australian Sport: A Profile*, Department of Sport and Recreation/Australian Sports Commission, AGPS, Canberra.

Dunstan, K. 1973, *Sports*, Cassell, Melbourne.

Haigh, G. 1993, *The Cricket War: the Inside Story of Kerry Packer's World Series Cricket*, Text Publishing Company, Melbourne.

Australia, House of Representatives 1908, *Debates*, vol. 44, p.1330.

Harris, A. E. 1990, *Australian Sports Commission Annual Report, 1988–89*, AGPS, Canberra.

Horne, D. 1964, *The Lucky Country*, Penguin, Melbourne.

House of Representatives Standing Committee on Finance and Public Administration 1989, *Going for Gold: The first report on an inquiry into sports funding and administration*, The Parliament of the Commonwealth of Australia, Canberra.

Jobling, I. 1974, 'A ministry of recreation and sport at the national level of government', *Report on British Commonwealth and International Conference on Health, Physical Education and Recreation*, University of Otago, Dunedin, pp.77–81.

—— 1980, 'The crumpled laurel wreath: international sport in disarray — Australia and the Olympic movement, 1894–1936', *Sport and the Elite Athlete — Proceedings of the 50th ANZAAS Congress, Sports Sciences Section, Adelaide*, pp.115–44.

—— 1982, 'Australia and the Commonwealth Games: the formative years', *Quest*, 33, pp.2–6.

—— 1988, 'The making of a nation through sport: Australia and the Olympic Games from Athens to Berlin, 1896–1916', *Australian Journal of Politics and History* 2, pp.160–72.

Jobling, I. and Barham, P. 1990, 'Early developments of women in Australian sport', in *Third Report of the National Sports Research Program*, ed. J. Draper, ASC, Canberra, pp.13–19.

Junior Sport in South Australia 1992, A Summary of the Research Findings commissioned by the Junior Sports Unit of the South Australia Sports Institute, Adelaide.

King, H. 1979, 'The sexual politics of sport: an Australian perspective', in *Sport in History*, eds R. Cashman and M. McKernan, University of Queensland Press, St Lucia.

Lawson, R. 1973, *Brisbane in the 1890s: a study of an Australian urban society*, University of Queensland Press, St Lucia.

McKay, J. 1991, *No Pain, No Gain? Sport and Australian Culture*, Prentice Hall, Sydney.

Mandle, W. 1973, 'Cricket and Australian nationalism in the nineteenth century', *Journal of Royal Australian Historical Society*, 59, pp.235–46.

Meade, K. 1994, 'Media fail to give women a sporting chance', *Australian*, 8 June.

Menzies, H. 1989, 'Women's sport: treatment by the media', in *Sportswomen Towards 2000: A Celebration*, ed. K. Dyer, Hyde Park Press, Adelaide.

Mulvaney, D. J. and Harcourt, R. 1988 *Cricket Walkabout*, 2nd edn, Macmillan, Melbourne.

Price Waterhouse and Co. Centenary, 1874–1974 1974, Price Waterhouse, Melbourne.

Recreation and Participation Survey 1987, Department of the Arts, Sport, the Environment, Tourism and Territories, Canberra, October/November.

Snyder, L. L. 1968, *The Meaning of Nationalism*, Greenwood Press, Westport.

Stoddart, B. 1986, *Saturday Afternoon Fever: Sport In The Australian Culture*, Angus & Robertson, North Ryde.

—— 1993, *Women, sport and the media: 1992,* A Report to the Standing Committee of Ministers of Recreation and Sport, SCORS, Canberra.

—— 1994, *Invisible Games: A Report on the Australian Media Coverage of Women's Sport,* ASC, Canberra.

Summers, A. 1975, *Damned Whores and God's Police: The Colonisation of Women in Australia,* Penguin, Melbourne.

Tatz, C. 1987, *Aborigines in Sport,* Australian Society for Sports History, Bedford Park.

—— 1992, 'Aborigines in sport' in *The Oxford Companion to Australian Sport,* eds W. Vamplew, K. Moore, J. O'Hara, R. Cashman, and I. Jobling, Oxford University Press, Melbourne, pp.1–5.

Twopeny, R. E. N. 1883, *Townlife in Australia,* Elliot Stock, London.

Victorian Health Promotion Foundation 1991, *Annual Report,* VHPF, Carlton.

Whitlam, E. G. 1972, **Australian Labor Party Policy Speech,** Blacktown Civic Centre.

Willee, A. W. 1972, 'Physical Education in Australia', *Physical Education Year Book, 1971–72,* P.E. Assn of Great Britain and Northern Ireland, London.

Women and Sport Unit 1993, *ActiveInfo, Australian Sports Commission Newsletter,* Canberra.

—— 1992, *ActiveInfo, Australian Sports Commission Newsletter,* Canberra, Spring.

13

MEDIA

....

John Henningham

After a decade's shake-up in ownership and structure, mass media in Australia are preparing for the challenges posed by satellites, computers, pay TV and the 'electronic super-highway'. In the midst of change, two factors are constant: the public's demand for media-supplied information and entertainment (although with changing preferences), and the capacity of the media to make money for their owners. It is significant that Australia's richest citizen, Kerry Packer (worth $5.5 billion), and richest ex-citizen, Rupert Murdoch, have made their fortunes primarily from mass media.

As a vast country with a small population, Australia has had more than its share of geographical constraints on media industries. Some of these have led to innovations that have subsequently been exported. For example, Rupert Murdoch's success in the 1960s in using emerging facsimile technology to publish a national daily newspaper has spread to Japan, Britain and the United States, while Australia's mixed mode of private and public broadcasting (commercial and ABC) together with its multicultural service (SBS) have proved to be pioneering approaches to problems created by distance and immigration.

The press includes two national daily newspapers, ten dailies in the state and territory capitals, and an additional thirty-eight dailies in provincial cities and towns. There are more than a hundred non-daily country newspapers (most published weekly but some published two or three times a week), and about 200 nationally published special-interest newspapers and magazines. It is significant that, as a result of Rupert Murdoch's becoming a United States citizen (in order to buy into United States television), and the successful purchases of newspaper companies by Canadian Conrad Black and Irishman Tony O'Reilly, most of Australia's print media are under foreign control. Table 13.1 shows ownership and circulation of metropolitan and national newspapers.

The broadcast area of the media is divided into commercial and public sectors. Commercial broadcasting includes 44 television stations and 166 radio stations. Most of the TV stations are linked with one of the three major networks — Seven, Nine and Ten — or with the main regional networks (Prime, Capital and TWT). Radio ownership is far more fragmented. Important groups include Village Roadshow (which took over Austereo for $120 million in 1994), Australian Provincial Newspapers (which paid $106 million for Wesgo), Rural Press, Lyndeal, Southern Cross Broadcasting and Bill Caralis's Super Network Radio.

There are different types of public broadcasting. The primary provider, which for most of Australia's broadcast history has been the only public broadcaster, is the Australian Broadcasting Corporation, responsible

Table 13.1 Capital city and national daily newspaper circulations by ownership groups (half year to September 1994)

	Monday–Friday	Saturday
News Ltd		
Australian (national)	113 654	313 360
Daily Telegraph Mirror (Sydney)	445 022	331 666
Herald Sun (Melbourne)	568 945	529 341
Courier-Mail (Brisbane)	225 019	330 634
Advertiser (Adelaide)	205 965	263 735
Mercury (Hobart)	50 865	63 069
Northern Territory News (Darwin)	22 020	28 113
Fairfax		
Australian Financial Review (national)	82 004	—
Sydney Morning Herald (Sydney)	227 683	385 669
Age (Melbourne)	204 948	361 204
Other		
West Australian (Perth)	239 087	379 526
Canberra Times (Canberra)	41 258	68 600

Source: Audit Bureau of Circulations, 1994

for an extensive network of radio and television stations throughout
Australia. Each capital city has an ABC television station and five radio
stations, with the emphasis on quality and 'middlebrow' broadcasting.
A second public broadcaster is the Special Broadcasting Service (SBS),
which runs an ethnically-oriented national television service as well as
four radio stations. A third group is community broadcasters, providing
services to such groups as the print handicapped, ethnic and indigenous communities, religious groups and educational communities.
There are now more than 200 community radio licences, with the list
growing by several dozen each year, and four community television
licences (Australian Broadcasting Authority, 1993).

To add to the broadcast spectrum, the 1992 *Broadcasting Services Act*
allowed for commercial 'narrowcasting' — low-power stations on the
FM band providing specialised services such as children's programs and
sports results. More than 400 short-term licences have been issued,
amidst concerns from traditional commercial broadcasters as well as
community stations that their audiences are being eroded (*Communications Update*, May 1994).

Residents of major urban areas (principally, the state capital cities
and adjacent regions) have access to the following configuration of
daily media outlets: two national dailies (the *Australian* and the *Australian Financial Review*); one daily metropolitan newspaper (two in
Sydney and Melbourne); three commercial television stations; an ABC
television station and an SBS television station; five to seven commercial AM radio stations; two FM commercial stations; three ABC AM
stations; two ABC FM stations; three to six public or community radio
stations (AM or FM), and in some cases one community television
station plus some narrowcast radio stations. Pay TV services, including
such programming as Cable Network News, are currently being added
to these outlets in major cities.

Significant changes have occurred over the last decade in the mix of
media types, with daily newspapers the principal victims. This chapter
will briefly survey the history of press and broadcasting, before
discussing current developments and issues.

DEVELOPMENT OF THE PRESS

Although Australia's press is almost as old as the country's written
history, it had humble origins, the first publication being a colonial
government gazette produced by a convict printer — the *Sydney
Gazette* (1803). In most colonies around the Australian mainland and

Tasmania the first publication was a government gazette, a fact that emphasises the authoritarian origins of the Australian press. It was almost forty years after British settlement that a genuine newspaper appeared in the colony of New South Wales — the *Australian* (no relation to the current title) in 1824. Its proprietors, lawyers William Charles Wentworth and Robert Wardell, adopted a relatively liberal policy (such as support for a low property franchise as well as legal rights for ex-convicts). The newspaper, like its rival, the *Monitor* (launched by Edward Hall in 1826), fell foul of the colonial governor, Ralph Darling, who jailed editors of both papers in the late 1820s for attacks on his authority.

The *Sydney Herald*, launched as a weekly in 1831, was to become a great newspaper in succeeding decades, with a role and influence similar to that of the *Times* in London. In 1840 it became a daily, and the next year was bought by Warwickshire immigrant John Fairfax, who renamed it the *Sydney Morning Herald*. When the *Australian* closed in 1848 the *Herald* became the colony's oldest newspaper, earning its nickname of 'Granny'. The paper was controlled by the Fairfax family until 1990. The first daily opposition to the *Herald* was politician Henry Parkes' *Empire* in 1851, but significant rivalry did not emerge until the launching in 1879 of the *Telegraph*, which was to overtake the *Herald*'s circulation lead.

An important Melbourne lineage was begun in 1840 with the launching of the *Port Phillip Herald*, which became an afternoon daily in 1869 and in the twentieth century was to be flagship of the Herald and Weekly Times (HWT) empire. One of Melbourne's most important newspapers was the *Argus*, established in 1846, a conservative organ for most of its history of more than a century. Its main rival was the *Age*, only eight years younger than the *Argus*, and owned by the Syme family (originally brothers Ebenezer and David) from 1856.

More than a century later, the *Age* was bought by the Sydney Fairfax family, but throughout the nineteenth century was a marked contrast to the conservative *Sydney Morning Herald*. The *Herald* 'equated democracy with "mobocracy" and argued for the representation of interests based on property rather than manhood suffrage. Later it also opposed votes for women and condemned the Eureka stockade as "the most wanton aggression against authority ever known in any country".' (Cummins et al., 1991, p.4). By contrast, as described by the biographer of David Syme, C. E. Sayers, 'the *Age* led almost every radical campaign for political, social and economic advancement. Under David Syme's ownership and control — from 1860 to his death in 1908 —

the *Age* was the mouthpiece of the popular movements of the time'
(Sayers, 1965, p.vii).

Other significant colonial papers that have flourished into the present
day are Hobart's *Mercury* (1854), Perth's *West Australian* (1833 as a
weekly) and the same city's first daily, the *Daily News* (1882–1990), and
Adelaide's *Advertiser* (1858), owned by the wealthy Bonython family for
almost forty years until 1929.

Three evening dailies also flourished in Sydney in the late nineteenth century; the most successful, the *Australian Star*, was relaunched
as the *Sun* when purchased by Hugh Denison in 1910 and was to enjoy
a long history.

Brisbane's first newspaper, the *Moreton Bay Courier*, was established
in 1846 by Arthur Sydney Lyon. Founded at the invitation of the Moreton Bay Progress Association, it was, as Cryle (1989) shows, strongly pro-
squatter and in favour of colonial expansion. Unlike equivalent
newspapers in Sydney and Melbourne, the *Courier* did not remain in the
hands of one family — there were various changes of ownership during the nineteenth century, and into the twentieth century. However,
a strong provincial press was to develop in Queensland, where family
domination became the norm (Kirkpatrick, 1984). In 1933 the *Courier*
finally merged with its rival the *Daily Mail* (founded 1903) to become
the *Courier–Mail*, owned jointly by Keith Murdoch and shady businessman John Wren.

Of a variety of weekly newspapers founded in New South Wales in
the late nineteenth century, two had a special role. The *Bulletin*, founded
in 1880 by two evening newspaper journalists, John Archibald and
John Haynes, provided an important outlet for local poets, authors and
essayists, while promoting such themes as republicanism, nationalism
and protectionism. The *Bulletin* survives as a news magazine. *Truth*,
founded in 1890, was used by editor and later proprietor John Norton
as a crusading newspaper, which supported both radical and racist
causes and specialised in smears and the sordid. Labour newspapers of
significance emerged with the growth of the labour movement in the
1890s (*Australian Workman*, 1890; *Worker*, 1892); significant titles in
the twentieth century (until the 1930s) were the *Labor Daily* and the
World. An interesting early feminist publication (1888–1905) was *Dawn*,
published by Louisa Lawson, whose son Henry was to become Australia's best-known writer.

The nineteenth century tradition of a variety of relatively small newspaper proprietors continued and grew into the first quarter of the twentieth century, but concentration began to emerge in the late 1920s.

There were 21 metropolitan dailies in 1903, in the hands of 17 independent owners. By 1923 the number of dailies had grown to 26, while owners numbered 21. But by 1950 there were 15 papers and only ten owners, while in the early 1970s there were 17 papers and just three owners, with even greater concentration to come (Mayer, 1980).

Australia's first newspaper empire was Associated Newspapers, headed by Hugh Denison, which included a range of daily and weekly newspapers including Sydney's afternoon *Sun* and morning *Telegraph* and Melbourne's *Sun News-Pictorial*. To emerge as main rival was the Herald and Weekly Times group in Melbourne, publishers of the afternoon daily the *Herald* and the rural *Weekly Times*. Two men who edited newspapers for these groups went on to manage the companies and establish their own empires — R. C. Packer in Sydney and Keith Murdoch in Melbourne.

Under Murdoch, the Herald group gained control of Adelaide's *Advertiser* and Perth's *West Australian*. R. C. Packer's son, Frank Packer, founded the very successful *Women's Weekly* in 1933. Frank Packer's and E. G. Theodore's Sydney Newspapers joined Associated Newspapers in 1936 to form Consolidated Press. Packer took control of the *Telegraph*, which had been in decline, and turned it into a popular and profitable newspaper.

John Norton's son, Ezra, challenged Sydney's established daily newspapers during World War II by launching Sydney's *Daily Mirror*, resulting in a circulation decline for Associated Newspapers' afternoon *Sun*, taken over by Fairfax in 1953. Five years later Fairfax also gained control of Norton's *Mirror* through a subsidiary company.

The 1950s also saw the loss of Melbourne's *Argus*, unsuccessfully revamped by its British Mirror owners. It closed in 1957 after 111 years. The *Age* fell into the financial control of the Fairfax group in 1966. The Fairfax company at its peak in the 1970s controlled a broad range of media, with particular strengths in quality publications. Its newspapers included the *Sydney Morning Herald*, Sydney's *Sun*, the *Sun-Herald*, the *Australian Financial Review*, the *National Times* (later *Times on Sunday*), Melbourne's *Age*, the *Newcastle Herald* and Wollongong's *Illawarra Mercury*. Other titles were magazines *Woman's Day*, *Cosmopolitan* and *People*, plus the Channel 7 television stations in Sydney and Brisbane, and the Macquarie radio network. The Herald and Weekly Times group until the 1980s owned the main morning and afternoon dailies in each state capital city except Sydney, the Channel 7 stations in Melbourne and Adelaide, and nine radio stations in four states as well as major magazines including *Australasian Post* and home improvement magazines. The

Packer family (Kerry succeeded his father Frank in 1974), although having sold the Sydney *Telegraph* to Rupert Murdoch, owned major magazines including *The Women's Weekly* plus the Sydney–Melbourne Nine network.

Newspaper circulations have declined in the post-World War II period. The *Sydney Morning Herald*'s circulation was well over 300 000 in the late 1940s but is now less than 230 000 on weekdays. Melbourne's once-mighty afternoon *Herald* sold more than half-a-million copies a day in the mid-1960s, but at its final audit in 1990 (before closure) was down to 175 000. The amalgamated *Herald Sun* in Melbourne is selling fewer copies than did the *Sun News-Pictorial* a decade ago, and the *Age* is also in decline. Brisbane's *Courier-Mail* reached a circulation peak of about 270 000 in the late 1970s and early 1980s: it is now well under 250 000, the level it had reached in the 1960s.

The decline in absolute numbers is more remarkable when matched with population levels. Brown (1986) calculated a decline of daily news-paper circulation from 576 per 1000 people in 1956 (the year television was introduced) to 400 in the early 1980s. It is now below 300. Circulation of dailies as a group has declined by 35 per cent in the past ten years (and by 43 per cent in terms of circulation per head of population). (See Table 13.2.)

Part of the decline may represent buyer resistance to newspaper price rises. The Communications Law Centre has found that between 1984 and 1994, newspaper prices increased at twice the rate of inflation (132 per cent compared with 68 per cent). From 1991 to 1994, newspaper prices went up by more than five times the rate of inflation (22 per cent compared with less than 4 per cent) (*Communications Update*, April 1994).

DEVELOPMENT OF BROADCASTING

Overseas developments in radio technology in the first two decades of the twentieth century were keenly monitored in Australia, and local engineers played an important part in the testing and improvement of long-distance transmissions.

A series of ad hoc decisions during the 1920s set the pattern for broadcasting policy, with influences from North America and Britain determining the development of a 'dual' system comprising both commercial and public broadcasting. Broadcasting in the United States, by

Table 13.2 Circulation change, 1984–94, capital city and national daily newspaper

	Average Monday to Saturday circulation	
	1984	1994
National		
Australian	119 010	146 938
Australian Financial Review	61 126	82 004
Sydney		
Sydney Morning Herald	252 006	254 290
Sun	347 441	—
Daily Telegraph	267 855	—
Daily Mirror	361 277	—
Daily Telegraph Mirror	—	426 129
Melbourne		
Age	238 327	231 676
Sun News-Pictorial	570 443	—
Herald	337 003	—
Herald Sun	—	562 344
Brisbane		
Courier-Mail	227 943	242 622
Daily Sun	161 040	—
Telegraph	141 922	—
Adelaide		
Advertiser	212 555	215 593
News	176 044	—
Perth		
West Australian	232 407	263 110
Daily News	112 027	—
Hobart		
Mercury	54 949	52 953
Darwin		
Northern Territory News	16 939	23 035
Canberra		
Canberra Times	45 181	45 662
Total	3 935 495	2 546 356
Circulation of metropolitan and national dailies per 1000 people (national population)	254	146

Source: Audit Bureau of Circulations, 1984, 1994

contrast, was entirely commercial, while Britain's system was entirely public, under the monopoly of the British Broadcasting Corporation. The Australian Broadcasting Commission (ABC) was set up in 1932 as a public corporation.

The broadcasting of news stirred up fierce opposition from powerful newspaper interests, as a result of which it was an underdeveloped resource for the first two decades of radio. Such news as there was consisted generally of readings from the day's newspapers. World War II caused a major reappraisal of radio's potential as an instant information medium, and limitations on news broadcasting were abolished. The ABC's independent news service did not, however, begin until 1946.

Television was introduced in Australia in 1956 after a royal commission set up by the Menzies government. Radio's dual formula was replicated, with major capital cities having two commercial television stations (or 'channels') and one ABC station. (Third commercial licensees began operating in major state capitals a decade later.) Despite some calls for policies to diversify media ownership, the Liberal–Country Party government did not object to the principle of newspapers having a major stake in the new medium. Thus the major newspaper publishers in each city, Frank Packer (Channel 9), John Fairfax in Sydney and the Herald and Weekly Times in Melbourne (Channel 7), and David Syme with the *Argus* in Melbourne (9), became major shareholders in the new commercial stations. The HWT group also secured licences in Brisbane and Adelaide, while Murdoch was granted one of the Adelaide licences (NWS–9). In 1960 Packer was given government approval to buy into Melbourne's Channel 9, giving him a Sydney–Melbourne network. When Murdoch later increased in power, he succeeded in acquiring the new commercial network. This comprised Channel 10 in Sydney and Channel 0 — later to be 10 — in Melbourne, acquired through joint control of Ansett with Sir Peter Abeles.

Far-reaching changes in broadcast ownership took place in the late 1980s following government policy changes that lifted earlier restrictions on the number of stations in which companies could have a significant interest (previously two), while also limiting, for the first time, cross-media ownership. The legislation did not force divestiture, restricting only future purchases, but was the catalyst for a major shake-up in the media industry, prompted by Rupert Murdoch's takeover of the Herald and Weekly Times group. All networks changed hands, some several times, with companies owned by entrepreneurs Christopher Skase (Qintex), Alan Bond (Bond Media) and Steve Cosser (Broadcom) gaining control of the Seven, Nine and Ten networks. But the received wisdom that owning a television licence was equivalent to a 'licence to print money' proved illusory for the new owners. Premium prices paid for the licences combined with rash overspending on American programs resulted in serious financial difficulties for all three owners, all of whom finally lost their coveted TV networks.

In 1993 the Seven network was publicly floated, with Murdoch's News Corporation ending up with 15 per cent of shares (the maximum allowable to a newspaper proprietor under revised cross-ownership laws), while Telecom holds 10 per cent. The Ten network, temporarily owned by the banker Westpac, attracted further controversy and an Australian Broadcasting Authority inquiry in 1992–93 when financial control went to a syndicate, 15 per cent of which was owned by a Canadian broadcaster, CanWest. Kerry Packer re-bought the Nine network from Bond for one-fifth of the $1.05 billion Bond had paid for it.

Insulated from the financial turmoil affecting the commercial broadcasters, but never far from controversy itself, the ABC was restructured by the Fraser government in 1982. Previously the Australian Broadcasting Commission, it became, on the recommendations of the Dix Report, the Australian Broadcasting Corporation. It remains a statutory corporation responsible, under the ABC Act, for providing public-funded radio and television broadcasting throughout Australia. The 1994 level of public funding was $515 million a year (with $566 million budgeted for 1995–96). This is supplemented by limited private enterprise activity, which brings in about $90 million. The ABC is prohibited from accepting advertising (to the delight of commercial broadcasters), but the decision in 1994 to permit sponsorship for the corporation's newly-launched Australian Television International service (beamed via an Indonesian satellite to southern Asia) may be the thin end of the wedge. The corporation has a board of eight directors, appointed by the federal government for five-year terms. The directors appoint a managing director, who is in charge of administering the organisation.

The multicultural public broadcaster, SBS, receives $76 million, supplemented by $13 million from limited commercial activities (including on-air advertising and sponsorship).

MEDIA DYNASTIES

The most extraordinary phenomenon in Australian media since the 1960s has been the growth in power of Rupert Murdoch. Murdoch is unique in publishing and the media generally, an Australian-born businessman who from a tiny base has built up an international media empire.

His father, Sir Keith Murdoch, had become a dominant force in Australia's newspaper scene in the 1930s and 1940s, as head of the Herald and Weekly Times group. The older Murdoch originally made his reputation during the First World War as the young maverick journalist who visited Gallipoli and was the first to publicise the military disaster affecting Australian troops.

Although a powerful newspaper executive, and the person largely responsible for expanding the HWT group into an empire, Keith Murdoch had limited financial interests in newspapers himself. He did, however, control Brisbane's *Courier-Mail* and Adelaide's afternoon daily, the *News*. Rupert Murdoch inherited these newspapers at the age of 21 upon his father's sudden death in 1952. Punitive death duties, unsympathetic bankers and powerful rival newspaper publishers forced the sale of the *Courier-Mail* (to the HWT). Young Rupert was left with the tiny *News* and might well have been expected to sink into obscurity. (His father had been concerned about the left-wing views he was developing while at Oxford.)

Rupert Murdoch demonstrated that his horizons were wider than Adelaide when he bought the run-down afternoon tabloid the *Daily Mirror* from Fairfax in 1960, and built this up to challenge the Fairfax *Sun*'s near-monopoly (and, within 30 years, to drive the *Sun* out of business). The visionary, if financially rather foolhardy traits of the young Murdoch were demonstrated by his 1964 launch of the first national daily newspaper, the *Australian*. But his successes with his metropolitan dailies enabled him to buy Packer's *Daily Telegraph* and *Sunday Telegraph* in 1972.

In 1969 Murdoch expanded to Britain, buying tabloids the *News of the World* and the *Sun*, which both proved enormously profitable, enabling him to move to the top end of the London market in 1980 with the purchase of the *Times* and *Sunday Times*, as well as the acquisition (less successful) of several American titles. His move into American television resulted in his renouncing his Australian citizenship to become a United States citizen in 1985. Other significant investments were the film-making company Twentieth Century Fox, the *New York Post*, *TV Guide*, *Village Voice*, the Boston *Herald* and Hong Kong's *South China Morning Post*. In the late 1980s he invested heavily in satellite broadcasting in Britain.

In 1987 Murdoch succeeded (after a failed attempt in 1979) in taking control of the Herald and Weekly Times group. He retained most newspapers in the HWT group, losing West Australian Newspapers to Robert Holmes à Court, who subsequently sold to Alan Bond. But rationalisations followed. Murdoch closed Brisbane's afternoon *Telegraph*, and in 1990 merged Melbourne's *Herald* and *Sun* and Sydney's *Telegraph* and *Mirror* into single titles in each city.

Also to close by early 1992, after short periods of Murdoch-sponsored ownership by former Murdoch executives, were the only remaining afternoon dailies in Adelaide and Brisbane (the *News* and the *Sun*).

Murdoch now controls two-thirds of Australia's metropolitan daily newspapers. Of the total circulation of capital city dailies, 66 per cent belongs to News Corporation, a degree of control and a paucity of titles unprecedented in Australian press history. Murdoch owns Sydney's *Telegraph Mirror*, Melbourne's *Herald Sun*, Brisbane's *Courier-Mail*, Adelaide's *Advertiser*, Hobart's *Mercury* and Darwin's *Northern Territory News*, as well as the national daily, the *Australian*. Murdoch also controls just over half the total circulation of Australian suburban newspapers, with a total of 66 titles. His suburban chains are in Sydney (16 titles), Melbourne (27), Brisbane (10) and Adelaide (13). The next biggest owner is the Fairfax group, with 16 titles.

The News group now has a relatively less significant role in the regional dailies market, half of which are in Queensland or northern New South Wales. The biggest proprietor is Irish businessman Dr Tony O'Reilly, who with his family owns Australian Provincial Newspapers, with 13 titles and 31 per cent of circulation. Murdoch, who under Trade Practices Commission pressure sold to O'Reilly, now has the second-biggest share, with five regional daily titles and 22 per cent of circulation (*Communications Update*, February 1994).

Murdoch retains significant magazine interests, including *New Idea* and *TV Week* (50–50 with Packer). Packer is the major magazine publisher: of the 22 magazines with circulations of more than 100 000, Packer owns 9.5 (Murdoch 4.5). Most popular are Consolidated Press's *Women's Weekly* and *Woman's Day*. Murdoch's Harper Collins is Australia's second biggest book publisher, with a $106 million turnover. (Imprints include Harper Collins, Angus & Robertson and Golden Press.) The largest publisher is the British group Reed International. Late in 1994 Kerry Packer merged his magazine publishing and television companies (Consolidated Press and Nine Network Australia) to form Publishing and Broadcasting Limited (PBL), valued at $2 billion.

Rupert Murdoch faced severe financial difficulties in the early 1990s, with a debt of more than $10 billion, as a result of recession in his major markets and losses from satellite broadcasting in Britain. He succeeded in negotiating a major financial restructuring, with the consequence of severe cost-cutting throughout his operations and the selling-off of certain assets. An earlier victim of the cost pressures was the *Sunday Herald* in Melbourne, a quality broadsheet established in 1989 as part of a Sunday newspaper 'war'. The amalgamation of his Sydney and Melbourne dailies in 1990 also indicates the cost pressures that the Murdoch organisation faced. Overseas titles sold included magazines and newspapers (such as *TV Guide* and the *South China Morning Post*), while Murdoch's satellite broadcasting company in Britain was merged with its competitor.

By 1994, News Corporation was again financially healthy, with an annual profit of $1.3 billion — joining BHP and the National Australia Bank as Australia's only 'billion dollar companies'. Recent overseas expansion includes satellite broadcasting based in Hong Kong, set to capitalise on the emerging economy of China.

Murdoch's success story contrasts with the riches-to-rags tragedy of Warwick Fairfax Jnr, whose rash attempt to privatise the Fairfax company cost him ownership of the company his family had controlled for just under 150 years. Fairfax, son of the late Sir Warwick Fairfax, who had been managing director of the company from 1930 until 1977, was the victim of personal stubbornness and dubious financial advisers. Borrowing heavily to buy shares in the company, he refused to call off his bid when the stockmarket collapsed in 1987. With the economic recession, interest bills on borrowings could not be met by revenue (although the Fairfax papers as a group operate at a comfortable profit), the banks refused further loan restructuring, and receivers were appointed late in 1990.

After controversial and long-drawn-out negotiations, involving attempts to buy into Fairfax by such media heavyweights as Kerry Packer and Tony O'Reilly, control of Fairfax was sold in 1991 to the Canadian owner of Britain's *Daily Telegraph*, Conrad Black, for $1.44 billion. Originally allowed 15 per cent of Fairfax, Black was permitted by the Foreign Investment Review Board (responsible to the federal Treasurer) to lift his holding to 25 per cent.

The only independent capital city newspapers are Perth's *West Australian*, which is unique as a publicly-listed company in which no individual has a controlling interest, and the *Canberra Times*, owned by businessman Kerry Stokes. It is relevant to note, however, that News Limited helped Stokes arrange credit to buy the *Canberra Times*, in return for an option (which subsequently lapsed) to have an interest in the newspaper (House of Representatives Select Committee on the Print Media, 1992).

Concerns within the Labor Party about concentration of ownership resulted in the Print Media Inquiry, which reported in 1992. It suggested little in the way of structural change, other than amending the *Trade Practices Act* so that 'substantial lessening of competition' rather than 'market dominance' became the test for print media mergers, with the Trade Practices Commission also to inquire into the impact of proposed mergers on free expression, fairness, accuracy and economic viability. It called for a restructured Press Council and for contractual extension of the journalists' code of ethics to proprietors and editors. None of the inquiry's recommendations have been put into effect.

PAY TV

After decades of governmental refusal to permit its development, pay television is being launched in Australia in the mid-1990s in a context of controversy and confusion, with rival groups using different technologies — satellite, cable and microwave — to offer services.

As with other forms of media, the leading mass communication magnates are at centre stage. In 1994, after losing to newcomer Australis Media in their combined bid with telecommunications corporation Telecom for satellite licences, Murdoch and Packer switched their interests to cable technology. Murdoch's News Corporation joined forces with Telecom (Telstra), which is spending $3.5 billion to lay an underground 64-channel fibre optic cable in metropolitan areas. News is providing the programming for the new network, drawing on links with News Corporation's Twentieth Century Fox network in the USA and its satellite pay-TV service, British Sky Broadcasting (BSkyB). Packer has shares in Optus Vision, which plans an alternative $3 billion cable, designed to carry telephone traffic as well as TV. US company Continental Cablevision has 47.5 per cent of Optus Vision, which has movie deals with Disney, MGM, Warner Brothers and Village Roadshow. Australis, which also bought microwave licences, has signed up Hollywood movie-makers Columbia, Paramount and Universal to provide movies and entertainment for three of its initial four channels under the Galaxy banner.

It is doubtful whether all three pay TV groups can survive in Australia's small market. With fierce competition, the key to success is the quality of programming available — principally Hollywood movies and major sport. Controversial issues include access by outside groups to pay TV, and the extent to which pay TV operators can gain exclusive rights over sport. Just as Packer transformed cricket into the commercially successful 'world series cricket', Murdoch's approach has been to develop a 'super league' for football and other sports in order to attract cable subscribers. The Fairfax group, concentrating on software rather than hardware, is developing a 24-hour pay TV news channel in conjunction with the Australian Broadcasting Corporation.

Technological advances in data compression foreshadow the potential of hundreds of channels to be distributed by pay TV methods, including, in the case of cable, interactive channels allowing consumers to 'talk back' to communication organisations.

Newspapers also have an uncertain future because of the means to transmit printed information directly to homes, either to computers, faxes or through new 'black boxes' which can print recyclable newspaper pages of interest to readers. 'Personalised' newspapers and television news bulletins are possible, with consumers being supplied with a diet of reading or viewing in predetermined categories (for example, lots of politics, but no sport — or vice versa).

Such developments will consign to dinosaur status the traditional means of manufacturing and distributing newspapers, particularly if advertisers switch to the new technologies. The revenue base of quality broadsheet newspapers, classified advertising (which accounts for two-thirds of the advertising revenue of the *Sydney Morning Herald* and the *Age*) will in particular be imperilled by the capacity of job-seekers or car-buyers to find the information they seek via computers and phone lines. This explains the interest of media entrepreneurs in buying stakes in the 'electronic super-highway'.

MEDIA PROPRIETORS AND POLITICS

Keith Murdoch was famous for his interactions with politicians of his day. In the 1930s he was known to summon the Australian prime minister, Joe Lyons, to his office. One report has Lyons standing before

Murdoch's desk, hat in hand, saying 'yes sir'. It is also reported that Murdoch said of Lyons, 'I put him there, and I'll put him out'. Before differences developed between them, Lyons recommended Murdoch's knighthood, and Murdoch gave detailed personal advice on the formation of his cabinet. Murdoch's son, Rupert, has been more subtle in his dealings with heads of government, but far less parochial: he has been a welcome guest at 10 Downing Street and at the White House (Bowman, 1988).

Mainstream newspapers have supported the conservative side of politics for most of this century. A temporary change in Fairfax loyalties came in 1961, when the *Sydney Morning Herald* supported Arthur Calwell's Labor Party, which came within one seat of defeating the Menzies Liberal–Country Party government. Subsequently Fairfax returned to its traditional loyalties. The *Age* under Ranald Macdonald's control took increasingly liberal positions, culminating in its support for Whitlam's Labor government in 1974. The Herald and Weekly Times group was always solid in its anti-Labor stance, as was Frank Packer's *Telegraph*. Newspapers have been more inclined to support Labor since the ALP's shift to the political centre in the mid-1980s.

Rupert Murdoch's political stances have varied: he liberalised his first paper, Adelaide's *News*, and took controversial and politically unpopular positions, including a campaign that saved a doubtfully convicted Aborigine from hanging. His Sydney afternoon tabloid, the *Daily Mirror*, was also a left-liberal foil to its Fairfax rival's *Sun*, while his national paper, the *Australian*, was left-liberal in its early years. Murdoch helped Whitlam personally and supported him editorially in the 1972 campaign that brought Labor to power, but turned dramatically against him in 1975 in a controversial campaign, which sparked strike action by journalists employed by the *Australian*. In Britain, Murdoch was renowned for his support for the Conservative government of Margaret Thatcher, and in the United States, for supporting Republican president Ronald Reagan.

Former Fairfax executive Max Suich claims to have evidence of then Treasurer Paul Keating's manoeuvres to help Murdoch and Packer and harm Fairfax and the Herald and Weekly Times group (Suich, 1991). Suich told his board that Keating's animosity to Fairfax was 'passionately held': an opinion based on what he saw as unfair treatment of himself, his family and his business friends in Fairfax publications.

Keating's dealings with media magnates became a public issue in 1994 following revelations by Conrad Black about discussions with Keating. The controversy led to an inquiry (dominated by Opposition and Democrat senators), which found, among other things, that the prime minister 'did attempt to improperly influence the political coverage of Fairfax newspapers by holding out to Mr Black the prospect of increased investment in Fairfax in return for balanced coverage' (Senate Select Committee, 1994, p.xviii). A key piece of evidence was a comment by Keating in an interview that, when asked by Black for approval of an increased stake in Fairfax, he had said: 'Well, we'll think about it, but we want a commitment from you that the paper will be balanced. And if there is any notion that, you know, of bias, that is that you barrack for the Coalition, on the basis of your conservative proclivities in other places, then there's no way you would qualify as the kind of owner we would like' (Senate Select Committee, 1994, p.124).

Governments try to influence media because of the power newspapers and other media have to influence public opinion about governments. As in other western democracies, Australian news media have a significant role, not only in reporting upon and evaluating government activities, but also acting independently to scrutinise politicians and government employees.

Journalism in Australia has taken its share of 'scalps', as public officials have been subjected to media probing. An important example of journalists' initiating the process of reform was the Fitzgerald Inquiry in Queensland, set in motion because of the investigative role of journalists with the ABC's 'Four Corners' and the Brisbane *Courier-Mail*. Chief editorial executive of the ABC and former Fairfax chief executive, Chris Anderson, has pointed to additional achievements by journalism:

> Joh Bjelke-Petersen has been ousted and Qld Inc exposed, initially by the activities of the ABC and the *Courier-Mail* . . . Mr Bond's, Mr Skase's and Mr Connell's tangles have been brought to light by the work (again) of the ABC, and also the writings in the *Sydney Morning Herald*, the *Australian Financial Review* and the *Australian*. The New South Wales police corruption stench was originally brought home by the work of Marian Wilkinson, Bob Bottom and Evan Whitton. The bottom-of-the-harbour tax scams were unearthed and detailed largely by the *Sydney Morning Herald* . . . Abe Saffron [crime figure], Murray Farquhar [former New South Wales chief stipendiary magistrate], Roger Rogerson [corrupt police officer] — and others — went behind bars because of the work of the Sydney press. (Anderson, 1990, pp.19–20)

The editorial cost-cutting of the 1990s has, however, resulted in a substantial diminution of the investigative role of the media, compared with the 1980s.

MEDIA REGULATION AND SELF-REGULATION

Despite an important role as a participant in the democratic process, mass media are subject to a variety of legal and quasi-legal controls. To some extent these restrain the media in their scrutiny of governments, and limit freedom of the press. Other restraints, however, set out to protect the public from the media, and to preserve other freedoms, such as the right to a fair trial or the right to privacy. The appropriate balance between conflicting rights is subject to continuing debate.

While enjoying a level of press freedom greater than that of most countries, Australia falls short of the USA, where freedom of the press is guaranteed in the Bill of Rights, which forms part of the nation's Constitution. More important than the constitutional provision *per se* is the fact that the US Supreme Court has, since the 1960s, interpreted the Constitution in the press's favour. Most significantly, public figures (especially government officials) are now effectively unable to sue news media successfully for defamation. The court has held that the functioning of democracy is a higher good than the privacy or personal sensitivities of those who are paid to serve the public. Even errors by the media in exposing wrong-doing by officials are protected — so long as the mistakes are made honestly and there is no malice involved. (Australia's High Court did, however, discern in 1992 an implied right of free speech when it ruled as unconstitutional Labor government legislation to limit broadcast political advertising.)

Australia has inherited from Britain a complex set of libel laws, which vary from state to state, but which generally involve the need for a specific public interest or public benefit to be proved, as well as the truth of allegations, for a successful defence of a libel suit. The attorneys-general of the three eastern states reached agreement in 1991 for steps towards uniform defamation law, but reforms fall far short of the American model.

However, significant developments in the extension of media freedom have come from the High Court, through its constitutional interpretation of the nature of representative government as permitting free political discourse. In 1992 the Court found that federal legislation to limit broadcast political advertising was unconstitutional. In 1994, when considering defamation actions brought by federal and state politicians against newspapers in Melbourne and Perth, the majority of the High Court determined that the Constitution involved a right of free political speech. Depending upon how lower courts interpret the judgment, it should mean greater freedom of news media to report and comment upon politicians' performance in their public duties, so long as media do this responsibly. In defending defamation actions by politicians, news media no longer have to prove the truth of allegations, but must show that they were unaware the material was false, did not publish it recklessly, and that publication was reasonable.

The effect of Australia's libel laws has been that many potential stories exposing politicians' or other officials' impropriety or illegal activities remain untold because of the risks of punitive damages awards. Even a relatively successful defence can cost millions of dollars in costs, as Channel 9 found in April 1991, in defending a libel suit from industrialist Sir Leslie Thiess, whose relationship with former Queensland premier Sir Joh Bjelke-Petersen was the subject of investigation by 'A Current Affair'.

On the other hand, the existence of complex libel laws may be the excuse for a largely quiescent media in not even initiating probes into suspected corruption. State and Commonwealth governments have enacted Freedom of Information legislation, a significant advance in government attitudes to the public's 'right to know' — but as Ricketson (1990) has pointed out, very few journalists make use of their newly-won freedoms.

One reason the United States has succeeded in elevating the claims of journalism over the more traditional claims of privacy may be the generally higher levels of responsibility demonstrated by US news media. Most daily newspapers throughout the USA take great pains to present information accurately and fairly, to correct errors, and to give right of reply to critics. They eschew the kind of sensationalism that dominates Britain's popular tabloids and that is evident in some Australian newspapers.

Most Australian journalists belong to a quasi-professional organisation that includes concern with ethical standards as one of its functions. Founded in 1910 as the Australian Journalists' Association (AJA), it amalgamated with other unions in 1992 to form the Media, Entertainment and Arts Alliance. Membership for journalists requires allegiance to a ten-point code of ethics, which codifies responsibilities and obligations. The alliance itself, however, faces the structural problem of being primarily a trade union: it represents rank-and-file journalists (and has done much to improve working conditions through arbitrated industrial awards), but thereby excludes the most senior and influential members of the occupation. Newspaper editors and other executives are exempt from union membership, and therefore are not required formally to subscribe to the code.

The best-known clause of the ethics code, which requires journalists to protect their sources, has since 1989 resulted in celebrated clashes between journalists and the judiciary, in trials where judges have demanded full disclosure of information. Journalists convicted of contempt of court for refusing to reveal sources have been jailed in Western Australia, Queensland and South Australia, and given a suspended jail sentence in New South Wales. An issue to be determined in the late 1990s is whether Australian journalists will be given legal protection (shield laws) to protect their sources' identity. Federal and state attorneys-general have signalled support for the principle of protection of sources, while the Senate Standing Committee on Legal and Constitutional Affairs (1994) has recommended amendments to state and Commonwealth Evidence Acts so that journalists will not necessarily have to reveal confidential sources.

Self-regulation of the press as an industry is a function of the Australian Press Council, established in 1976 as a voluntary watchdog to receive and adjudicate on complaints about editorial material (news stories, features, columns, leading articles) appearing in the press. It was largely modelled on the now defunct British Press Council (established after World War II on the recommendation of a royal commission into the press). Establishment of the Australian council followed lengthy lobbying by the AJA, and came together rather suddenly in the wake of government rumblings about statutory controls on the print media. The council at its formation included representatives from the participating publishers, the AJA and the public. Complaints are adjudicated by the council, with newspapers expected to publish adjudications concerning themselves. The council has published a statement of principles, which sets out ethical guidelines against which it tests newspapers' performance (APC, 1989).

The council was considerably weakened with the withdrawal of the AJA in 1987. This was the result of the AJA members' dissatisfaction with the majority members' refusal to call for a government inquiry into press ownership, following the Murdoch takeover of the Herald and Weekly Times group. The council's chairman, former judge Hal Wootten, who agreed with the AJA's position, also resigned. The AJA described the council as 'a publisher's poodle'.

In a report on itself in 1994 the council said it had received 429 complaints in 1993–94, more than double the number of five years previously. Major areas of complaint concerned claims of unfair treatment, inaccuracy, bias, poor taste, sexism, racism and invasion of privacy.

About 40 per cent of complaints are upheld, and almost all adjudications are published by the newspapers concerned. However, as a result of applying its own guidelines rather narrowly, the council has failed to carve out any reputation as a meaningful antidote to newspaper excesses. There is arguably a conflict of interest in the council's activities, for it also acts on behalf of the press in general by organising public conferences on media issues, making submissions to government inquiries, publishing press releases and actively promoting classic liberal concepts of freedom of the press.

Melbourne's *Herald Sun* set an example to other newspapers in 1993 when it developed its own comprehensive code of conduct for its journalists.

Broadcasting is more heavily regulated than is the press, as a result of the federal government's powers to allocate broadcasting frequencies. The Australian Broadcasting Authority (ABA) has the power to issue licences and to monitor industry codes of practice. It determines standards for minimum levels of Australian content and children's programming on television.

Important areas in which the ABA's predecessor, the Australian Broadcasting Tribunal, was involved included advertising time and television violence. The rapid turnover in broadcast ownership in the 1980s resulted in considerable activity by the tribunal in its function of approving share transactions (including keeping an eye on cross-ownership implications), while a famous inquiry in the late 1980s was its probe into whether Western Australian entrepreneur Alan Bond was a 'fit and proper person' under the terms of the Broadcasting Act to be a licensee. (The tribunal found in the negative.) The main direction of broadcasting policy in the 1990s has been towards self-regulation by industry.

Although required, like commercial broadcasters, to lodge its code of practice with the ABA, the Australian Broadcasting Corporation is self-regulating, subject ultimately to the control of its board of directors appointed for fixed terms by the government of the day. However, it is also subject to the budget set by the federal government. Under its charter, the ABC is required to provide educational and cultural programming as well as news and current affairs. The issue of regulation of the ABC arose during the 1991 Gulf War, when critics, including government ministers, accused the ABC of being insufficiently supportive of Australia's involvement. Similar controversies have embroiled Britain's BBC. (The ABC is, however, resistant to outside scrutiny: an attempt by a consortium of interest groups led by the National Farmers Federation to have ABC coverage of the 1993 election analysed by the University of Queensland foundered when the ABC reversed its original decision to cooperate.)

CONCLUSION

Like many Australian institutions, mass media are undergoing major change — largely as a result of technical advances and deregulation. Amidst the change is continuity. The two most powerful media proprietors in Australia are Rupert Murdoch and Kerry Packer. Turn the clock back fifty years, and we find a great deal of the press under the control of these two men's fathers. But in the space of a few years, the traditional owners of some of the country's leading media groups have disappeared, ownership of major groups has shifted offshore, and commercial imperatives have spread to the once sacrosanct area of public broadcasting. Meanwhile, the long-term future of the press is in doubt, as readership declines and as new technologies are set to render the traditional means of manufacturing and distributing newspapers obsolete. There remains, however, no doubt that mass media's prospects are bright. Hence, major entrepreneurs are investing in the rapidly developing technologies and applications of satellite, optical fibre and pay television. Journalists and other media professionals face the challenge of adapting to the skills requirements of the new technologies while maintaining or improving their professional and ethical values.

FURTHER READING

Details of the history of Australia's press can be found in Walker's two books on New South Wales press history, Cryle (1989) on Queensland's colonial press, Kirkpatrick (1984) on the provincial press of Queensland, Sayers (1965) on David Syme and Souter (1981) on the Fairfax company. Holden (1961) gives a useful thumbnail sketch of major dailies' histories. My bibliographical review of historical studies of the press and other media (Henningham, 1988) has been overtaken by major biographies and histories that have emerged since 1988. Shawcross (1992) has written the best biography of Rupert Murdoch, while Chadwick (1989) presents the definitive analysis of the Murdoch takeover of the Herald and Weekly Times and the ensuing turmoil, as well as giving an invaluable chronology of media ownership, government policy and political manoeuvres since 1922. The Fairfax collapse is detailed in Carroll's and Souter's books of 1991, while Conrad Black's (1993) autobiography gives the perspective of the successful purchaser. Barry (1993) has written a biography of Kerry Packer, which grew out of a television documentary. Inglis (1982) has written the history of the ABC's first 50 years, while Petersen (1993) has completed the first volume of his history of the ABC's news service; Lloyd (1985) records the AJA's first 75 years. Tiffen (1989) has written the best contemporary book on politics and the media, while Mayer's *The Press in Australia* (1964) is a classic in the field. A range of contemporary issues are canvassed in Bowman's *The Captive Press* (1988) and my *Issues in Australian Journalism* (1990). The journal, *Communications Update*, published by the Communications Law Centre at the University of NSW, gives a detailed account of current media ownership in its February issue each year. *Media Information Australia* is very useful in the field of mass media and communication generally, while *Australian Studies in Journalism* and *Australian Journalism Review* have given considerable attention to professional issues in recent years. Geoff Turner's annual chronicle in *Australian Studies in Journalism* outlines major events affecting news media.

REFERENCES

Anderson, C. 1990, 'The media: why the critics are wrong', *Communication Law Bulletin*, 10 (3), pp.19–20.

Australian Broadcasting Authority 1993, *Annual Report*, ABA, Sydney.

Australian Press Council 1989, *Aims, Principles, Constitution and Complaints Procedure*, APC Booklet no. 4, APC, Sydney.

Audit Bureau of Circulations 1984, *Summary*, no. 94, 1 April–30 September, Audit Bureau of Circulations, Sydney.

—— 1994, *Summary*, no. 114, 1 April–30 September, Audit Bureau of Circulations, Sydney.

Barry, P. 1993, *The Rise and Rise of Kerry Packer*, Bantam, Sydney.

Black, C. 1993, *A Life in Progress*, Random House, Milson's Point.

Bowman, D. 1988, *The Captive Press*, Penguin, Ringwood, Vic.

Brown, A. 1986, *Commercial Media in Australia*, University of Queensland Press, St Lucia.

Carroll, V. J. 1991, *The Man Who Couldn't Wait*, Heinemann, Sydney.

Chadwick, P. 1989, *Media Mates: Carving Up Australia's Media*, Macmillan, Melbourne.

Cryle, D. 1989, *The Press in Colonial Queensland: A Social and Political History, 1845–1875*, University of Queensland Press, St Lucia.

Cummins, C., Shand, A. and Ward, P. 1991, 'Flaws in the Fairfax formula', *Australian*, 23 April, p.4.

Henningham, J. P. 1988, 'Two hundred years of Australian journalism: a history waiting to be written', *Australian Cultural History*, 7, pp.49–64.

Henningham, J. P. (ed.) 1990, *Issues in Australian Journalism*, Longman Cheshire, Melbourne.

Holden, W. S. 1961, *Australia Goes to Press*, Melbourne University Press, Melbourne.

House of Representatives Select Committee on the Print Media 1992, *News and Fair Facts: The Australian Print Media Industry*, AGPS, Canberra.

Inglis, K. 1982, *This is the ABC*, Melbourne University Press, Melbourne.

Kirkpatrick, R. 1984, *Sworn to No Master: A History of the Provincial Press in Queensland to 1930*, DDIAE Press, Toowoomba.

Lloyd, C. 1985, *Profession: Journalist*, Hale & Iremonger, Sydney.

Mayer, H. 1964, *The Press in Australia*, Lansdowne, Melbourne.

—— 1980, 'Media', in *Australian Politics: A Fifth Reader*, eds H. Mayer and H. Nelson, Longman Cheshire, Melbourne.

Petersen, N. 1993, *News Not Views: The ABC, the Press and Politics, 1932–1947*, Hale & Iremonger, Sydney.

Ricketson, M. 1990, 'Why journalists should use and cover Freedom of Information laws', *Australian Journalism Review*, 12: pp.9–15.

Sayers, C. E. 1965, *David Syme: A Life*, F. W. Cheshire, Melbourne.

Senate Select Committee on Certain Aspects of Foreign Ownership Decisions in Relation to the Print Media 1994, *Percentage Players: The 1991 and 1993 Fairfax Ownership Decisions*, Parliament of the Commonwealth of Australia, Canberra.

Senate Standing Committee on Legal and Constitutional Affairs 1994, *Off the Record: Shield Laws for Journalists' Confidential Sources*, Parliament of the Commonwealth of Australia, Canberra.

Shawcross, W. 1992, *Rupert Murdoch: Ringmaster of the Information Circus*, Random House, Milson's Point.

Souter, G. 1981, *Company of Heralds*, Melbourne University Press, Melbourne.

Souter, G. 1991, *Heralds and Angels*, Melbourne University Press, Melbourne.

Suich, M. 1991, 'What did the Labor Party do for you?', *Independent Monthly*, March, pp.21–3.

Tiffen, R. 1989, *News and Power*, Allen & Unwin, Sydney.

Walker, R. B. 1976, *The Newspaper Press in New South Wales, 1803–1920*, Sydney University Press, Sydney.

Webster, M. 1990, 'Book publishing', in 'Forum: foreign ownership of media', *Communication Law Bulletin*, 10 (3), pp.8–9.

CONTRIBUTORS

Professor Greg Bamber, director of QUT's Australian Centre in Strategic Management, has published many articles and books, including *Militant Managers, Managing Managers* (with Ed Snape and Tom Redman), *Organisational Change Strategies Case Studies of Human Resource and Industrial Relations Issues* (with Margaret Patrickson and Val Bamber), and, with Russell Lansbury, *International and Comparative Industrial Relations: A Study of Industrialised Market Economies* and *New Technology: International Perspectives on Human Resources and Industrial Relations*. He is currently president of the Australian and New Zealand Academy of Management.

Dr John Biggs is Postgraduate Medical Dean at the University of Cambridge and the Anglia and Oxford Regional Health Authority in the United Kingdom. A specialist gynaecologist by training, he has been increasingly involved in medical education at all levels. Formerly Dean of Medicine at the University of Queensland, he was a member of the Medical Board and of the South Brisbane Hospital Board. He has a particular interest in the delivery of medical education and how students and doctors learn.

Dr Adrian Bower, head of the Office of Graduate Medical Education within the Queensland Medical Education Centre, is a Deputy Dean of the Faculty of Medicine and a Senior Lecturer in Anatomy at the University of Queensland. His research interests lie in developmental neurobiology and he has always been keenly interested in medical education. He was awarded a foundation Harvard Macy scholarship to attend Harvard University in 1995 to study aspects of change in medical curricula.

Dr Colin Brown is Lecturer in Agricultural Economics in the Department of Agriculture at the University of Queensland. He has been a research officer with the Australian Bureau of Agricultural Economics and senior research officer with the Danish Institute of Agricultural Economics. His special fields of interest are agricultural policy, rural marketing and international trade.

Dr Brian Costar is Associate Professor of Politics at Melbourne's Monash University. A graduate of the University of Queensland, he has published widely in the fields of Australian federal and state politics, especially in relation to elections and political parties. He co-edited, with Mark Considine, *Trials in Power: Cain, Kirner and Victoria*, a study of the Labor government in Victoria in the decade 1982–92, and recently edited *For Better or For Worse: The Federal Coalition*.

Dr Russell Cowie is Senior Lecturer in Education at the University of Queensland. He teaches courses in History Curriculum Study, Pedagogics and Instructional Practice, and Principles of Curriculum Design. He has taught in secondary schools in New Zealand, England and Australia, and is known nationally as the author and editor of numerous history textbooks for secondary schools.

Professor Edward Davis is director of the Labour-Management Studies Foundation, Graduate School of Management, Macquarie University, Sydney. He is author of *Democracy in Australian Unions* (1987) and editor of several books, including *Democracy and Control in the Workplace* (1986), co-edited by Russell D. Lansbury. His current research includes a study of the power and influence of the Australian Council of Trade Unions.

Dr Donald Gifford is Reader in Law at the University of Queensland and was Deputy Dean of the Law School from 1991 to 1993. He currently teaches courses in Administrative Law and Pollution Control Law and has written extensively on town planning law and on statutory interpretation. His PhD (Cantab.) deals with the unreasonableness doctrine of administrative law, and he has addressed various international conferences on that and other topics. He is an associate member of the American Bar Association.

Dr Ian Gillman was Senior Lecturer in Studies in Religion at the University of Queensland from 1975 to 1992. Originally a civil engineer, he studied theology in Sydney and Princeton and was ordained a Presbyterian minister. He was closely involved from 1960 to 1977 in planning for the foundation of the Uniting Church in Australia and has been a minister of the Uniting Church since 1977. He has been Professor of Theology and Church History at Queensland Presbyterian Theological Hall. His publications include the Bicentennial volume *Many Faiths — One Nation* (1988).

Professor John Henningham was appointed to Australia's first Chair of Journalism in 1989 at the University of Queensland. A graduate of the University of Sydney, he worked on metropolitan and national newspapers, and for the ABC as a journalist, won a Mombusho Scholarship to Tokyo University's Institute of Journalism, and has been a research fellow at the Institute of Culture and Communication, East–West Center, Honolulu. Awarded Australia's first PhD in Journalism in 1984, he is the author of *Looking at Television News* and editor of *Issues in Australian Journalism*. He edits the academic journal, *Australian Studies in Journalism* and is currently undertaking national surveys of journalists in Australia and Great Britain.

Dr Ian Jobling is Associate Professor in Human Movement Studies at the University of Queensland. His main teaching and research interests are the socio-historical aspects of sport in Australian society, especially the Olympic Games, gender issues and sport education. He is president of the Australian Society for Sports History and a member of the editorial review board of the Society's journal, *Sporting Traditions*. He is also a member of the editorial review board of *Olympika — The International Journal of Olympic Studies*, regional director (Australia/Oceania) of the International Council for Sports Science and Physical Education, and former chair of the Australian Olympic Committee's Education Commission and Olympic Academy.

Professor John Longworth is Pro-Vice-Chancellor (Social Sciences) at the University of Queensland and is Professor of Agricultural Economics. In recent years his research has concentrated on investigating the economic and socio-political factors influencing Australian export markets in Japan (for beef) and in China (for wool). He has published *Beef in Japan* (1983), *China's Rural Development Miracle* (1989), *The Wool Industry in China* (1990) and *China's Pastoral Region* (with Greg Williamson in 1993), as well as more than 100 professional articles and research papers. He is a Fellow of the Academy of Social Sciences in Australia and a Farrer Medallist.

Dr Tony Makin is Senior Lecturer in Economics at the University of Queensland, specialising in international macroeconomics, monetary economics and Australian macroeconomic policy. He has previously served as a senior economist in the federal departments of the

Treasury, Finance, Foreign Affairs and Trade, and Prime Minister and Cabinet, and has published widely on aspects of the international and Australian economies. He is a regular media commentator on national economic issues.

Mr John May is Lecturer in Social Policy and Administration at the Department of Social Work and Social Policy at the University of Queensland. His teaching and research interests are in social policy, human services administration and the non-government sector. He is a Board member of the Australian Council of Social Service (ACOSS) and is a regular media commentator on social policy and social issues. He is co-author of *Working in Human Service Organisations* (1992).

Mr Doug Tucker, Senior Lecturer in Public Administration within the Department of Government at the University of Queensland, has research and teaching interests in administration theory and in local, urban and regional government. He has acted as a consultant to the (Australian) Advisory Council for Inter-government Relations and the Electoral and Administrative Review Commission of Queensland (EARC), and has been a member of various committees appointed by the Brisbane City Council and by the Director of Local Government to advise on legislative, policy and management problems.

Dr Ian Ward is Senior Lecturer in Government at the University of Queensland, where he teaches courses in Australian politics and politics and the media. He is the author of various articles and chapters about the Australian Labor Party, rural conservatism in Australia, mass media and political parties, and is co-author of a textbook on Australian politics, *Politics One*.

INDEX